ON THE LEVEL

ON
THE
LEVEL

WITH SELF

FAMILY

SOCIETY

G. HUGH ALLRED

Brigham Young University Press   Provo, Utah 84602

Library of Congress Cataloging in Publication Data

Allred, G   Hugh
On the level: with self, family, society.

Includes bibliographies.
1. Interpersonal relations.   2. Interpersonal relations—
Case studies.   I. Title.
HM132.A36   301.11   74-14721
ISBN O-8425-1412-0
ISBN O-8425-1400-7 (pbk.)

LCN: 74-14721
ISBN: 0-8425-1400-7 (pb); 0-8425-1412-0 (hb)
Brigham Young University Press, Provo, Utah 84602
© Brigham Young University Press. All rights reserved
First edition
Printed in the United States of America
74 4.5M pb .5M hb   2994

To my wife, children,
and New Zealand friends

CONTENTS

viii

PREFACE

How often do we ask ourselves these questions: How can I increase my positive feelings toward myself, loved ones, and other people? How can I achieve a peaceful and serene life?

This book is dedicated to helping you find answers to these vital questions. It presents for your consideration a way of relating to loved ones, friends, and neighbors that tends to bring about harmony, happiness, and meaningful productivity; that is, it presents guides for helping you to understand and influence yourself and other people in a positive manner. Being on the level with other people may be considered the process of moving with one's fellowmen rather than against them, working with them rather than competing, and being concerned about their welfare rather than using them for one's own selfish purposes.

The text contains numerous case studies of parent-child, husband-wife, and neighbor-neighbor relationships, with suggestions for how the participants might become happier with themselves in their relationships with other people. Each case represents in some way real-life situations. But because life is dynamic, complex, and ever-changing, probably no life situation will exactly duplicate any of the cases presented, for no two situations are exactly the same, though they may be similar. Cases are representative of not one but many situations whose stories have been woven together. The names and events themselves have been changed to protect identities.

The primary purpose for presenting the cases as contained in parts 3, 4, and 5 is to help you increase your understanding of people and your repertory of effective relationship responses. In order to get the greatest benefit from this book, you will need to read many cases. Such reading can help you develop an artistic feel for how you can better respond to members of your family and other people. It can enable you to relate flexibly as you appropriately draw upon all you have learned through your readings and experiences with yourself and other people. Moreover, you should become better prepared to deal more effectively and creatively with people in general as you add the ideas in this book to your already existing reservoir of understanding and effective behaviors.

There is no easy answer to many situations. Most difficulties with others require courage, persistence, knowledge, skill, and the creativity and sensitivity that enables you to use the right principle with the right response in the right situation with the right person at the right time. Put another way, being able to relate positively with other people requires proper matching of one's behavior with the situation, time, place, and other person(s).

The theoretical position taken in this book is very similar to that of the Third Force group. This term refers to those who are devoted to a holistic, phenomenological (subjective), teleological (purposive), field-theoretical and socially oriented approach to understanding man. I have also included many ideas from learning and communication approaches and from social systems. In addition, behaviorists' methods for tallying, charting, and graphing behavior have been helpful in identifying an individual's progress, and one such strategy is included. I do not stress stages of development, for I believe that such concepts have too often been used to excuse irresponsible, unconstructive, and even destructive behaviors: e.g., "the terrible two's."

On the Level with Self, Family, Society attempts to give the reader insights into basic concepts and principles of human behavior that are of great worth in effecting change. For those who wish to study these concepts and principles further, the following recommended writers are a few whose ideas are generally consistent with those of the Third Force: Alfred Adler, Albert Bandura, William Barrett, Arthur W. Combs, Don Dinkmeyer, Rudolph Dreikurs, Viktor Frankl, William Glasser, Karen Horney, Don Jackson, Abraham Maslow, C. Moustakas, Carl Rogers, Jurgen Ruesch, Virginia Satir, H. S. Sullivan, Thomas Szasz, and Paul Watzlawic.

While a book can provide insight into situations, there are times when family members or couples in difficulty need the assistance of a competent, professional therapist. There should be no hesitation in getting such help when and if the need for it arises. One way to insure the receiving of competent assistance is to contact local school, university, religious, or other recognized institutions and find out the names of those residing nearby who belong to such organizations as the American Association of Marriage and Family Counselors, or a clinical division of the American Psychological Association, or the Academy of Certified Social Workers. Acquiring the services of a therapist who belongs to one of these organizations will help you obtain the kind of help you may want and need. After you have the names of several who are recognized professionally, you can then narrow your search by investigating their reputations in the community. It is important that you discover which ones seem to offer the most constructive help and which ones have values and ethics similar to your own.

I am greatly indebted to the many individuals, couples, and families in Canada and the United States with whom I have counseled from 1960 to the present. They have taught me much of what I know about people. I am especially indebted to the Maoris of New Zealand who opened their homes and hearts to me. They have served as catalysts for many of the ideas presented herein.

I am very grateful to Ruth Benedict for her illuminating concepts of high and low synergy and to Lydia Sicher and Rudolf Dreikurs for their writings on vertical and horizontal movement. These people have provided me with the basic framework for my analysis throughout the book.

I am also grateful to the specialists in human behavior who were appointed by Brigham Young University Press to critique a rough draft of the manuscript and also to Dr. Burton C. Kelly who critiqued a part of the manuscript. Their suggestions were most helpful. I am also indebted to Carolyn Green and Carol Ellsworth who edited a later draft. Many individuals, including Sue Gregory, Karen Brooksby, Linda Draper, and my sister, Orvilla Stevens, typed the various drafts. I also thank Margo McDougald for her efforts and Marilyn M. Miller for her enthusiastic encouragement and support.

I express thanks to MaCrae Magleby, Jr., and Raymond C. Morales who have designed the book so appropriately. Kerril Sue Rollins has edited the manuscript and provided many valuable suggestions. I express special appreciation to her for her many hours of cooperative, friendly, and skilled association. Many other people at Brigham Young University Press have also contributed to the final product. To all of these, and to those previously mentioned, I express deep appreciation.

My hope is that you, the reader, will be able to enhance the happiness and richness of your life with self, loved ones, friends, and neighbors as you work to apply the ideas presented in *On the Level.* From the wide variety of situations discussed in the book I hope that you will be able to get a workable feel for the principles and that you will thereby be able to apply them in creative and common-sense ways to your own life situations.

GUIDE FOR READING AND USING THE BOOK

At times we all have problems in our relationships with other people and find the need to improve our understanding and skills. This book can be a valuable aid as it provides how-to suggestions for many different situations. Our needs differ from time to time and each of us has unique preferences. Hence, you may benefit from skipping around in the text, reading parts out of sequence. At the end of each case, under *Concepts you may want to review,* are suggestions for integrating ideas with behaviors. Those who may benefit from reading *On the Level* include:

- Couples preparing for marriage
- Husbands and wives
- Parents of young children
- Parents of adolescents
- Marital-study group leaders and members
- Parent-study group leaders and members
- Teachers and students in family life, human relationships, mental hygiene, social work, and home economics courses.
- Therapists and counselors and their clients
- Community, religious, and business leaders
- Family physicians and their patients

Depending on the setting, the concepts and case situations might be used for:

- Increasing the optimism and courage of an individual by fostering these ideas: I am not alone. Others have similar problems. There are things that I can do to work through my relationship difficulties.
- Increasing a person's knowledge and perception about people and relationships.

- Increasing a person's ability to apply concepts to relationships.
- Increasing a person's alternatives for improving relationships.
- Warming up individuals to simulate and role-play real-life, personal relationship situations.
- Stimulating discussion and critical thought on values and ethics in relationships.
- Stimulating discussion and practice in working through relationship problem situations.

The uses of *On the Level* are many and varied. The creativity of the reader will insure its worth.

And a youth said, Speak
to us of Friendship
And he answered saying:
Your friend is your needs answered . . .

Kahlil Gibran

ONE

CONDITIONS
OF MAN

1
THE
CHALLENGE

Most of us have experienced difficulties and have been hurt in relationships with other people, whether they are members of our families or society in general. We know the feeling of being unaccepted or rejected, of being alone, of being apart from others who are loved and valued. We realize that it is a major challenge to understand such experiences, learn from them, and then have the courage to do those things that will bring us closer to our fellowmen. For example, many men and women seek help when they are considering divorce. The following is a simulated, rather typical story which presents a number of reasons why this is such a common occurrence.

"He is a good man," she began. "I was attracted to him initially, not only by his good looks but by his diligence. He works hard and I am sure he will succeed. I guess that is another reason why I was so attracted to him. He made me feel secure. I felt if I married him I would never have to worry about feeding and clothing myself and my children. This part has come true. He is so good in so many ways that I feel guilty about the way I sometimes feel.

"You see, I was the baby in our family and I guess people had taken care of me all my life, and when he came along, so handsome, strong, and sure of himself, I fell for him completely." She had tears in her eyes; now her voice took on a higher pitch and she lisped slightly. "Anyway, I fell hard.

"Our honeymoon was exciting. I remember I felt so secure, so loved, so wanted; but that soon changed. I guess the first time I found myself getting angry with Craig was during the second week of our marriage. He came in the house and found me resting. I had just finished mopping the kitchen floor and doing all the dusting and vacuuming." She lifted her face and a look of defiance flashed through her tears. "He took my feet and swept them with his arm off the couch on-to the floor. He shook me by the shoulders, put his face next to mine, and almost shouted that no wife of his was going to be known as a lazy housewife. I guess I was too shocked to say anything. He stomped out of the house and I bawled for an hour after. I guess he felt bad about it too because he was exceptionally kind to me that evening. That is what makes it so hard. He can make me so angry one minute, and the next he is so kind. If he were mean all the time, I think it would be easier for me."

Shauna shifted her position, gave a helpless little girl shrug and continued her story. "I found myself becoming resentful of Craig. It bothered me because the feeling didn't just come and go. It seemed to be continually with me. About six months after our marriage, I guess, I became aware that this feeling was, it seemed to me, eating me alive. It got so bad I found I couldn't respond to him sexually. Oh, I didn't realize it was affecting me this way at first. That realization came to me over a period of time. This feeling of resentment became all pervasive. I found it crowding out other thoughts. I'd be doing dishes or sweeping the floor, and my mind would wander away from what I was doing to thinking about Craig. I'm not very proud of my thoughts at such times. I'd find myself wishing he were dead, or I were dead.

"It was four years after our marriage, when our baby was about a year old, that I began to really see what Craig was doing. Seeing what he was doing to our baby made me realize what he was doing to me. Craig is one who believes in making kids behave. He is very critical of the way other people raise their kids. I've often heard him say, 'No kid of mine would do something like that. Those parents don't care what their kids do.' Well, anyway, he has tried to make sure that little Craig doesn't grow up like some of the neighborhood kids. He gave our baby his first spanking when he was six months old. It made Craig angry to see him knock the spoon out of my hand and get baby cereal all over my dress. He justified spanking him at the time by saying that no kid of his was going to be disrespectful to his mother and that the best time to train him was when he was young.

"I felt terrible. Right after Craig spanked him, he went to work. It took me an hour of cuddling and rocking little Craig before he would quiet down. That is the story of our lives. Craig spanks him and

I have to quiet him down. It's getting harder and harder. He cries more now. Last month Craig began spanking him for crying. He says he is not going to raise a crybaby.

"I feel like I've portrayed Craig as a monster. He's really not. I know he loves our little son. He plays with him much of the time and will fondle and kiss him and is really proud of him when we go out in public—when he's not crying. You see, Craig Jr. is a really handsome little boy, like his father. Craig's a good man. He's just so stubborn. He thinks he is so right in everything he does. He won't listen to me at all.

"That's what makes it so hard. He is so good to us in so many ways. I guess I'm beginning to sound like a broken record.

"When our baby started crawling Craig said that he was not going to babyproof the house like so many of our friends. He insisted I leave everything in place, for this, he said, was the way to train our son to respect other people's things. The last six months have been like a nightmare to me. I believe Craig has spanked our baby at least once every day for the last few weeks. He is determined to train him to stay out of our things. Our son has begun crying more and more, and it is harder for me to comfort and settle him down again. It's hard on our baby boy, frustrating for Craig, and terrifying for me.

"As I said before, it was our troubles with our son that caused me to look closely at our relationship. When I discovered what was really going on between us, it was impossible for me to accept it any longer. That is why I'm here. It is a last ditch effort to save our marriage.

"I began to write things down, and this is what I discovered. Craig is good in whatever he does. When he comes home from work, he asks me what I have done all day. I feel like I am reporting to a father. He usually finds things not to his satisfaction and lets me know about it. He criticizes me for the way I cook. Very often he will move me aside and finish cooking our meal. He criticizes the way I discipline little Craig and will often move in. It's got so I hate to do anything with our son while Craig is around. Craig insists on buying my clothes; and the few times I have bought my own, he has criticized my choices. It's easier to let him do it. I used to drive before I got married, but it was so painful to hear his criticisms that I just gave it up. He manages all the money, and whenever I need any, I have to go to him. I feel like a little girl. He always asks me what I need it for and will usually find some reason why I don't need it or can get along on less.

"What am I to do? I don't want to leave Craig. He's a good man. I know he means well, but I can't take it any longer. I can no longer stand this smothered feeling and all the hurt. There has to be a better way for our son." She clasped her hands tightly. She looked up and waited—expectantly.

The following day Craig came in, tall, broad-shouldered, and good-looking. He moved with the confident grace of one who is sure of his own worth and sat easily in the chair indicated for him. After we introduced ourselves and talked for a few minutes, he began to express how he felt.

"I can't understand Shauna anymore. She used to be so appreciative of the things I did for her. Now nothing I do seems to please her. I have a good income for a young man and she hasn't lacked for anything. I really don't know what's gotten into her the last while. She won't even speak to me for two or three days at a time. I once thought we had a good marriage. I've done all I can to make her happy. I've tried so hard, but the harder I try the more distant she becomes.

"I guess she told you we have a little boy. She's spoiling him rotten. I try hard to make a little man out of him. Everything I do she seems to undo. I'm firm with him. She's too soft. If she keeps it up, she's going to ruin him." A touch of anger crept into Craig's voice.

"Shauna has always been 'scatter-brained.' She is a lovely person, but she needs a strong hand to guide her. She does not know how to budget money or how to manage the home. I've even set up work schedules for her to follow to improve her efficiency, but she is too irresponsible to follow them. Sometimes I get very impatient with her. She has a hard time making up her mind about anything. I'm afraid little Craig is going to be just like her. Oh, if he were a girl, it wouldn't be so bad. But my sons are going to be hard workers, decisive, and responsible.

"I guess I get a little hot under the collar when I talk about these things. You see there are so many people in the world who just don't seem to give a damn. I want my sons to grow up to be worth something—to be somebody and to contribute something worthwhile to humanity. Don't get me wrong. I love Shauna very much even though

I don't agree with the soft way she handles our boy. She is an attractive and talented young woman. I am proud of her. I think the world of her. I'd do anything for her. I just wish I could train her to be more responsible." Craig sighed and dropped his hands into his lap.

"Do you think it's too late?" Craig asked searchingly.

If Shauna and Craig were to discover what each of them does to hurt the other and then learn to think new thoughts and practice new ways of relating, they would have a much greater chance for achieving happiness. This is generally true of all people who sincerely desire to improve their relationships with others, whether they be loved ones, friends, or associates.

The following chapter provides a way of viewing destructive interpersonal relationships and includes, in a final section, a description of Shauna and Craig's destructive patterns with a discussion of their consequences. Chapter 3 presents a way of viewing constructive relationships, the last section providing some possible alternatives for Shauna and Craig to use in an attempt to improve their interactions.

2
VERTICAL INTERACTION

Many specialists who spend their lives studying people are continually impressed by the complexities of the human condition. Presently, there is a wealth of information pouring forth in bits and pieces from professional and nonprofessional sources. In order to make sense out of this mass of information and facilitate its application to the nitty gritty where, in the final analysis, life is lived, it is often useful and even necessary to build general models of behavior. No word, phrase, or sentence can completely portray a particular thought, feeling or action, and of course no paradigm, or model, can completely and without some distortion represent the human condition. But such models can help communicate rather esoteric knowledge in a simplified, meaningful, and useful manner and thus enhance our basic understanding of people.

The vertical and horizontal models of relationships found in Chapters 2 and 3 are some basic ways of viewing and understanding important aspects of the human condition. Vertical movement in relationships is viewed as being primarily movement *against* one's fellows. It is movement that leads to much of the misery and unhappiness people experience. In contrast, horizontal movement occurs *with* one's fellows. It is a way of relating that tends to bring about greater satisfaction and happiness.

The figure on page 10 illustrates a basic error made by those who are vertical in their relationships with others. They believe that in order to get ahead they must appear superior to other men. This attitude is easy to learn in our present society. Prestigious persons who relate vertically are often held up as people whose actions should be imitated. For instance, the mass communication media are filled with vertical movement of countless variety. Advertisements often portray users of their products as being superior to any others and those who do not use them as inferior, naive, or even stupid. Such vertical behavior is so

Characteristics of Vertical Movement

deeply ingrained in our society that we learn it easily, quite unaware of what it is we are doing and the inevitable consequences that follow.

The figure demonstrates how those caught up in the practice of vertical movement view themselves—on a ladder climbing over each other to become successful. There is room for only one person on each of the ladder's rungs. Each figure that is situated precariously above another illustrates the attempts in life of some who raise themselves at the expense of others. It is figurative of the common dog-eat-dog relationship. Some people compete and push against others or climb over their backs in their desperate scramble to get ahead. Individuals who fall from the ladder are representative of those so pushed against and trodden on in the game of life that they become discouraged, lose their grip, and fall off. These are the ones who give up. The ground of life is littered with such wreckage.

Often those who climb a vertical ladder in their relationships do it not so much to be good as to appear superior. Their outward manifestations of caring for their fellows are merely techniques for acquiring acclaim and a following, the prestige and status that they have long dreamed about. They may not even feel the smallest semblance of warmth for the people whom they constantly push against. They often do the right things, not so much for the joy of doing right, but to prove how much better they are than other men.

Those who give themselves to such endeavors in order to prove their superiority often move into the game of one-up-manship. In this game they keep their eyes fixed on those next to them; and whatever they do, they attempt to top and demean others' accomplishments.

The person who practices vertical behavior may even be dishonest in his relationships. The great pressure he puts himself under to appear better than his fellows and to acquire status and prestige may influence him to distort information so that he will appear in a favorable light. The flim-flam con artist is typical. He may even distort information to cause his *imagined* competitors to appear unfavorable. He may be dishonestly ruthless in his economic negotiations with his fellows in order to gain an advantage that will add to his material wealth, power, and status.

Greed is another characteristic basic to the behavior of the vertically oriented person. He is often found to spend vast amounts of time and energy designing and executing schemes to diminish other people's possessions, services, and status in order to add to his own. Thus he piles up for himself a vast rubbish heap from which he stands and casts his exalted eyes on those who are around—and below—him. His is a lonely and fearful perch. He must guard his pile with his very life, for he fears that others, as he has done, will take from his pile as they build their own and thereby he will lose his prestige and status. He is thus ever wary of his fellowmen, whom he views as his eternal enemies.

Another characteristic possessed by the vertically oriented person is the tendency to criticize others in a negative, destructive manner. He also tends to be critical and intolerant of himself. He is mistake and fault oriented. The errors and mistakes of others loom large before his eyes and crowd out their effective and responsible works. He may also become sorrowful, pessimistic, and depressed.

One of the greatest character calamities to beset the vertically oriented man is that he tends to measure his own progress against what he perceives as being the progress of his fellows. This measurement is full of distortion, for if he starts out ahead of them in a certain area, he will tend to judge that all is well with himself and he will not progress. Or if he is behind at the start, he may decide he does not have the abilities to move ahead as they do, and he will tend to work half-heartedly or else give up. He may become so threatened by the progress of other people that his major objective becomes putting obstacles in their paths to slow them down. In reality, the vertically oriented person tends to do all three of the above, depending on the situation, the people involved, and the time and place.

Finally, a characteristic of the vertical movement that invites desperation is its yo-yo quality. One can never be sure of his being up or down. In one minute, he could be higher than his fellows; in the next, the same fellows could be climbing up and over his back, pushing down on him as they surge upward. Even the person at the top can be pulled down by others and tomorrow find himself at the bottom. There is no sure place. There is no safety. All is unstable. Each person is a potential enemy.

CONSEQUENCES OF VERTICAL MOVEMENT

Such characteristics of vertical movement as those previously described lead to a number of rather bitter consequences. The vertically oriented person can never be sure he is high enough or good enough because he has no stable measuring device that will tell him where he has been and the progress he has made. Because of his critical posture toward himself and others, he will more than likely immerse himself in self-criticism, self-abasement, and the abasement of those about him.

His fear that others will overtake him, abuse him in their climb, or knock him off his rung makes him suspicious and fearful of them. He therefore experiences much tension and anxiety. His capacity for love may become poor and that which he may be able to give, hesitant and distorted in its expression.

Another typical consequence is stunted growth. Learning and progression contain an element of risk because they require a person to make decisions based on the choices available to him. This results in the possibility of his making a bad decision. The vertically oriented person may become terrified because of an intense fear of making mistakes, for he feels that when he makes mistakes he loses love, prestige, and status. He feels that he will no longer belong, that others will move in and take over his place. He may even become mesmerized by the fear of making mistakes and refuse to risk making decisions. He, therefore, holds tight to the status quo. To the degree that an individual's learning becomes tied to his degree of belonging, his learning and progression tend to suffer in some way.

Thus the vertically oriented person may exhibit extreme caution. His constant fear of failure makes him focus on his mistakes, and he tends to fulfill them by making them come true. It is as if we were to walk a foot-wide path placed five hundred feet in the air. Most of us would fear falling, and that focus on falling would help make us fall. But if the narrow path were on level ground, most of us could walk it with no problem. So it is with those who are vertically and horizontally oriented. The vertical individuals focus on failure and mistakes and tend to make them because those are all they see, while the horizontally oriented tend to be full of confidence and faith. They focus on the positive and make their positive thoughts come true.

Feelings of being small, deficient, worthless, and of no good are common in those who relate vertically. But the complete opposites of these feelings may also be manifest. The individual may feel better than all other people and refuse to be concerned with the common folk. He may even develop delusions similar to the megalomaniac. He may feel he has the right, because of his belief that he is superior, to dictate to others. He may also feel that others are obligated to obey him and help him build higher and higher his pile of goods from which he can look down on them as they sink ever lower and lower.

A typical consequence of a person's taking the vertical stance is his emphasis on competition rather than cooperation. Competition tends to become a god. He emphasizes the win-lose concept. In order to win, he must be sure that his competitors fail. Hence, he may deliberately structure his environment and the games he plays so that other people readily fall into his trap by playing the game of life his way. Where he wins, they fail.

A life filled with complexities is a common consequence for the person who behaves in a vertical manner. For example, he may be dishonest as mentioned previously. His communication is very likely indirect, with hinting qualities about it. He may also speak the typical half-truths and falsehoods. One who is false must always remember his false statements, for, of course, there is the danger that he could be caught in his lies. Such behavior leads to caution, confusion, insecurity, and a life filled with complex transactions with others.

There is also at least one other consequence that those who are vertically oriented must face. To the degree that they relate vertically with each other, they will tend to have cliques and divisions in their families and communities. They will also tend to experience alienation and perhaps bitter feelings of loneliness and anxiety. Fear may encompass them. Feelings of separateness may engulf them as they feel there is no one to whom they can turn. Misery and unhappiness will become their common companions. Apathy may follow as they lose interest in other people. And if they have no interest in others, they will more than likely have little or no interest in life; for without people life is of little value.

My clinical experiences suggest to me that much of so-called psychosomatic illness and what is commonly called mental illness can usually be traced to vertical interpersonal relationships. Many people experiencing such things as headaches, neck aches, stomach problems, fatigue, depression, hallucinations and delusions could be caught up in the whirlwind of a vertical world.

Perhaps the final, ultimate consequence to the person who extensively involves himself in the world of vertical movement is a kind of spiritual death wherein he becomes separated from his fellowman and perhaps even his God. He stands alone and naked, fearful and trembling, and may eventually enter a vacuity that makes him a nonbeing who shuts himself off from human experiences.

PRIMARY INSTITUTIONS

Our primary institutions contribute a good deal to the development of vertical movement among people. Many schools tend to produce hundreds of failures for every few winners. How many people delight in learning after they leave the formal classroom? Too often homes produce similar results. How many look to their families with deep love and affection? Or how many experience intense feelings of frustration and bitterness because of the hurtful experiences they encountered in ruthless competition with their brothers and sisters for favored status and prestige with their mother and father? How many vertically oriented programs are there in religious institutions and service organizations that are so structured that the win-lose philosophy prevails? How much of the inactivity in churches is a result of vertical relationships?

The vertically oriented person has, down through the history of man, been found in religious settings, and is in fact found at present in practically all such settings as well as various religious groups. It is often here that he can be especially effective in his superiority games, for in the religious setting he has available many subtle and powerful techniques. He who is caught up in proving himself more pious, righteous, and moral than his fellows may aspire to a high office from which he can survey and dominate them. He may present a solemn countenance and be eager to express, through facial expressions and tones of voice as well as words, criticism of his brothers. He may even be ever ready to build straw men of hearsay from the utterances of others and then knock them over as he plays the champion of his god or gods. He in effect becomes the good knight who fights imaginary dragons. Of course, the well-adjusted, horizontally oriented person can be of great value in religious settings as he works to help his fellowmen attain a harmonious, full life.

GOALS OF THE VERTICALLY ORIENTED

One meaningful way of achieving greater understanding of vertical behavior is to identify its characteristic goals. Four such goals can be defined as the *A, B, C,* and *D* goals, primary goals of getting *A*ttention, becoming *B*oss, *C*ounterhurting, and appearing *D*isabled.

The following discussion is concerned with a number of rather typical behaviors and descriptive phrases used by those engaging in vertical relationships as they might be classified according to each of the *A, B, C,* and *D* goals. Each goal from *A* to *D* indicates a greater degree of discouragement. Those who are striving for the goal to be boss are often more discouraged by the feeling that they can belong by being cooperative than those who strive to get attention, and those who strive to counterhurt are often more discouraged than those who strive to be boss. In most cases the most discouraged of all are those striving to appear disabled. In this discussion the behaviors and phrases listed are classified according to the goal which indicates the most discouragement. For example, a husband may be trying to boss and also hurt his wife. The goal that most likely indicates the greatest discouragement is goal *C,* to counterhurt, and the husband's behavior would thus be labeled accordingly.

The vertical behaviors that are presented are those used by adolescents and adults as well as by children. Modification has been allowed for each person's particular subculture. For example, a husband may have grown up using tears—water power—to boss others; but since he has become a grown man and the culture puts great pressure on men not to cry, he conforms by screaming and yelling at his family instead. Vertically oriented adolescents and adults generally use the same kinds of behaviors as do most children in order to achieve their goals. The main difference is that they have refined their skills and have become more subtle and covert. *Many adults are, in reality, often still children of yesteryear.*

To label a relationship as being vertically oriented because of one vertical interaction would, of course, be unwise. But when such behavior is exhibited repeatedly and occurs as a pattern, it should be changed.

Anyone who attempts to change this kind of behavior must be aware that *the target of a person's goal can be displaced*. For example, a husband may be hurt by his wife. He may be afraid, however, that if he hurts her, she will hurt him again. Thus he attempts to get even with her by hurting their young son who is less capable of revenge.

GOAL A: GETTING ATTENTION

When an individual's goal is to get the attention of others in a vertical way, he usually competes for that attention, working continually to be noticed. He may be afraid that others will not give him their attention as a free gift and that he has to buy it with his antics. He often will work to draw the focus of others to him rather than to his fellows, feeling the need to be in the spotlight. He may also strive to get loved ones to do things for him which he should be doing for himself.

Some rather typical attention-getting behaviors are listed here. If they occur as a general pattern in an individual's behavior, they are probably vertical attempts to belong. They may be executed with a variety of approaches: humor, charm, complete seriousness, flattery, to name a few.

- See what I've done.
- Get me a drink of water.
- Do you know what happened to me?
- Help me with my coat.
- I can't do it. Help me.
- Only I could have done it so well.
- Turn on the T.V. for me.

- Dressing in clothes that set one apart
- Wearing makeup that sets one apart
- Accumulating and displaying material goods
- Teasing
- Telling shocking stories
- Being indecisive
- Acting helpless
- Talking continually
- Asking questions continually
- Banging pots and pans together

- Eating gruesome concoctions
- Being charming
- Being shy
- Being lazy
- Tattling
- Parading one's accomplishments
- Dawdling
- Entering meetings late
- Eating in a picky manner
- Monopolizing conversation
- Trying to please

GOAL B: BECOMING BOSS

The vertically oriented person whose goal is to boss tends to feel that he is worthwhile and important only to the degree that he has power over other people and can get them to do what he wants. As he achieves this goal, he gets the necessary attention as well, for others tend to focus on him as he strives to boss and to have power over them.

Common bossing behaviors are listed below. Again, if these occur as a general pattern, they are more than likely signs of vertical behavior. As with goal *A,* the variety of approaches is numerous.

- Let me do it for you.
- Speak only when you are spoken to.
- Think before you jump.
- Leave him alone.
- Is that the way I taught you?
- I told you at least ten times to do it.
- Be careful.
- Do it to please me.
- Mother knows best.
- That man is watching you. You'd better shape up.
- If you want my love, you'll . . .
- You make me happy when you do what I say.
- I'm older; therefore . . .
- No allowance until . . .
- None of your lip now.

- Quit complaining.
- Respect your elders.
- You really don't believe that!
- You'd better tell me all about that. I'll find out anyway.

- Arching an eyebrow
- Staring
- Pointing a finger
- Shaking a fist or finger
- Holding one's head high in the air, then marching away
- Curling one's lip
- Baring one's teeth
- Sticking out one's tongue
- Drawing one's head down between one's shoulders
- Hissing
- Pounding one's fist on the furniture
- Sitting apart from another person(s)
- Clicking one's tongue
- Looking at one part of a larger group in a knowing way
- Keeping a rigid posture
- Refusing to notice one's acquaintances
- Looking disinterested
- Averting one's eyes
- Walking away
- Gritting or grinding one's teeth
- Standing on higher ground than another person
- Redoing something done by another person
- Whining
- Crying
- Scaring another person
- Lying
- Pouting
- Building alliances and cliques
- Running the streets
- Structuring for competition
- Quarreling
- Disobeying

- Being stubborn
- Helping dress another who is capable
- Straightening another's clothes
- Picking lint off of another person
- Rearranging another's personal articles
- Deflecting
- Scolding
- Yelling
- Screaming
- Being sickly
- Throwing temper tantrums
- Acting triumphant
- Acting better than another person
- Acting lower than another person
- Acting the *poor me* attitude
- Trying to subdue someone else
- Initiating and/or perpetuating crises
- Admonishing
- Dominating
- Ordering
- Commanding
- Exhorting
- Moralizing
- Preaching
- Advising
- Lecturing
- Analyzing
- Probing
- Rewarding
- Bribing

GOAL C: COUNTERHURTING

The vertically oriented individual who counterhurts does so because he feels that others have hurt him. In his desire to get even with them, he seeks some sort of revenge. And this revenge usually enables him to achieve the vertical goals of getting attention and bossing. These first three goals tend to be summative, for a person's behavior is accumulative. A list of rather typical counterhurting behaviors follows. As with the *A* and *B* goals, the general pattern is to be considered and also the variety of approaches.

- Must you be so stupid?
- Does Ruth dress as sloppy as you?
- Do you want me to hit you?
- You're just plain bad.
- You should be ashamed.
- Grow up.
- You're a dummy.
- You are cheap and no good.
- I hate you.
- You're worthless.
- A child could do that; why can't you?
- Once a thief, always a thief.
- Quit being a baby.
- You're a spoiled brat.
- If you had any brains at all, you would . . .
- You were born to be a failure.
- Why can't you be like . . .
- Don't be a fool.
- You never were any good.
- Everybody looks down on you.
- You're the laughing stock of the whole neighborhood.

- Hitting
- Slapping
- Scratching
- Biting
- Smirking
- Laughing derisively
- Thumbing one's nose at another person
- Looking down one's nose at another person
- Looking another person up and down
- Snickering
- Sneering

- Comparing
- Being disloyal
- Using sarcasm
- Getting revenge
- Emphasizing mistakes and inadequacies
- Punishing
- Rejecting affectionate responses of another person
- Rejecting sexual responses of spouse
- Being sexually promiscuous
- Having extramarital sex
- Stealing
- Becoming sloppy and dirty
- Defecating or urinating in clothes or in bed
- Ignoring another person while flirting or playing up to other people
- Withholding food
- Embarrassing someone in front of other people
- Throwing up mistakes of the past
- Suffering in a martyrlike manner
- Judging
- Criticizing
- Ridiculing
- Shaming
- Spanking
- Beating
- Gouging
- Twisting
- Kicking
- Cutting
- Burning
- Committing suicide
- Committing homicide

GOAL D: APPEARING DISABLED

Usually the most discouraged of the vertically oriented individuals is he whose goal is to get other people to believe he is disabled. He typically is so discouraged and low in self-esteem that he wants others to demand nothing of him, for he believes that any relationship with them will bring him more failure. His way of defending himself is to send out signals which in essence communicate "Leave me alone. I'm a hopeless case." This person should not be confused with the shy or dependent individual whose goal is to get attention. The attention-getter's eyes may dance and sparkle while the disabled person's eyes may show no interest and even be lifeless.

The following are again some of the rather typical behaviors that can help us identify the individual whose goal is to appear disabled. He will also very likely use a variety of approaches.

- Saying nothing
- Withdrawing into the background
- Not working
- Not doing assignments
- Avoiding other people
- Showing no interest
- Appearing apathetic
- Giving up
- Committing suicide

SUMMARY

The vertical model is one way of viewing destructive interpersonal relationships. It is characterized by movement against others and includes striving to appear superior, competing for favored positions, and exhibiting dishonest, greedy, critical, and one-up-manship behaviors. The consequences of vertical movement may include low self-esteem, fear, suspicion of others, stunted growth, cliques and divisions, alienation, loneliness, misery, apathy, and even emotional illness. The home, school, and religious institutions too often become training grounds in vertical relationships and encourage the four goals: to get attention, to boss, to counterhurt, and to appear disabled.

IMPLICATIONS FOR CRAIG AND SHAUNA

In behaving vertically toward Shauna, Craig is being critical of her housekeeping, cooking, driving, money managing, decision making and disciplining methods. He learned some of these behavioral patterns in his original family as he found his place by bossing his younger brothers and sisters and mother. Hence, his goal with Shauna is to boss her and assert his power over her because he feels this is again the way to find his place. He probably also feels that he is not being a good husband unless he is *helping* her by criticizing her efforts and telling her what to do.

Shauna's destructive vertical methods include not telling Craig what she really feels when he bosses her, interferes with her discipline of the baby, or criticizes her. Her refusals to speak to him for two or three days at a time are especially destructive. Her purpose is to punish him and make him hurt as she feels he has hurt her. She, of course, is most likely not conscious of this at first. She also engages him in power contests, for the more he criticizes such things as her housekeeping the worse she performs in this respect. Thus she defeats him in his efforts to improve her.

The consequences of such vertical behavior include Shauna's resentment for Craig, her desire to give up in doing things for herself, her dissatisfaction with life, and her daydreams of another, more pleasant life elsewhere. Shauna also overcompensates for what she perceives as Craig's brutal behavior with their baby by comforting little Craig and demanding almost nothing of him. And as Craig observes what he considers to be her undermining of his authority with his son, he becomes more harsh and demanding than he otherwise would be.

Craig and Shauna have become caught up in an ever spiraling destructive relationship in which each one's response seems to trigger even more destructive vertical interpersonal behavior from the other. These patterns must be broken if they are to achieve greater happiness and rear their son to have a secure, productive, and happy life. Learning and applying horizontal behavior in their relationships with each other can enable them to achieve this greater satisfaction.

REFERENCES

Allred, G. Hugh
　　1968　　Mission for Mother: Guiding the Child. Salt Lake City: Bookcraft.

Brosnan, Jim
　　1971　　"What we're losing by our craze for winning." Today's Health (May): 17-19.

Davidson, Henry A., et al.
　　1960　　"Should Johnny compete or cooperate?" NEA Journal 49 (October): 30-32.

Dreikurs, Rudolf, et al.
1971   Maintaining Sanity in the Classroom. New York: Harper and Row.

Haines, Donald Bruce, and W. J. McKeachie
1967   "Cooperative versus competitive discussion methods in teaching intro-
ductory psychology." Journal of Educational Psychology 58 (6) (December):386-390.

Holt, John
1966   "The fourth r—the rat race." The New York Times Magazine (May 1):
146-151.

Kennedy, John L.
1971   "Simulation study of competition in an 'open world.'" Journal of Applied Psychology 55 (1):42-45.

Kogan, Mathan, and Julia Carson
1969   "Difficulty of problems attempted under conditions of competition and
group consensus." Journal of Educational Psychology 60 (3):158-167.

Madsen, Clifford K., and Charles H. Madsen, Jr.
1972   Parents Children Discipline. Boston: Allyn and Bacon.

Maslow, Abraham H.
1971   The Farther Reaches of Human Nature. New York: The Viking Press.

Nelson, Janice D., et al.
1969   "Children's aggression following competition and exposure to an aggressive model." Child Development (December):1085-1097.

Reed, William F.
1972   "An ugly affair in Minneapolis." Sports Illustrated (February 7):18-21.

Sage, George H.
1968   "Team morale and the problem of intra-squad competition." Athletic
Journal 49 (November):44-45, 61.

Schollander, Donald A., and Michael D. Savage
1971   Deep Water. New York: Crown Publishers.

Sicher, Lydia
1955   "Education for freedom." The American Journal of Individual Psychology 11 (2).

Smith, Judith M., and Donald E. P. Smith
1966   Child Management: A Program for Parents. Ann Arbor, Michigan:
Ann Arbor Publishers.

"The fanatics"
1970   Newsweek (May 4):67-68

Weinberg, Carl
1965   "The price of competition." Teachers College Record (November):
108-114.

3
HORIZONTAL INTERACTION

Peace and true friendship with loved ones and neighbors can be realized through the horizontal approach, for it is a type of interaction that enables us to relate cooperatively with other people.

The horizontal, or level, plane in the figure below suggests that all men are equal in their rights to progress and develop unhindered by any type of vertical interaction. The plane itself is an infinite one with no end to either side. Hence, there is a respectable place for each individual within his groups. He is not pushed down and away or treated as inferior because of his name, sex, occupation, race, nationality, or economic status. Each person belongs to his various family, neighborhood, church, and national groups without attempting to make his fellowman less a person than he makes himself. His place is not dependent on making others feel that they do not belong.

The attitude of touching in the figure represents the concept that each of us is partly responsible for the well-being of his fellowmen. A

Characteristics of Horizontal Movement

man must of course be responsible for his own behavior first; but if he cares about another person's happiness, he usually feels concern for the way he can and does influence him. Most people feel the need to receive and give cheerful encouragement to each other so that they can work together, progress, and develop. The movement of those functioning in this horizontal manner is with and toward their fellows. They experience a feeling of togetherness and are aware that whatever happens often influences all people around them and possibly many others. Their stance is one of cooperation and concern for the welfare of all people.

The horizontally functioning individual measures his own progress and development over time in relation to fixed standards which he has come to understand and accept, either consciously or unconsciously. He does not allow himself to become bogged down in the fruitless, neurotic, and confusion-breeding attempts to base his judgment or measure his progression on the basis of how well he performs in relation to other people. He realizes that to do so would either lull him into a false sense of security or else so discourage him that he would tend to give up. He is very much aware that he would be subjected to a distorted measurement which would hinder his real personal development.

The horizontal attitude allows the individual to consciously choose the direction he wishes to follow, his objectives, and his friends without worrying about what others may be doing or thinking. He is able to base these decisions on his interests and what he believes to be right and good rather than on how what he does affects his popularity with others. He is also tolerant of the rights of others to make decisions for themselves, as long as these decisions do not cause harm for other people. He allows a wide latitude for idiosyncratic behavior that is not harmful.

An additional characteristic of people who function horizontally is their mutual respect for one another. Their relationships are free from demeaning critical comments. Each is secure in his belonging and is therefore free to risk learning new ideas. He progresses quickly for he is freed from fear of failure. Failure means only a momentary setback or a new attempt at the solution of a problem, not the loss of respect and affection of loved ones. Love is not tied to success or failure; it is ever present.

In the horizontal relationship, love and affection tend to be expressed freely, with little reserve, for there is no fear of rejection. Trust in one another encompasses those relating horizontally. They tend to be open and spontaneous in their responses and exhibit a zest for living. Though the horizontal society is a rather ideal one and though very few if any groups function horizontally all of the time, an awareness of and a knowledge of this kind of interaction enables an individual to move meaningfully and successfully in the horizontal direction.

Horizontal movement is not to be confused with sameness. Each individual in a horizontally relating group can develop his own interests and unique abilities or areas of expertise, and others may look to him as a resource person who can supply needed information and skills. He therefore becomes a knowledgeable, competent person in a particular area or areas. He offers his ideas for consideration and volunteers his skills. He never imposes them. In a vertically oriented group, the person with expertise tends toward authoritarianism, to impose his ideas. And anyone who rejects his expertise is often made to look stupid or naive by this expert.

In the society moving in a horizontal direction each individual's contribution is respected for what it is. The teacher, for example, is respected because without him society would move toward ignorance and eventual oblivion if the education of youth became severely restricted. The policeman is respected because without him no one would be safe. The medical doctor is respected because he enables society's members to achieve a high level of health. And the garbage man is respected because without him society would find itself deep in its own rubbish. Each is equally respected because society depends on each for a healthy, secure existence. The teacher as he fights ignorance and the policeman as he fights crime prevent disintegration of civilization, while the garbage collector and the medical doctor as they fight disease in their unique ways, prevent epidemics that could wipe out much of civilization as we know it. Each is necessary for the survival of civilization. As people are not accepted on the basis of name, sex, nationality, race, or creed but on their basic character and behavior in the society that is moving in a horizontal direction, so its members respect a man because he does his job well, whatever it is, not because he follows a prestigious occupation or profession. The conscientious carpenter merits and receives respect equal to that accorded the conscientious medical doctor or lawyer.

CONSEQUENCES OF HORIZONTAL MOVEMENT

The consequences of both vertical and horizontal movement tend to be somewhat predictable. Life is often simplified for those who move horizontally with others. Because they are open and honest with their fellows, their social transactions are usually clear and simple, and they escape many of the complexities brought about by the practices of those who relate vertically.

As they function in a horizontal manner with one another, people feel secure in belonging with their fellowmen and thus are free to make the maximum and most efficient use of their individual uniquenesses. They progress rapidly in increased love for one another. They have great faith and trust in each other. Not only do they do these things in an efficient manner, but they tend to do them with a zest, spontaneity, and joy that make them attractive people.

It seems fairly safe then to say that mankind as a whole will find harmony, peace, and happiness when all people relate to each other in a horizontal manner. In this way only will all men become equal.

SUMMARY

The horizontal model is one way of viewing constructive interpersonal relationships. It is characterized by limitless opportunity for each person to progress as rapidly as he chooses and his abilities allow. The horizontal society has room for all as each has a place of respect among the others. Also, each person assumes responsibility for his own behavior and its possible influences on his fellows. The horizontally oriented individual measures his progress against his own previous performance or basic standards of personal excellence. He also gives equal respect to all occupations and professions, as long as they are not harmful. He judges a person on the basis of how well he does his job, not on the status and prestige it brings.

The consequences of horizontal movement with others tend to be simplified social transactions, feelings of security, rapid growth and development, harmony, peace, zest for living, and concern for other people.

In reality, few if any real-life situations are completely vertical or horizontal. Most have elements of both. It is important, however, that the people involved clearly discern the vertical and horizontal elements in a situation if it is to be improved. They can then actively work to decrease the number of vertical elements and increase the number of horizontal elements to bring about desired harmonious consequences.

When you first become aware of how you relate to other people and the implications of this behavior, you may feel happy and successful or frustrated, discouraged, angry, and even depressed. This is probably a healthy sign, for it may be indicative of your having gained greater insight into the strengths and weaknesses of your relationships. You more than likely realize that your relationships could be better and that you want to improve them. You might even discover that you feel a good deal of anger toward your parents because you wish they had not allowed you to grow up with certain behavior patterns that limit, at present, your ability to relate more successfully with your spouse, your children, or your friends and neighbors. Most parents of course have had to wrestle with the particular traditions and patterns that were passed on to them by their parents as they attempted to help their children grow into happy, responsible people.

It seems then that negative patterns of behavior can be overcome and replaced with positive ones in a horizontal manner when people work together with a large element of forgiveness and the ability to even laugh at themselves in a healthy, positive way. It is wise to focus on strengths as you work to change only one or two weaknesses at any one given time. Your success with overcoming these will bring about habitual positive patterns and result in greater motivation to change other behaviors. The first attempts are usually the most difficult, but an optimistic attitude combined with success will reassure you that you can relate more satisfactorily with other people and at the same time be helpful to your spouse, your children, your parents, and your friends as they try to change their behavior for the better.

IMPLICATIONS FOR CRAIG AND SHAUNA

Shauna and Craig can strengthen their marriage and their relationships with their son by becoming aware that their vertical relationships are destructive, deciding to replace them with constructive interaction, and consistently learning to think and behave more horizontally. For example, Craig will improve their interaction a good deal if he reassures and encourages Shauna as she makes her own decisions, cleans house, cooks, and disciplines Craig Jr. He will then more than likely realize that criticizing her in a patronizing way is no help at all, but rather a barrier to horizontal interaction. When Shauna wrings her hands, looks at him expectantly, or delays making a decision in order to pressure Craig into making it for her, he will be of more help to her, himself, and their relationship by being firm with himself so that he will not give in to the pressure to decide for her what is rightfully hers to decide. He will find a worthwhile place as her comrade rather than as her critic. By shopping in the hardware department of a store while Shauna is shopping in the women's department, Craig can prevent himself from deciding what she should buy when he finds himself slipping back into his old behavior. When Shauna is disciplining Craig Jr., Craig can walk into another room if he feels that he is getting ready to criticize her. Shauna can also do the same thing when she disapproves of Craig's behavior with their son and she finds herself wanting to intervene. Of course the ideal situation is for them to eventually come to some agreement on discipline methods. During this time of change, it is very important for Craig and Shauna to explain to their son that they will be acting differently toward each other for a while in an attempt to make a better home for all of them. He may be confused for a while, but he will come to like the change. The types of behavior discussed are usually necessary while Shauna and Craig work together to reach an agreement. Such respectful horizontal movement tends to free them from negative emotions toward one another so that understanding and agreement become possible.

Words spoken sincerely—such as "That's a neat handbag you bought"; "You really work hard"; "You really try hard"; "I love you very much"—can do much to encourage Shauna to attack life's problems with gusto. And thoughtful, spontaneous, warm interaction, such as Craig's putting his arm around Shauna, kissing her, and holding her close can do much to help her feel loved and wanted.

Shauna can learn to relate in a horizontal manner with Craig by communicating honestly and directly with him. As she learns to give him corrective feedback when he forgets himself and criticizes her, she will most likely find that she has less need to punish him. She will also have to work at being courageous in making her own decisions and refusing to manipulate Craig to make those decisions for her that she should be making for herself.

In order to let Craig know how he makes her feel when he criticizes and bosses her or is harsh with their son, Shauna might say something like this: "Craig, I love you very much, but when you criticize me with that superior tone and that fatherly look, as you have just done, I get resentful and it makes me feel far removed from you. Please stop it. I want to feel close to you." When she catches herself trying to manipulate him to make personal decisions for her, she might say: "I just now realized that I am trying to force you to make the decision for me. I was getting scared that you would not approve, and I slipped. Please don't give in to my pressures to get you to tell me which coat to buy."

As Craig and Shauna practice behaviors such as those specified above, they will tend to experience a greater degree of harmony, peace, and happiness in their relationships with each other and with their son.

REFERENCES

Adler, Alfred
    1964   Social Interest: A Challenge to Mankind. New York: Capricorn Books.

Allred, G. Hugh
    1968   Mission for Mother: Guiding the Child. Salt Lake City: Bookcraft.

Ansbacher, Heinz L., and Rowena R. Ansbacher
    1956   The Individual Psychology of Alfred Adler. New York: Basic Books.

Maslow, Abraham H.
    1971   The Farther Reaches of Human Nature. New York: The Viking Press.
    1962   Toward a Psychology of Being. New York: D. Van Nostrand Co.

Sicher, Lydia
    1955   "Education for freedom." The American Journal of Individual Psychology 11(2).

TWO

ON UNDERSTANDING PEOPLE

4

PREREQUISITES
FOR UNDERSTANDING
PEOPLE

The ancient mariner steered his ship safely home by the light of familiar stars because he was committed to a definite direction and course. Likewise, he who would diminish the number of vertical elements and increase the number of horizontal elements in his interpersonal relationships must be committed to understanding and using powerful principles of human behavior and learning as vehicles to help him relate harmoniously with his fellowmen. These principles, when wisely applied to the task of improving relationships with other people, can help us achieve a greater degree of equality and oneness and the subsequent harmony, serenity, and happiness that are its concomitants. The purpose of this chapter is to identify and describe these principles.

PRINCIPLES OF HUMAN BEHAVIOR

AGENCY

Each individual is his own agent. In other words, he has the *creative power* to make choices that enable him to behave horizontally rather than vertically in most if not every situation in which he finds himself. He has the potential to make the most of each situation by choosing to behave horizontally, provided he has the desire and courage to make such choices. He need not be at the mercy of past or ongoing vertical experiences, or the feeling that behavior is but a result of heredity.

The principle of agency has far-reaching implications for interpersonal relationships. It includes the concept that each of us has the creative power to change himself, to influence those about him, and to be influenced by them. It is impossible for a person to exert no influence, nor is it possible for him to remain uninfluenced. This is indicated in the following figure, which graphically presents the creative power of the individual. The arrows in the figure represent the in-

The Child/Adult In His Environment: All Influence and Are Influenced

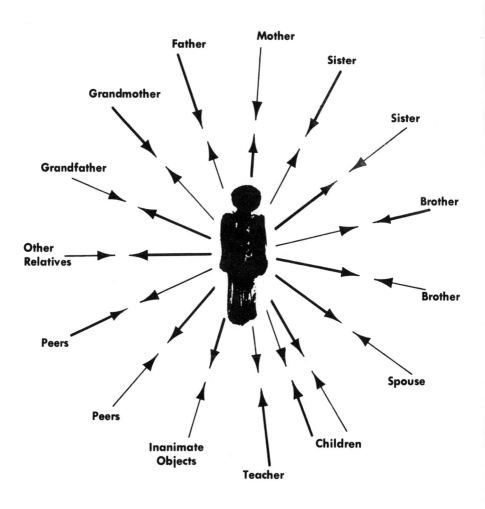

fluences or manipulations going on in the life space (area within which he can influence and is influenced) of the individual. The boldface arrows represent the lines of greatest influence at a particular time in the individual's life.

The pattern may vary depending on the individual and others in his life space, as well as on time and place. The figure suggests that there are times when the individual, whether he is a child or an adult, may be more influential in modifying others' behaviors than they are his, due to his creative power. Also, the concept of agency suggests that the individual's behavior will be fluid and dynamic and not totally predictable. The implication of regarding the growing individual as having creative power is that parents, teachers, and other influential figures will have to be continually on their toes if they are to help him acquire those behaviors that will enable him to be a happy, productive human being.

Questions that can help us understand ourselves and others relative to the principle of agency are numerous. The following list includes some of the more general ones:

- Do I believe I can make changes in my present situation?
- Do I have the desire to take the responsibility for making choices and acting upon them?
- Do I allow others to influence me to the detriment of my progression and theirs? How?
- Do I influence others for good? How?

PURPOSE

A second principle basic to human behavior is *purpose*. Behavior, whether it be conscious or semiconscious, has purpose. Each of us behaves with the desire to achieve certain goals. Some of these goals are naturally more essential to life and well-being than others. The following schematic drawing, based on the works of Alfred Adler and Abraham Maslow, suggests that the individual works to achieve his general goals in a somewhat hierarchical manner. He seeks to satisfy his physiological goals before he makes much of an attempt to achieve his safety goals (such as a predictable, familiar world free of harm from others, and protection from extremes in temperature). Furthermore, he

General Goals of the Individual

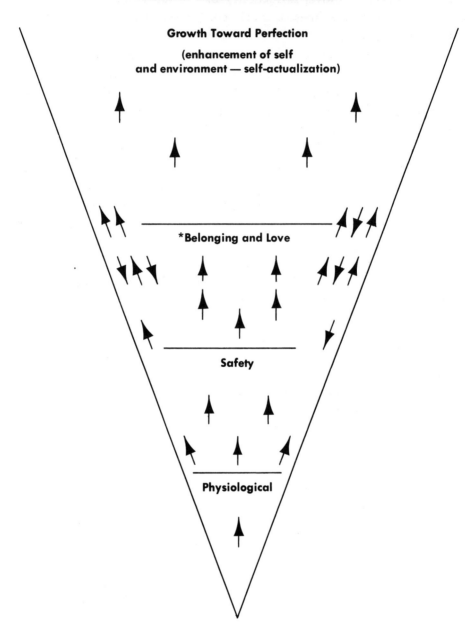

Growth Toward Perfection

(enhancement of self
and environment — self-actualization)

*Belonging and Love

Safety

Physiological

*The primary focus of most people, especially of those experiencing difficulties.

tends to satisfy his safety goals before he expends much energy on his goals to belong, to love, and to be loved.

As he turns his attention to these latter goals, he strives with great intensity to achieve a place with those who are of significant value to him. He desires more than anything else to achieve this goal at this time. He may even forget the times he was hungry and/or afraid and felt that loving, being loved, and belonging were not too important. It seems that the goal to belong is the goal for which most of us are still striving. Most children as well as adults in difficulty are probably thwarted in their quest for self-actualization and perfection by their inability to satisfy this central goal. It is the responsibility of everyone—and part of the process of becoming a loving human being —to relate to each other in such a manner that each person feels he is accepted and loved and has a secure, positive place among those with whom he lives, works, and plays.

The drawing also suggests that an individual will achieve, to some degree, all of the lower order goals before he concentrates his efforts on striving for perfection, which includes his desire for enhancement of self and environment. This may include the pursuit of such aesthetic qualities as beauty, order, closure, systematic approaches, structure, and symmetry. Moreover, the individual strives to create, to discover or arrange new relationships from among known elements. This implies that the poet will write new poetry, the musician will compose or perform music in new ways, and the artist will paint with new techniques. As each produces poems, songs, or pictures, he becomes more completely in that particular area what he is capable of becoming. Thus, the individual enlarges himself. This is indicated in the drawing by the ever-expanding outside lines, which are funnel-shaped with the top area becoming infinite in its dimensions.

The goal of perfection is not to be confused with the neurotic goal of becoming perfect now. We perceive the neurotic as intolerant of himself and others. He compares himself with others and evaluates his progress as never good enough. He is the opposite of the healthy, fully functioning individual.

The movements of the individual from goal to goal do not necessarily occur in a systematic upward fashion. As indicated by the arrows, there is usually movement back and forth from goal to goal, depending on the time and place. However, the progressing individual will grow generally in the direction of perfection, becoming less and less concerned with lower level goals as he is able to achieve them.

A concept of critical importance to those who would diminish vertical behavior and increase horizontal elements in relationships is that of *payoff*. Whenever someone achieves a particular goal, he achieves payoff. This encourages repetition of the behavior that led to achieving that goal when the same goal is desired again. This behavioral pattern is exemplified by the child who cries when he wants a piece of candy. When someone gives him candy at such times he achieves payoff, which increases his tendency to cry whenever he wants candy again. The purpose or goal of any particular behavior is to achieve payoff.

When horizontal, constructive, and cooperative behavior leads to payoff there is a tendency for that horizontal behavior to be repeated whenever the same goal is desired again. Conversely, when vertical, destructive, and competitive behavior leads to payoff there is a tendency for that behavior to be repeated when the same goal is sought again.

The chart on page 43 shows the four goals of vertical behavior as discussed in Chapter 2, with suggestions for how the individual may be encouraged to relate more horizontally.

If we believe that our behavior influences others, then it is important that we understand the chart so that we can apply its concepts and hence behave responsibly in our relationships. We help other people achieve their goals when they behave horizontally by giving them positive payoff. On the other hand, we also help them by not giving payoff when they behave vertically. When we work to pay off the horizontal behavior of others and to withdraw payoff when they behave vertically, we become responsible in our relations with them.

Studying the chart carefully and reading the many cases in parts 3, 4, and 5 will help you understand and use the concept of payoff as you work for harmonious interaction with other people.

Questions that can help you understand the principle of payoff are listed here:

- Do I attempt to achieve my goals with others by using vertical behavior? Do I cry, pout, punish with silence, or scream and yell?

A Guide for Responding to the Individual When He Behaves Vertically*

Vertical Goals: A,B,C,D→	To Get Attention	To Be Boss	To Counterhurt	To Appear Disabled
Typical Vertical Behaviors →	Individual may pull faces, talk long and loud, tattle, tell shocking stories, continually ask questions, not be able to hear others, leave things around for others to pick up, kick and poke others.	Individual may scream, yell, shout, throw self on floor, throw objects, criticize, whine, cry, display stubbornness, disobey, act superior.	Individual may destroy property, strike others, steal, say such things as: "You're stupid," "You're no good," or "I hate you."	Individual doesn't participate, doesn't answer questions, avoids looking at others, keeps eyes downcast, is alone most of the time.
Evidence for Determining Goals of Vertically Behaving Person (tends to pay off vertical behavior) →	Others give individual undue attention and/or service. Others are annoyed and irritated and often express this in words such as: "You take so much of our time."	Others fight individual for control, to be boss, and feel angry, often expressing themselves in words such as: "You can't get away with that." They may also feel sorry for him or even pity him.	Others feel hurt by individual and want to hurt him back; they may think, "I'll get even with you." Others may also feel guilty.	Others leave him alone, feel hopeless, don't expect anything of him, and often think, "I don't know what to do."
Behavior That Will Tend to Stop/Diminish Vertical Behavior →	Ignore individual at this time, say nothing, and do nothing. Control facial expression, tone of voice, and body movements that would indicate he has achieved his goal. When he demands service, say, "You can do it yourself," then focus on others.	Refuse to engage in power contest with him and say, "You could be right." Continue whatever you are doing, focus on others, keep cool, walk into another room. Refuse to feel pity for him.	Refuse to engage in battle of retaliation with him. Show no hurt or guilt in words, tone of voice, facial expression, body movement, or any other way. Say calmly such things as: "It may be so," and focus on others.	Refuse to give up in the relationship and keep encouraging him.
Encouragement of Horizontal Behavior →	Have positive experiences with him when he is not demanding vertical involvement, not trying to defeat or hurt you. Relate to him in a warm, accepting manner (e.g., smile at him, put your hand on his shoulder, invite him to participate). Initiate positive relationships when he is behaving horizontally.			Set your expectations so that the individual can have many success experiences and learn that effort is valuable in and of itself. Concentrate on having a warm, friendly, nonthreatening relationship with him.

*Based on a design developed by Rudolf Dreikurs. Revised by G. Hugh Allred.

- What is he (the other person) getting out of his . . . (state the behavior, e.g., crying)?
- What do I do when he is . . . (again state the behavior, e.g., constantly sad, complaining)?
- Do I pay off his inappropriate behavior and thereby influence him in an irresponsible way? How?
- Do I pay off his constructive, appropriate horizontal behavior and thereby influence him in a responsible manner? How do I encourage him as he attempts to relate horizontally?

COMMUNICATION

Communication is the vehicle through which man achieves his purposes. The definition of *communication* here includes all of the verbal and nonverbal signs we make to achieve these purposes. These signs include words, tone of voice, facial expressions, body stance, and physical distance. Most emotional and most significant interpersonal communication seem to occur at the nonverbal level. For example, we have the greatest impact on others, and they on us, through such things as a friendly or sarcastic tone of voice, a smile or frown, and physical proximity (see Chapters 5 and 6).

Here are a few questions which can help you reach a better understanding of the results of certain behaviors:

- What am I saying with my words?
- What am I saying with my eyes, tone of voice, and body posture?
- Are my words and body signs saying the same thing?
- If they are not saying the same thing, why? (What is the real message I wish to communicate?)
- Am I responding to the other person's words or to his nonverbal signs?

SOCIAL LINKAGE

All men are *socially linked*. Important questions surrounding our behavior appear to be in the final analysis social questions. In some way or other they have to do with man's humanity or his inhumanity to his own kind. We are as mountain climbers roped together on a perilous climb. He who is roped to his comrade cannot do anything that does not affect his comrade, nor can his comrade do anything that does not affect him. As it is in mountain climbing, so it is in life.

There is a great implication in this principle, however, that can help us relate horizontally. We can increase our overall understanding of an individual to the extent that we understand his movement, his purposes among his fellows, and their purposes with him. In order to do so, we need to know something about an individual's order of birth, the atmosphere of his family of origin, what people significant to him may expect of him, and how he learned to achieve his goals with them.

Relevant questions to help us understand this concept of social linkage include:

- Do I consider myself responsible for the way in which I link myself to others?
- How do I influence others in a responsible horizontal manner?
- Do I attempt to truly understand another person by observing how he is linked to others and how these social links influence him to behave either vertically or horizontally?

BELONGING

The general, basic striving of the individual appears to be *to have a place—to belong*—with those who are significant to him (see Purpose above). One who feels he does not belong to those important to him may suffer great anxiety and pain and spend all of his energy and time attempting to gain a place. Many find their place with other people by being cooperative and by being helpful to them; but there are others who, in discouragement, feel they cannot find a satisfactory place in this manner and are content only with such things as notoriety or infamy—vertical ways of belonging.

Too often we as family and community members respond to the discouraged person by not paying off his horizontal efforts. Instead we attend to and pay off his vertical behavior. Parents, teachers, and other people who are in positions of influence have a particular responsibility to actively work at paying off horizontal efforts. To the degree that this is not done, and payoff is given for vertical, uncooperative efforts to belong, we exhibit a lack of concern for the welfare of the person who needs help.

On the other hand, when we have a loved one who relates vertically, it is often helpful to remember that such behaviors may be his misguided attempts to belong. We may be very important to him even though he may embarrass or hurt us. If we were unimportant to him, he would very likely not spend his energy relating to us.

Some questions that can help us achieve an understanding of this principle are listed here:

- Do I recognize and pay off the cooperative efforts to belong of each family member? How?
- Do I approach my spouse and each of my children several times a day when they are moving horizontally and give my love as a free gift through words and touch?
- Do I act responsibly toward my fellowmen by not attending to—not paying off—their unconstructive and uncooperative vertical efforts to belong?
- Do I recognize and pay off the constructive efforts of my fellowmen? How?

HIGH SELF-ESTEEM

Closely related to the principle of belonging is the principle of *high self-esteem,* a principle which is essential to an individual if he is to have the self-confidence and courage necessary to attack life's problems with zest. It provides him the greatest motivation for development and progression. He must take risks as he makes choices which he hopes will help him find a full life. High self-esteem with its concomitants of self-confidence and courage enable him to take these risks and to progress at a healthy rate. He has little fear of making mistakes, for he knows love from those significant to him will not be diminished if he should err for a time.

High self-esteem is also an essential ingredient for happiness and love. If an individual does not have a high level of self-esteem, he may find it difficult to like himself or other people. Without love of self and love of others one cannot really experience actual happiness.

Questions which can help us apply the principle of self-esteem include the following:

- How can I improve my own self-esteem? Do my behaviors match my basic beliefs and values? Do I associate with other people who like themselves and stimulate me to like myself?
- Do I pace myself so that I experience success in most things I try? Do I encourage my children to do the same?
- Do I communicate to my children and spouse the high esteem I have for them? How?
- What words do I use to describe my spouse and children? Do my words stimulate them to think well of themselves?
- What words do my children use to describe themselves?
- Do they attack life's problems with zest?

COMMUNAL INTEREST

At the very core of the horizontal attitude is *communal interest*. Without this interest, an individual lacks the desire and ability to be concerned about the welfare of his fellows and to behave cooperatively with them. Every individual is born with the innate potential to work harmoniously with his fellowmen. But this potential must be carefully nurtured. He is also born with the innate potential for cooperation, but he must learn the skills for cooperation and effective, horizontal living with others in order to develop fully.

It is possible that communal interest is a critical element lacking in the lives of neurotics, psychopaths, perverts, and criminals. They do not appear to be interested in the welfare of their fellows nor do they appear to have developed interpersonal skills for cooperative living. We see then that man also has the potential to learn to be interested in his fellows in order to achieve his own selfish purposes and to move competitively against them, the essence of vertical movement. Those who would teach the individual to move horizontally must take care that they do not teach him to move vertically.

It may be said that our concern for the welfare of others and our belonging to their groups offer the ultimate meanings in life, those things that make life worthwhile.

Questions which can lead you to a better understanding of communal interest include the following:

- Do I like people in general?

- Do I strive to understand others?
- Can I walk in their shoes?
- Do I emphasize cooperation and deemphasize competion in my relations with others?
- Do I cooperate or compete with my spouse?
- Am I training my children to develop cooperative rather than competitive interpersonal skills?

LIFE-STYLE

A man's *life-style* is formed by the guidelines which he creates for himself and by the patterns of responding which he develops. The infant first seems to learn randomly by trial and error, but soon creates certain beliefs, attitudes, and principles for living that guide his future actions. Thus, the basic life-style of an individual may be formed during infancy, probably before age three.

The guidelines that he creates may be quite logical or illogical depending on his own unique, subjective view of life. Whatever the case, he acts as if they are true and tends to make them come true, thus fulfilling his own prophecy. For example, the person who believes himself unable to speak in public will consciously or semiconsciously manipulate his environment to avoid it. He will as a result not practice this skill, will say to himself: "I am the kind who cannot talk in public," and will make this belief come true. Conversely the person who believes himself capable of public speaking will search for opportunities to do so. His skill will improve with practice and he will say to himself, "Yes, I am the kind who can do it." As a result, it will come true.

Birth order (position in the family), age and sex differences or sex similarities among siblings, parental expectations, and the emotional climate in the family all appear to influence the development of an individual's life-style. It is often found that the eldest in a family will tend to be rule-, authority-, and past-oriented, protective of and too responsible for others, conservative, bossy, nosy, a high achiever, and dependable. He may also be intolerant of himself and others. When parental expectations are perceived as too high to be attainable, the eldest may rebel by adopting values and behaviors completely contrary to his parents'. The second or middle child tends to be quite different from the eldest. This is especially true in a competitive family atmosphere where birth order takes on added significance. He will often be very active, rebellious, subtle, liberally oriented, a martyr, and creative. He is the one parents seem usually most concerned with when they come for family counseling. The youngest child is often spoiled as a result of excessive parental and sibling pampering. He may be considered cute and therefore be able to manipulate service from others through his charm.

The only child may be in an extremely disadvantageous position if his parents pamper, indulge, and overcaution him about life's problems and dangers. He may develop a life-style of pessimism, timidity, low self-esteem, and low competence. However, when wise parents stimulate the only child to a high level of independence and courage, they may rear a child who becomes highly competent, experiences success, and thinks well of himself and others.

The only boy in a family of girls may become feminine as he models after his sisters or very masculine as he struggles hard to achieve a masculine identity. His chances of being masculine appear to be greater if he is the eldest, less if he has many older sisters. The only girl in a family of boys may have problems similar to the only boy in a family of girls as she becomes submerged in a world of masculinity, or she may struggle to achieve femininity and overcompensate, thereby becoming extremely feminine. A girl reared in an all-girl family might view boys as strangers and may feel uncomfortable around them. Similarly, a boy from a family where all of his siblings are boys may grow up viewing girls as foreign objects to be avoided, and he may not develop the understanding and skills necessary to get along well with them.

Twins may respond extremely competitively in the competitive family. One may become highly aggressive and dominant while the other becomes passive and submissive to the point of giving up his identity to the other. Foster children may develop great manipulative skills in bossing others and getting service from them when parents, feeling sorrow and pity, pay off their disturbing, demanding behavior. The handicapped child often appears to develop a life-style similar to that of the foster child.

The impact of birth order and special conditions (e.g., being handicapped) appear to be kaleidoscopic, depending in part on parental expectations, sex, ages and number of siblings, and the emotional climate in the family. It is in the vertical, highly competitive family that birth order appears to take on added significance as children often enter the game of power politics in order to achieve preferred places with their parents.

Wise parents will refuse to pay off the power plays of a child who attempts to appear better than others in the family. Instead, they will work consistently to pay off his constructive endeavors and tend to rear an eldest child who is reasonably responsible and productive, a second child who is constructively creative, a youngest child who develops great skills in constructively working with groups of people, and a handicapped child who develops great courage, optimism, and high self-esteem and becomes effective in stimulating others to greater courage. In other words, effective parenting tends to stimulate the child to take advantage of his unique situation to develop a positive and constructive life-style. Of course, no two eldest children who are raised in horizontally oriented homes will be exactly the same.

The situation in which the growing individual finds himself, with all of its vicissitudes and opportunities, is generally not nearly as important as how he learns to successfully overcome the vicissitudes and take advantage of the opportunities.

Questions that can help us come to a better understanding of life-style include the following:

- Do I believe people are basically good?
- Do I view people in general as friends or enemies?
- Do I see myself as a worthwhile person?
- Do I view myself as a person who can learn to do almost anything with practice?
- Do I feel that I can succeed only if I push others down, or do I feel that I can succeed by responding horizontally?
- How does my birth order affect my attitudes and behavior?
- What am I doing to rear my children to have a logical, courageous, and optimistic life style?

WHOLENESS

The individual should be viewed with a *holistic* approach—as a whole person who functions within his total environment. All aspects of an individual and all significant aspects of his environment appear to be related and to interact in a continuing dynamic manner. Each of us functions within a system of self and within a system of interacting others. We are all part of a cosmos of influencing interactions. It is by viewing a person we wish to understand in his entirety, functioning within a system of complex interbalancing relationships of people and things, that we come closest to a real understanding of him.

Answering the following questions may help us achieve greater understanding and appreciation for the totality and complexity of the interacting and interbalancing situation of man in his cosmos. You may find it helpful, as well as interesting, to select people you wish to understand better and then apply the questions to them as they seem appropriate.

- How does his behavior influence his attitudes toward man's place in the universe?
- How does his lack of knowledge influence his behavior toward educational institutions?
- How does his poverty affect his chances for acquiring a good formal education?
- How does his social and economic status affect my attitude toward him? How does it affect his attitude toward me?
- How do his own feelings of insecurity affect his behavior?
- How does his birth order affect his attitude toward authority figures?
- How do my responses to my child's tattling affect him and other members of the family?
- What does it do to my children's relationships with each other when I settle their quarrels? What does it do to my relations with them?
- What does it do to my relationships with my fellowman when I disagree unkindly with him in public? What does it do to his relationships with the others who are present? What does it do to my relationships with them?
- What does it do to my children's attitudes toward leaders when I habitually criticize them? What does it do to their attitude toward public institutions? What does it do to their feelings for me? How does it affect their feelings toward themselves?

- How am I contributing to the achievement of a better life for generations which follow me?
- How am I affecting the human and material ecology of the earth?

PRINCIPLES OF LEARNING

In the previous section, nine principles of human behavior have been discussed. This section is concerned with several powerful principles of learning that are vital to those who desire to eliminate vertical elements and increase the horizontal elements in their relationships with others. By using such principles, they should find that behavior can be efficiently changed.

BONDING

Whenever two events occur simultaneously, there is a tendency for the individual to connect the two, a process called *bonding*. For example, when a teacher punishes a child in school by embarrassing him, speaking harshly to him, and/or spanking him, the child will generally feel angry, revengeful, sad, and/or humiliated. He will tend, to the extent these experiences recur, to get these same feelings whenever he attends school or thinks about it or anything associated with it.

In contrast, the child who experiences many loving touches and friendly words when he is in school tends to feel joy and contentment. For him these feelings become bonded to school itself, his lessons, teachers, and classmates. His feelings for school will tend to be warm and friendly.

The following questions can help us better understand the principle of bonding:

- How does discipline at school or church affect my children's attitudes toward these institutions?
- How does my behavior with my spouse while we are in public affect his/her attitude toward being in public with me?
- How do my relationships with my children during family get-togethers affect their attitude toward these occasions?
- How do my discipline techniques affect my children's feelings toward me?
- How does my behavior with ———— affect his/her attitude to-

ward the neighborhood? (Insert here the name of a recent new arrival, widow, someone not of your own age group or race, someone with whom you are having difficulty.)

PAYOFF

When we achieve any particular goal, we attain our objective and thus receive *payoff* for our efforts. We tend to repeat again those behaviors which we believe have helped us achieve our goals. When we achieve our goals, we retain the behavior that preceded and resulted in the payoff.

For example, an individual who, when he gets stomachaches, is able to get much love and concern and at the same time get out of his chores around the house, will sometimes tend to get stomachaches whenever he wants the attention of others or wants to get out of his responsibilities. In contrast, the individual who does his chores and then receives recognition for his helpful contribution to the welfare of the family will enjoy doing his chores. The assumption here, of course, is that the principle of bonding is taking place while he is in the process of doing his work.

Questions that can aid us in understanding the principle of payoff include:

- How do I respond to my children when they misbehave?
- How do I respond to them when they are being peaceful or cooperative? Do I attend to them then or am I too busy doing other things?
- How do I handle my martyr daughter, who is always complaining and finding fault? Do I attend to her at such times or do I ignore her then and attend to her when she is being optimistic and courageous?

MODELING

People tend to repeat those behaviors they see in other people, especially when these people are of significant value to them. For instance, if a person wants to acquire a particular skill, he will most likely select other people who possess this skill as appropriate models. *Modeling* has special relevance to those working with young people, for it is the young who are generally most aware of their lack of knowledge and skills and are eagerly looking to others whom they can imitate. Be-

54

cause of this, it is extremely important that those in authority positions select as leaders of young children and youth those who are horizontally oriented, good models. It is also important that authorities assign men as well as women to teach even the very young children. This will help young boys model after male behavior. Hearing stories from good books related to them by male teachers who emphasize, as well as exemplify, horizontal, masculine qualities of idealism will assist small boys to identify with such attitudes and behaviors.

Most parents serve as the primary models for their children. Many have come to realize that words they speak to their children are not nearly as powerful a teaching device as their total behavior. Possibly the best single teaching device parents can present to their children is the example they set of self-respect, love for themselves, and love for their fellowmen. Parents who model well, and effectively apply these principles of learning, will tend to rear children who themselves will also rear respectful, responsible children.

Questions which can help us better understand the principle of modeling include:

- What kind of adults will my children grow into as they model my behavior?
- Do my sons have sufficient time with male models to learn their masculine roles?
- Do my daughters have sufficient time with female models to learn their female roles?
- How can our public and religious schools maximize the use of male and female teachers so that both boys and girls can identify more fully with those things we value?
- Who is skillful in —————? (Identify an area where you wish to develop a skill.) What skills would I like to learn from him/her and become proficient in through practice?

PRACTICE

Whether an individual is learning about things of a cognitive nature (e.g., ideas), developing certain body movements, or developing social skills, *practice* is a necessary prerequisite to the attainment of high levels of understanding and skill. Rehearsing how to respond effectively to a dominating, angry spouse or a discouraged daughter is as important as practicing follow-through with a golf club. The old adage "practice makes perfect" tends to be valid in all areas where change to a new or different behavior is desired.

Questions that can help us more fully understand the principle of practice include:

- If I am the kind who finds it hard to express affection to loved ones, do I take the time and energy to practice doing it?
- If I use anger to get my own way, do I practice keeping it under control and dealing reasonably and justly with others?
- If I have a hard time being assertive and standing up for myself, do I practice being assertive and expressing my opinions?
- If I am the type who has developed great skill in monopolizing the attention of others, do I sincerely practice the art of sharing this attention with others?
- Do I sincerely want to change the way in which I handle conflict with others? Do I practice and rehearse with others in simulated life situations the skills and techniques of successful conflict resolution?

PERSONALITY TRAITS

There are certain *personality traits* of a teacher that appear to facilitate the teaching-learning processes. And since we all influence and teach others in some way or other, these traits are important to each one of us. Essential, time-tested traits of the effective teacher include being sincere, empathic, warm and friendly, relaxed, easy-going, flexible, simple and approachable, confident, consistent, and well organized. Some research indicates that the most important attribute of those who would help another learn is friendliness. This also includes friendliness toward one's self when self is the learner.

The effective teacher is also able to communicate well. He is direct, succinct, and congruent in his communication. The effective teacher avoids being dogmatic, preachy, cold, abrupt, quick-tempered, patronizing, or coercive. Criticism and discipline that is overly strict and coercive tends to produce rigid conformity, shyness or aggression, anxiety levels that impede learning, or deference to authority figures. As a result, learning tends to become threatening and therefore something to be avoided.

Here are a few questions that can help us better understand personality traits:

- If I were one of my children, what adjectives would I use to describe me as I teach my children?
- How do my children respond to me when they are in a learning situation? Are they excited and eager or are they frustrated and angry, and do they work to avoid learning situations?
- What is the emotional atmosphere of my home/class?

ADDITIONAL PRINCIPLES

The following are additional principles of learning that you may find helpful and of interest.

When a desirable new horizontal behavior occurs, it is important that it be paid off immediately, and every time it occurs, until it is well established. This is know as giving continuous payoff. Once it is well established, payoff should be given in a random fashion. Random payoff is given for the second, third, fourth, or fifth time the behavior occurs to keep the individual responding at a high rate.

The individual needs to be successful in learning if he is to have the courage to continue. It may be that the typical person needs at least three success experiences to one failure if he is to keep trying. Teachers and parents should structure the experiences of children in a manner that will enable them to experience much success. The adult should also structure his own life so that he will be able to experience much success.

Shaping is another helpful principle, one based on the idea that it is beneficial in training to pay off any behavior that more closely approximates the desired behavior. For instance, as the child makes his bed and for the first time tucks in one corner, he is paid off for that behavior. And, if two days later he tucks in a second corner, this too is paid off. By applying this method, one can gradually shape his behavior until he becomes skilled at making the bed.

The most rapid learning tends to occur during infancy and early childhood. Because of this, parents and teachers of early grades are extremely important influences. If learning is to occur at a rapid but healthy rate, the idea or skill to be learned should generally not be too easy or too hard. It is generally best to distribute education and training over an appropriate period of time. Each person is somewhat different, and will therefore learn at his own unique rate, depending in part on his experience and past learning.

For successful learning to take place, the learner must have the desire to learn, for he will decide what is motivating (what is payoff) and what is not. Novel, fresh, and stimulating experiences in which the individual is an active participant tend to encourage him to learn.

SUMMARY

Those who desire to decrease the number of vertical elements and increase the number of horizontal elements in their relationships need first to understand principles of human behavior and learning. They also need to commit themselves to the application of horizontal approaches as they attempt to make desired changes. Agency, purpose, communication, social linkage, belonging, high self-esteem, communal interest, life style, and wholeness—nine fundamental principles of human behavior—have been identified. Important principles of learning that have been discussed are bonding, payoff, modeling, practice, and personality traits. Several additional principles of learning have also been identified.

REFERENCES

Adler, Alfred
    1954   Understanding Human Nature. Greenwich: Fawcett Publications.
    1958   What Life Should Mean to You. New York: Capricorn Books.
    1964   Social Interest: A Challenge to Mankind. New York: Capricorn Books.
Allred, G. Hugh
    1966   A study of the personality traits and classroom verbal behavior of senior high school student teachers. Doctoral dissertation, University of Oregon at Eugene, Oregon.
Ansbacher, Heinz L., and Rowena R.
    1956   The Individual Psychology of Alfred Adler. New York: Basic Books.
Bandura, Albert, and Richard H. Walters
    1963   Social Learning and Personality Development. New York: Holt, Rinehart and Winston.
Beier, Ernst G.
    1966   The Silent Language of Psychotherapy. Chicago: Aldine Publishing Co.

Buckley, Walter, ed.
1968   Modern Systems Research for the Behavioral Scientist: A Sourcebook. Chicago: Aldine Publishing Co.

Chaplin, J. P., and T. S. Krawiec
1960   Systems and Theories of Psychology. New York: Holt, Rinehart and Winston.

Cochran, Andrew A.
1966   "Mind, matter and quanta." Main Currents in Modern Thought (March-April) :79-88.

Dreikurs, Rudolf, et al.
1971   Maintaining Sanity in the Classroom. New York: Harper and Row.

Fagan, Joen, and Irma Lee Shepherd, eds.
1970   Gestalt Therapy Now: Theory, Techniques, Application. Palo Alto: Science and Behavior Books.

Haley, Jay
1963   Strategies of Psychotherapy. New York: Grune and Stratton.

Hilgard, Ernest R.
1956   Theories of Learning. New York: Appleton-Century-Crofts.

Hill, Winfred F.
1963   Learning: A Survey of Psychological Interpretations. San Francisco: Chandler Publishing Co.

Maddi, Salvatore R.
1970   "Alfred Adler and the fulfillment model of personality theorizing." Journal of Individual Psychology (November) :153-160.

Maslow, Abraham H.
1954   Motivation and Personality. New York: Harper and Row.
1962   Toward a Psychology of Being. New York: D. Van Nostrand Co.

Mehrabian, Albert
1970   Tactics of Social Influence. Englewood Cliffs, New Jersey: Prentice-Hall.

Ruesch, Jurgen, and Weldon Kees
1956   Nonverbal Communication: Notes on the Visual Perception of Human Relations. Berkeley: University of California Press.

Staats, Arthur W., and Carolyn K. Staats
1964   Complex Human Behavior: A Systematic Extension of Learning Principles. Chicago: Holt, Rinehart and Winston.

Szasz, Thomas S.
1961   The Myth of Mental Illness: Foundations of a Theory of Personal Conduct. New York: Harper and Row.

Watson, Goodwin
1963   "What do we know about learning." NEA Journal 52 (March):20-22.

Watzlawic, Paul, et al.
1967   Pragmatics of Human Communication: A Study of Interactional Patterns, Pathologies and Paradoxes. New York: W. W. Norton and Co.

5

COMMUNICATION:
VEHICLE FOR
ACHIEVING GOALS

In previous chapters we have discussed a husband-and-wife case, a way of viewing destructive relationships—vertical movement against others —and a way of viewing constructive relationships—horizontal movement with others. We have also identified important principles that must be understood and used by those who desire to work in a thoughtful and active way to diminish vertical and increase horizontal interaction in their relationships. This and the following chapter present an in-depth analysis of communication, a previously stated activity of critical importance in interpersonal relationships.

Historically, students of human behavior have attempted to understand the individual by investigating what goes on inside him. Recently, however, it has been found even more profitable to emphasize an individual's interactions with others. For it is within the social context that communication takes on added significance.

Man is a social being by nature. His basic striving is to belong and to have the esteem of his fellows. The means by which he jockeys for position, either in vertical or horizontal ways, as he strives to belong and gain their respect and acceptance is actually communication. This means then that communication is a social process. It is the basic process in human life that molds and shapes the individual as he relates with other people. It may be that an individual is actually the way he communicates. Personality is the impression, in total, that the individual manages to communicate to others. Thus the individual's personality is also more or less equal to his communicative skills and techniques.

It may be assumed that all interpersonal interaction is, in reality, communicative interaction. In other words, communication may be defined as all behavior that is interpersonal in nature. This includes not only words, but body language and nonlanguage sounds as well. Apparently then, there is no such thing as not interacting in one's interpersonal relationships. Husband and wife, parent and child, neighbor and neighbor cannot keep from communicating.

Every individual's activity and inactivity have communicative value. The child who sits at the TV, looking straight ahead at the picture even though his father has told him in a loud voice to take out the garbage, is communicating. He may be saying in effect, "You can't tell me what to do." The daughter who, while doing dishes, bangs them against the sink is also communicating. She is probably communicating to her mother such thoughts as "I don't want to do your old dishes. If you keep asking me to do them, I'll probably break a few, and then you'll be sorry."

Communication between parent and child, husband and wife, and neighbor and neighbor has a mutuality of effect. Each influences the other. Perhaps a relationship is best described in terms of the patterns of communication, communication being viewed as the procedures and activities by which one person works to influence another.

STRUCTURE OF COMMUNICATION

Communication involves three things: a sender, a message, and a receiver. The message is the bond between the sender and the receiver. Communication is the bond between parent and child, husband and wife, and neighbor and neighbor.

THE INDIVIDUAL'S COMMUNICATION SYSTEM

Communicative behavior of the individual is fluid, ongoing, and multi-moded—in other words, verbal, tonal, gestural, postural, each of which may affect the meaning of the other. At any one time the individual may be saying the same thing with all of these modes of communication, or he may be giving many different messages simultaneously. A child, for example, may say "I hate you, Father!" at the same time he is crying; and the crying may be communicating "Feel sorry for me." Thus, no single piece of communication can be really understood if it is considered in isolation, because the individual does not communicate piecemeal.

It is generally a mistake to think of communication as having a beginning and an end. For example, consider the following situation: Mother asks Mary to shut the door. Mary goes over to the door and slams it. Mother asks Mary to shut the door again and this time to do it quietly. She says it in an angry voice. Mary throws herself on the floor and begins to scream and kick her heels into the floor. Mother goes over to Mary, slaps her, and tells her to get up immediately. Then Mother goes over and shuts the door herself. Soon Mother feels guilty about slapping Mary and a little while later offers her a dish of ice cream. There is a vague beginning to this sequence of interactions. Mary probably left the door open in the very expectation, because of past experience, that her Mother would tell her to shut it. Neither does the episode end with Mother giving Mary a dish of ice cream. This response actually pays off Mary's behavior and stimulates her to repeat the same temper tactics in the future, in the expectation that her Mother will feel guilty and make amends with a treat.

At any one time, any specific communication is influenced by all of the communication that went before and by the participants' expectations of what comes after. Hence, interpersonal behavior, or communication, seems to definitely be a complex system of interactional behavior. Because of this, in order to understand the behavior of another, we need to analyze and define it within its total system or context.

METACOMMUNICATION: COMMUNICATION ABOUT COMMUNICATION

Messages may be broken down into two channels. One channel carries the *content* aspect of the communication: for example, the content of the request "Help me with my coat." This is the overt message, the one others are most conscious of. But there is another aspect of this message—the *relationship* aspect—that which communicates something about the relationship. This is called *metacommunication.* It is usually subtle, covert, and primarily sent by nonlanguage means. Generally, the way the individual looks at others when he makes his request, his tone of voice, bodily posture, gestures, facial expressions, and the sequence, cadence, and rhythm of his words themselves will communicate what he feels about the relationship he has with them and will influence their responses to him. If his voice is a whine, if he droops his shoulders, and if he has a hound dog look on his face, he is probably communicating, besides the overt message, "Help me with my coat," such a covert message as "Feel sorry for me so that I can manipulate you to give me service." Or he may also be expressing, "This is the only way I have to keep you involved with me and know that you know I am around."

Most of us are aware of the content aspect of messages, but relatively few of us are sensitive to the covert messages individuals send out about relationships. Even a very careful observer must make a good deal of effort in order to read and understand the powerful metacommunication of others. The significance of this aspect of communication is evidenced by how strongly people are influenced and controlled by the individual as he uses nonverbal attempts to achieve his purposes with them.

Most often when a person feels that he does not belong successfully with others, when he feels that he cannot be accepted by behaving constructively and cooperatively, he relies on nonverbal communication techniques to influence and control responses in more vertical ways. It is at this time that we need to be sensitive to and aware of his nonverbal communication in order to resist being manipulated by him into behaving in ways that pay off his vertical behavior, and thus help him to achieve his goals through our responses.

CHANNELS OF COMMUNICATION: VERBAL BEHAVIOR

Verbal methods of communication are primarily used to express the content aspect of communication, the statement proper of the message. Signals suggesting interpretation and defining the ongoing relationship are given nonverbally. The words used in communication appeal primarily to the receiver's ear; being transmitted in words, the content aspect is received by the receiver aurally.

CHANNELS OF COMMUNICATION: NONVERBAL BEHAVIOR

We are usually surprised when we first realize that loved ones are talking to us nonverbally. Some of us have difficulty grasping the idea that much of the communication going on between us and others, indeed the most important, is through nonverbal channels. The implications of this are great and essentially mean, for example, that if parents want to truly understand their children, if husbands and wives want to understand each other, and if neighbors also desire to relate harmoniously with each other, they need to concentrate less on the words that are used and much more on nonverbal responses.

Some of the nonverbal methods of communicating which we need to recognize are voice intonation, length of speech, frequency of pauses, bodily posture, eye contact or lack of it, facial expressions, body distance of the person speaking in relation to the person listening, tightness of muscles, body odors, and dress.

It is important for us to remember that it is usually through the nonverbal channel that an individual expresses his greatest concerns and attempts to influence the responses of those whom he loves the most. Also, the greater the risk involved in a relationship, the more an individual will tend to relate vertically and feel the need to influence the behavior of the loved one, again using the nonverbal channel to send his important messages.

COMMUNICATOR AWARENESS

In order for each of us to feel secure we usually need to be able to predict what will happen in our environment. An individual may, as he strives for security, attempt to influence and control the responses of others in order to make his world more predictable. He may attempt to control the responses of others or influence their responses through the medium of metacommunication. It is usually through subtle, covert, hinting cues or messages that the individual relating vertically most urgently attempts to control the responses of his fellows. In this way, the risk of having to accept the responsibility of his intent is minimal. Any individual may function in this manner, depending on the time, the place, and those with whom he is communicating.

As a child, parent, spouse, or neighbor attempts to control or influence another's behavior, he does not always understand that his attempts often occur with or without his awareness of himself or other participants in the communication.

THE CONSCIOUS MANIPULATOR

When the individual consciously attempts to persuade, influence, or control another's behavior to achieve his goals, he becomes a conscious manipulator of the other person.

One person may often consciously attempt to manipulate the

responses of another through covert and subtle means in order to test him, without accounting for what he is attempting to do. For example, in an insecure marital relationship the wife, while watching TV, may put her head on her husband's lap, giving this covert message, "Put your arms around me and hug me, because I'm not sure you love me." She is more than likely, however, sending subtle messages which she hopes will reduce her husband's awareness that she has set him up to be influenced or controlled by her behavior.

The purpose of the wife's message is to create an emotional climate or environment favorable to achieving her goals. To do this effectively, she must structure the situation in such a way that her husband is made to feel and not to think. If she is successful, her husband will believe that he has decided to behave in this way of his own free choice. If her husband asks, "Are you trying to get me to say that I love you?" she is safe to say, "Certainly not. I'm not saying that at all. I'm just sleepy." She thereby protects herself from the hurt of possible rejection. The more vertical the relationship, the more often individuals will tend to communicate in such hinting ways.

THE UNCONSCIOUS MANIPULATOR

In many cases, the individual is unaware that he is attempting to manipulate or influence others to respond in certain ways in order to achieve his goals. As a result, he often manipulates responses from others of which he is not aware.

It is generally through this type of semiconscious communication that a person actually maintains his current life style—his consistency of personality. With his messages he creates the behaviors in others which enable him to confirm his own biased apperception of people. As they respond to his influences, he continually obtains proof that his biased perception is a true perception. It is necessary for him to interpret his relationships accordingly. An example of this is the individual who feels that the world is full of people who will not pay any attention to him unless he competes for their attention. He may become a show-off, continually clowning at parties as well as in his close interpersonal relationships. He tends to wear people out with his maneuvers. As a result, they often become so tired of him that even when he is not showing off they will not move toward him on their own. They do not have the desire or the energy left to relate freely with him. Hence the pattern becomes set, and when they do not get involved with him when he is behaving normally, he can say to himself, "Yes, just as I expected. People don't care for me and won't relate to me unless I clown around." In reality he has arranged his own failure.

COMMUNICATION AND PAYOFF

If an individual, through horizontal behavior such as respectful words and smiles, brings about the desired behavioral responses from others, he achieves payoff and will tend to continue to use these horizontal communicative techniques.

The converse is also true. When a person through his nagging, continual talking, yelling, screaming, pouting, ridiculing, or physical punishment is able to bring about desired changes in another, he achieves payoff and will tend to continue this vertical communicative behavior.

There is also another way that payoff can affect behavior. An individual may train others to talk about what interests him and use many techniques in order to do so. If we look at another in an interested way, the effect is to pay off his behavior and encourage him to continue talking about the same things in which we are showing interest. But if we lose interest and communicate this by looking away from him, we train the speaker to talk about other things. An audience who is listening closely is powerful payoff for the person discussing a particular topic.

COMMUNICATION AND THE MALADJUSTED PERSON

The more inferior or inadequate an individual feels and the more he feels he does not belong, the more skillful he will tend to be in affecting the emotional responses of others. For example, when a person feels that he does not belong, he may develop skillful, vertically communicative techniques for keeping others involved with him. Whining, crying, banging pots and pans around, jabbing, and bugging other people may serve his purpose effectively.

The individual who feels inadequate or inferior may continually elicit supportive responses from loved ones by using vertical communications such as "I'm no good," or "I have no friends." He may also find that the hangdog look is usually effective in getting responses. The more others support such vertical communicative behaviors—pay them off—the more the individual will tend to keep using them. On the other hand, when an individual receives payoff for communicating about himself in positive ways—moving horizontally with himself and people who are significant to him, he will tend to keep those positive behaviors.

SUMMARY

In this chapter we have attempted to demonstrate that communication is the vehicle for interaction between and among people. In fact, it is suggested that a person achieves his social goals through communication and that all social behavior is communicative behavior. The individual is continually communicating with others and represents a part of a communicative network within small and large units of society.

Communication can best be understood as a system wherein all parts are related and influence one another. To better understand interpersonal behavior, we must look at the patterns of ongoing communication rather than at isolated pieces of a message. A person is always communicating, and he is always influencing the behavior of others around him. In other words, he is in part molding the behaviors of others through his communication, as are those others, in part, molding his behaviors through their communication.

An attempt has also been made to identify certain aspects of the communicative process. Communication may be considered a complex system of ongoing, continuing, interactive behaviors interrelated in varying degrees. Any message contains a content and a relationship aspect. Generally, by far the most important part of the message is the relationship aspect. It is herein that the individual attempts to manipulate the responses of others in order to achieve his goals. He may be consciously aware of what he is attempting to obtain from others, but generally he is not.

Communication proceeds through two primary channels, verbal and nonverbal. In interpersonal relationships such as those between child and parent, husband and wife, and neighbor and neighbor, non-verbal communication is considered to have much greater communicative power and emotional impact, and it is usually through the non-verbal channel that messages about the relationships are sent.

Moreover, when the individual through his communicative techniques is able to effect the desired response in the behavior of another, this acts as payoff for the one sending the initial communication and tends to stimulate the sender to keep the same behavior. To the extent that he achieves his purposes through vertical behavior he will tend to keep that behavior; and to the extent that he achieves them with horizontal behavior, he will tend to maintain that behavior.

The maladjusted person will more than likely be skillful in manipulating the responses of others. But those of us who would behave responsibly with such an individual must be perceptive in seeing what is happening in relationships with him and courageous in not paying off his vertical attempts to belong. Effort must be made to pay off his horizontal attempts.

REFERENCES

Adler, Alfred
    1969   The Science of Living. New York: Anchor Books.

Allred, G. Hugh
    1968   Mission for Mother: Guiding the Child. Salt Lake City: Bookcraft.

Beier, Ernst G.
    1966   The Silent Language of Psychotherapy. Chicago: Aldine Publishing Co.

Buckley, Walter, ed.
    1968   Modern Systems Research for the Behavioral Scientist: A Sourcebook. Chicago: Aldine Publishing Co.

Haley, Jay
    1963   Strategies of Psychotherapy. New York: Gruen and Stratton.

Loeffler, Dorothy
    1970   "Counseling and the psychology of communication." The Personnel and Guidance Journal 48 (8) (April):629-636.

Parry, John B.
    1967   The Psychology of Human Communication. New York: American Elsevier Publishing Co.

Ruesch, Jurgen, and Weldon Kees
    1956   Nonverbal Communication: Notes on the Visual Perception of Human Relations. Berkeley: University of California Press.

Watzlawic, Paul, et al.
    1967   Pragmatics of Human Communication: A Study of Interactional Patterns, Pathologies and Paradoxes. New York: W. W. Norton and Co.

6
HORIZONTAL COMMUNICATION

Individuals who successfully communicate with others learn to immerse themselves in the total ongoing communication process, much as they would if they played a violin in a symphony. They do not isolate certain details or parts from the whole.

Communication at any one given time may be viewed as a measure of how much the same thoughts, ideas, and feelings are shared. A message is accurately communicated to the extent that the receiver understands what the sender actually intends, whether the intent is conscious or semiconscious. Good communicators develop great sensitivity to all of its characteristics. They are especially sensitive to the nonverbal cues that are emotionally laden and have the greatest communicative value. Through study and practice almost anyone can learn to use these cues to strengthen his relationships with those important to him—his children, spouse, and neighbor.

One approach that is often helpful as we work to understand the communication of others is the gaining of an acute and sensitive understanding of our own communicative techniques. This suggests that we observe and carefully analyze all of the nonverbal behaviors we use to achieve our goals with others, including our spouse, children, and neighbors. This study of self will help us better understand our responsibilities in any communicative system.

CHARACTERISTICS OF VERTICAL COMMUNICATION

Vertical communication between parent and child, husband and wife, or neighbor and neighbor is typically characterized by competitive struggles in the relationships (see Chapter 2). Vertical communication is also often characterized by more indirect forms of communication. There tends to be a hinting quality about much of it. This generally occurs because the relationship is viewed as risky or hurtful. The participants feel they cannot communicate directly and openly to one another about the most important aspects of the relationship because they fear this would make them more vulnerable to hurt. The child, for example, is too afraid to ask his mother and father in a straightforward manner if they love him. They might say no, and this would be too painful. This same child may run the streets at night to see if his parents care enough to set limits. If they do not set limits, he may then interpret such lack of action as their not caring for him. However, because he is using the hinting type of behavior, he can continue to think, "Maybe they do love me." If he asked them directly about their love and they said, "No, we do not love you," he would be faced with the awful, final truth. Hinting is much less dangerous to one who is uncertain of the love of a person whom he values highly, even though he runs the risk of not being understood or of not understanding.

A lack of trust can also do much to interfere with horizontal communication and is typically found in vertical communication. When family members have consistently hurt each other, whether the hurt has been between parents or between parents and children, family members may choose not to communicate with each other about things most important to them for fear of being hurt again. This results in much chaff being blown about and very little real communication taking place.

Vertical communication may also occur when anyone or all in a communication network lack skill in listening, expressing themselves, or interpreting accurately what is being communicated. When parents come from homes where accurate communicative skills were not developed, they are often handicapped somewhat in communicating horizontally with their children and with one another. However, parents can develop horizontal communicative skills by acquiring more knowledge about them and then conscientiously practicing these skills to improve their communication.

CHARACTERISTICS OF HORIZONTAL COMMUNICATION

Since vertical communication is characterized by hinting, sarcasm, ridicule, humiliation, and dishonesty, horizontal communication is its inverse. Following are some characteristics of healthy horizontal interpersonal communication.

NONPOSSESSIVE WARMTH AND RESPECT

Horizontal communication between individuals tends to occur when they exhibit nonpossessive warmth. For example, parents who are nonpossessively warm usually share a friendly, affectionate relationship with their children. They sincerely like them as individuals and are interested and concerned about them. Because their affection is non-possessive and thus not exclusive, they do not selfishly try to isolate the child from the affections or interests of other people. They do not exploit their child as a means for fulfilling their own unrealized dreams. They respect his interests, abilities, and rights to progress in independence, for they realize that he is a person of great individual value. Warmth and respect are some of the most important character-istics necessary for effective horizontal communication.

GENUINENESS

Horizontal communication also tends to develop and thrive within a context of genuineness. Individuals who are horizontal communicators tend to exhibit traits of genuineness, sincerity, honesty, and congruence. They do not try to bluff others. They do not verbalize one way and then behave another. If they do not know something, they openly admit it rather than trying to bluff their way through. They trust themselves, are honest and open about their own feelings, and will often admit, "We don't know," or "We're confused." Warmth be-tween people usually helps build trust; but without genuineness, trust is quickly destroyed. Open, authentic communication can take place only between and among people in an atmosphere of honesty.

ACCURATE EMPATHY

Horizontal communication is greatly facilitated by the person who is able to empathize accurately. He is able to put himself in another's shoes and understand his thoughts and feelings. He understands and feels with his heart as well as with his head. He has a sense of what the other person is going through. This does not mean, however, that he pities or feels sorry for the other person, which emotions would tend to make him vulnerable to undesirable manipulations and tempt him to pay off vertical behavior. He can understand and appreciate what another person is feeling because he has experienced similar feelings or because he realizes that the other person is feeling real emotions. He does not, however, have to feel the exact emotions of the other person in order to empathize.

FACILITATING PHRASES AND BEHAVIORS

Many phrases can be used to stimulate more horizontal communication. In the following list the phrases and questions tend to indicate to spouse, child, or neighbor that the speaker is open to what he has to communicate. Of course, the tone of voice and all nonverbal responses must be congruent with the verbal content.

- What is going on between us?
- What are you feeling now?
- What do you mean?
- Please help me to understand.
- Do I understand? This is what I think you mean . . .
- Please go on. I am confused, will you help me to understand what you mean?
- What do you think would happen if . . . ?
- Could this be what you're saying . . . ?
- How did that make you feel?
- What happened?
- Could you have done it differently?
- Could you have said it differently?
- What was he feeling when you said that?
- Could you have done anything to make him angry?
- What could you do differently to make him feel differently toward you?
- What is your responsibility in the relationship with him?
- What am I doing that makes you feel angry?
- What could I do differently to make you feel differently?
- What could I do differently to help you feel better towards me?

This is only a partial list of a multitude of phrases and questions that you can use to help other people communicate honestly with you. These phrases have certain characteristics that tend to facilitate horizontal communication rather than thwart it. Such phrases help one avoid being judgmental. They allow the other person to feel secure as an individual. They lead him to evaluate himself and his circumstances and stimulate him to think independently. These phrases can help a parent train his childern to analytically evaluate their relationships with other people. They can also lead the child to discover that he has responsibilities in these relationships.

Such phrases as those listed tend to bring forth from the other person his honest thoughts, feelings, and attitudes. When he sincerely responds to such phrases, he exposes his real self and thereby risks a good deal. He becomes more vulnerable to the rejection or criticism of other people when he exposes his real self rather than a false self. It is vitally important that he who asks the questions also reveal his real self by expressing his honest thoughts, feelings, and attitudes on the topics under discussion if the other person is to feel free to continue to respond honestly. Otherwise, the respondent is the only one taking a risk. Moreover, when one exposes himself by expressing himself openly and honestly, it is important that he do it in such a manner that he does not make the other person appear wrong or stupid if he disagrees. Always to be avoided is the type of interaction in which a participant feels backed into a corner where, rather than dealing with the issue under consideration in a problem-solving manner, he believes that he must fight you to preserve his self-respect.

Vertical phrases that tend to attack another's self-respect and cause him to withdraw or fight include the following:

- Well, anybody knows . . .
- The more intelligent agree with me.
- People with experience agree with me that . . .
- Don't be so stupid. I know that . . .
- I know I'm right. Other people . . .
- I know you . . .

These phrases are often stated in a nonverbal vertical context of authoritarianism. They may be delivered in a harsh tone of voice, accompanied by stern facial expression, rigid body posture, and finger pointing.

The following phrases can assist one to express to others his beliefs, thoughts, and feelings in a respectful, nonthreatening attitude.

They are best received when expressed in a nonverbal context of warm tone of voice, accompanied by relaxed facial muscles, relaxed—even sloppy—body posture, and a friendly smile, when appropriate. Each phrase contains a qualifying element that allows one to express himself honestly and yet communicate that the truth may be other than what he may believe or support. Much conflict is thus avoided and respect for the other person's ideas is implicitly communicated. The other person can as a result differ without appearing to be wrong or stupid.

- It appears to me that . . .
- My feelings at the present time are . . .
- My thinking at present is . . .
- My ideas may change on the matter, but now I feel . . .
- From the information I have, I am led to believe that . . .
- When you do/say that, I feel . . .

It is highly important for parents to be aware that they thwart the desire of a child to communicate when they criticize, reject, and dominate his behavior. What he needs is reassurance as they work actively to pay off his horizontal attempts to relate. Parents can do this, for example, by looking at him, listening to him, hugging him, smiling at him, patting him on the back, and saying something like "Uh huh. You could be right." This must be done with genuine interest for him as an individual, however. If parents respond horizontally to him when he is communicating, the child will tend to believe that his parents are interested in what he is saying, and this should stimulate him to communicate responsibly. This is also true of communication between adults.

It is important that we give payoff immediately if we desire more communication. Payoff should be given as soon as a person shows interest in communicating, with attention focused on him as he communicates. This, of course, assumes that we wish to encourage the other to communicate and that he—for example, a child—is not just keeping us busy giving him our attention.

If a loved one has a difficult time relating, it is especially important that we provide a safe environment for him devoid of any hint of sarcasm or ridicule and full of much nonverbal payoff, such as that described above. It is also important to give him payoff as soon as he shows the slightest interest in communicating. If he looks as if he is going to say something, we should stop what we are doing and encourage him in an appropriate manner. As a result, he will feel that he is important enough for someone to listen to.

It is important that we be aware, however, that it generally is a mistake to interact by using even horizontal communicative methods with an individual, child or adult, when he is behaving vertically in pattern (similar behavior that occurs over and over again), as any interaction at such time tends to pay off his efforts. The methods discussed in Chapter 4 are often more appropriate for such situations. The methods suggested in this chapter may be used effectively with people who exhibit *new* vertical behaviors or with those who are *sincere* in their desire to change.

Horizontal communication is the lifeblood of positive interpersonal relationships; therefore, it is the lifeblood of happy families. To the extent that communication is vertical, family members probably feel the negative consequences of such relationships (see Chapter 2).

HANDLING POSITIVE EMOTIONS

Positive emotions include love, happiness, gratitude, contentment, warmth, and self-confidence. These are the emotions exhibited by growth-oriented individuals who feel positive towards themselves and their fellowmen. These are generally productive emotions and should be encouraged. Sometimes adults are embarrassed or threatened by children who are self-confident and happy, and they wrongly try to discourage them. However, it is very important that adults do all they can to encourage positive emotions in children, by showing no hint of sarcasm or ridicule and by exhibiting behaviors indicating that the children can achieve their belonging and love goals through the use of positive emotional behaviors.

HANDLING NEGATIVE EMOTIONS

The negative emotions include anger, hurt, frustration, hopelessness, guilt, resentment, fear, depression, disgust, antagonism, rebellion, rejection, hostility, and loneliness. Many times when a child or spouse responds with such emotions, other family members become defensive and attempt to get him to deny his emotions by making him feel wrong for having them. They very likely do so because they do not know how to handle such emotions; therefore they try to put them out of their minds and the mind of the one experiencing the emotions as they work at not dealing with them. But because the child is somewhat dependent on his parents, he needs their help in analyzing his own feelings and the possible reasons for his having them. He needs them to also help him understand his responsibility to do whatever needs to be done to change them.

It is important that we communicate friendliness, warmth, empathy, and sincerity when we get involved with others exhibiting such negative emotions. However, it is important that we do not get caught up with their emotional intensity. When we do become caught up, we render ourselves useless to them by falling prey to the same problems they have; we can no longer remain objective.

One of the first things we can do to help someone who is exhibiting negative emotions is to help him understand and possibly even label what it is that he is feeling. Asking him "What do you feel?" can help him analyze his own emotions. A second step is for us to help him define the origins of his feelings, perhaps by asking, "What did he do to influence you to feel this way?" A third step is for us to help him understand his responsibility in the interaction with questions such as "What can you do about it?" Again, we should feel no hint of ridicule or of blaming him for feeling the way he does; otherwise we will be relating to him in a vertical manner. The purpose of the questioning is to help him analyze what is going on and resolve the difficulties. Nagging, preaching, scolding, and shaming tend to cut off communication and should be avoided.

Many times when an individual is feeling negative emotions, especially such emotions as guilt or fear, he will verbally deny that this is taking place. At this time we can be most helpful by describing back to him in a friendly way some of the nonverbal cues we are picking up. We might respond in this manner: "Gee, Becky, you say that everything is all right, but your face is flushed and you're gripping the chair hard. Can you help me understand what is going on?" This must be done within a safe, warm, friendly context in order for the individual to respond. There must be no hint of "Ha ha, you say nothing's wrong, but I can see your face is flushed and you're gripping the chair." Our response should not be one of "I've caught you in your inconsistency," but one of "I don't understand. Will you help me?"

We must be aware of two cautions, however. First, it is important that our nonverbal as well as verbal messages communicate real interest in listening and communicating. For example, many times we, in the hurry of the day, will say to another, "Please tell me what you want to say. I'm listening." However, as we are speaking, we continue to read the paper or scrub the floor. This communicates that we are more interested in world events and keeping a clean house than in really listening. The person may interpret this as rejection, feel hurt, and clam up. Second, we must be careful not to probe or demand that the other talk. In order to be helpful and communicate openly, we must if at all possible stop what we are doing and focus on the other person in a warm, accepting manner when he is in need of communicating and relating with us. This assumes, of course, that he is sincere and has not set a pattern of keeping us involved with his vertical behaviors.

WORKING THROUGH CONFLICT

Horizontal interaction allows people to work through conflict in a manner that brings about productive results, whereas vertical interaction tends to bring about unproductive results. Vertical conflict may be viewed in four ways. First, there is the destructive conflict in which the primary purpose of those individuals involved in the relationship is to hurt one another rather than to work out problems. Second is the spiraling conflict, in which tempers get higher and higher. Here the hostility increases and the problems enlarge as the individuals interact. A third form of unproductive conflict is the habitual conflict. Here it appears that the parties involved respond habitually with antagonism. For some it is a familiar way of relating. There is little attempt to resolve the tension, for the primary purpose of the interaction appears to be to continue the conflict. Fourth is the hidden conflict. It never really breaks out in the open. There is much hinting. Subtle messages are sent out that suggest anger, hurt, sarcasm, and ridicule. Real problems are not expressed openly. There is a tense undercurrent in the air. Subtlety in conflict is difficult for most participants to handle effectively.

The following are guidelines that you can follow to horizontally and productively resolve conflicts. First, *recognize that a problem exists.* Helpful questions may include "What is going on?" "What is happening?" "What are your feelings?" "I am feeling. . . ," "What is going on between us?"

Second, *identify the problem in existence.* Questions that focus on the problem at hand include "What is it that is concerning you?" "What is it that makes you feel the way you do?" "What is our problem?"

Third, *stick to discussing and solving the problem at hand.* This is one of the most difficult tasks in a conflict situation. We may ask ourselves, "Are we sticking to the subject?" "Could we be wandering away from the major concern we have identified?" "What are we doing now, and does this have relevance to the problem at hand?" "How does this relate to the problem that we have identified?"

Fourth, *avoid counterhurting one another.* This suggests avoidance of red flag, negative, and emotional phrases such as "To think that, you would have to be awfully stupid," "How can you be so selfish?" "That's a rather dumb way of thinking." When one person uses these red flag phrases, other people often work actively to counterhurt rather than to work in a productive manner to resolve the conflict with which they are faced.

Fifth, *explore the alternatives available* in order to find good solutions to the conflict. It is important that each member be open to any available alternatives. Questions which may stimulate us to think of other alternatives include "What else can we do?" "Are there other ways in which we can handle this?" "How else might you/I respond?" "What could I do differently that would make you feel better about the situation?"

Sixth, *actively select from among available alternatives.* All persons involved must agree on a choice of the more effective alternatives facing them if they are actually to resolve a conflict. They may ask themselves and each other, "What do I/you think is the most effective way of responding to this situation?" "After considering the advantages and disadvantages of each alternative, what do I/you think would be the best way to handle it?"

One of the more difficult tasks is for everyone to agree on an alternative in such a manner that all participants in the conflict feel good about the alternative. There are ways of reaching a decision, however, that increase the probabilities that horizontal behaviors and good feelings will occur. Some of these ways may be obvious to some. However, this is usually not the case when parties are emotionally involved in conflict. At such times, feelings of frustration, anger, and hurt may block reasonable attempts unless those involved have at their finger tips a repertory of effective strategies. Possibly the most desirable strategy is for those involved in conflict to work until they find an alternative that is satisfactory to all. If they are able to do so, they achieve consensus. Accommodation occurs when each party voluntarily agrees to let the other(s) pursue his own desires. Compromise takes place when the parties move toward an alternative that partially satisfies the desires of all. Concession occurs when one party gives in to the desires of the other(s) with a voluntary action. Taking turns in having one's desires met and flipping coins or drawing straws can also be helpful in making decisions that are fair to all.

Seventh, *commit yourself to making the selected alternative work.* If a decision has been reached in a fair, horizontal manner, it can usually be made to work if each party in the conflict verbally commits himself to the others to do all that is possible to make it work.

Eighth, *communicate with other people in an open, spontaneous manner.* All of the questions on pages 71 and 72 have been worded in such a way that they should help keep the lines of communication open between parents and child and husband and wife. There is no attempt to make judgments, to ridicule, or to humiliate. If communication is to remain open, it is important that family members actively work to encourage one another to express feelings, desires, and needs in a safe, unthreatening environment. This may be accomplished by using the above-mentioned questions and following the guidelines presented in this chapter under the section titled Characteristics of Horizontal Communication.

SUMMARY

In this chapter, horizontal communication, message by message, has been discussed as containing the building blocks necessary for healthy, satisfying, interpersonal relationships. Vertical communication includes such characteristic behaviors as competitive struggles, indirect messages, sarcasm, ridicule, humiliation, dishonesty, lack of trust, and lack of skill. Horizontal communication includes behaviors that are expressed with characteristic warmth, respect, genuineness, sincerity, honesty, congruence, and empathy. The appropriate expressions of positive emotions such as affection, love, and happiness should be paid off spontaneously and quickly so that other people can achieve their belonging goals through horizontal behavior. Negative emotions including anger, hurt, guilt, and fear should be responded to with *differential behavior,* depending on how appropriate or inappropriate the emotion is to the situation and whether or not the individual has set a pattern of responding with negative reactions.

People who engage in vertical, unproductive ways of working with conflict tend to use destructive, spiraling, habitual, and covert forms of behavior. The process of effective problem solving includes recognizing that a problem exists, identifying the problem, finding a workable solution to the problem, avoiding counterhurting behavior, seeking and selecting alternatives, committing oneself to making the selected alternative work, and communicating openly.

One should remember that it is usually best to behave in a reassuring, encouraging manner with people when they are sincere in their efforts to communicate.

REFERENCES

Beier, Ernst G.
    1966   The Silent Language of Psychotherapy. Chicago: Aldine Publishing Co.

Berenson, Bernard G., and Robert R. Carkhuff, eds.
    1967   Sources of Gain in Counseling and Psychotherapy. New York: Holt, Rinehart and Winston.

Bergin, Allen E., and Hans H. Strupp
    1972   Changing Frontiers in the Science of Psychotherapy. Chicago: Aldine Publishing Co.

Blood, Robert O., Jr.
    1969.   Marriage (2nd ed.). New York: The Free Press.

Cannon, Kenneth L.
    1968   What You Bring to Marriage. Provo, Utah: Brigham Young University Press.

Haley, Jay
    1963   Strategies of Psychotherapy. New York: Grune and Stratton.

Parry, John B.
    1967   The Psychology of Human Communication. New York: American Elsevier Publishing Co.

Ruesch, Jurgen
    1961   Therapeutic Communication. New York: W. W. Norton and Co.

Sicher, Lydia
    1955   "Education for freedom." The American Journal of Individual Psychology 11 (2).

Watzlawic, Paul, et al.
    1967   Pragmatics of Human Communication: A Study of Interactional Patterns, Pathologies and Paradoxes. New York: W. W. Norton and Co.

THREE

APPLICATION: ACHIEVING HORIZONTAL INTERACTION WITH MY CHILDREN

7
HORIZONTAL
TRAITS
AND METHODS

The individual who functions horizontally with other people demonstrates a high level of self-esteem, a high degree of courage and spontaneity, and the desire to continually increase his repertoire of cooperative, democratic behaviors. His main interest and concern is the welfare of others as well as himself. He is sensitive to the workings of groups and responsibly contributes to making them function horizontally rather than vertically. He bases his actions on what he believes to be right rather than on the capricious pressures of others. He sees with clear eyes the bad as well as the good and behaves responsibly to what he sees. He is honest and congruent: his verbal and nonverbal communication are consistent with each other. He tends to have much common sense, to be relaxed, and to be somewhat easy going. He usually has a sense of humor that facilitates the horizontal functioning of people involved in group activities. His humor is never designed to elevate himself at the expense of others; however, it can be and is often used to dissipate tension so that others can work more effectively through their difficulties. The horizontally oriented individual often has deep spiritual roots. His relationships with others and his attitudes toward them and himself are often profoundly affected by the spirit that emanates from him.

Principles of learning such as bonding, modeling, payoff, practice, and effective teacher personality traits (discussed in Chapter 4) are powerful concepts that should be understood, respected, and wisely applied by parents if they are to help their children develop horizontal traits described in the previous paragraph.

One of the most effective childrearing principles is the use of *natural consequences.* When parents do not intervene between the child and the consequences that naturally occur as a result of his behavior, they allow him to learn from his mistakes. Usually parents need to intervene only if a situation could be a dangerous one. An example of the wise use of natural consequences is the father who does not pay the installment payment on his son's bicycle when the son has set a pattern of not budgeting wisely. The father even allows it to be repossessed so that his son will be able to suffer and thus learn the consequences of his irresponsible behavior. Such behavior on the part of the father demonstrates real concern for the development of character. Possibly one of the greatest errors of many affluent parents is their taking upon themselves the consequences of their children's irresponsible actions.

When parents structure the environment in such a way that their children experience the reasonable and logical impact of their irresponsible behavior, they are implementing *logical consequences.* For example, the mother who puts her child to bed early after he was late for school is using this principle. The mother acts on the logical assumption that if her child is too sleepy to get to school on time, he must need more rest.

In order for logical consequences to work effectively, a good relationship must exist between parents and children. The children must have a say in determining the consequences of their behaviors. Otherwise the use of logical consequences can stimulate battles and thus vertical interaction between parents and children. There must be no hint of sarcasm, ridicule, humiliation, or revenge on the part of parents. The emotional content must be calm and matter-of-fact.

Natural and logical consequences are major principles that are suggested for your use as you work to prepare your family to relate horizontally. There are, however, certain intangibles that are also vitally important which have to do with the total personality that emanates from parents and is communicated to their children. It is from such emanations that children model their own behavior, and either interact harmoniously or resist and rebel.

The following questions can help you define and understand these intangibles:

- Am I truly committed to the principles of individual agency?
- To what degree do I let my children have a say in making decisions affecting them and the family?

• How do I demonstrate my belief that my children have the same rights for growth and happiness that I have?
• How do I demonstrate my respect and love for my children? For my spouse? For my fellowman?
• How do I demonstrate that I like who I am and that I have a high level of self-esteem?
• How do I demonstrate my love for the aesthetic and divine?
• As my children model after me, how will they demonstrate their love and zest for life?
• As I mingle with members of my family, to what extent do I demonstrate those traits of character possessed by the effective teacher (see Chapter 4)?

REFERENCES

Allred, G. Hugh
    1968   Mission for Mother: Guiding the Child. Salt Lake City: Bookcraft.

Dreikurs, Rudolf, et al.
    1971   Maintaining Sanity in the Classroom. New York: Harper and Row.

Glasser, William
    1965   Reality Therapy: A New Approach to Psychiatry. New York: Harper and Row.

Maslow, Abraham H.
    1962   Toward a Psychology of Being. New York: D. Van Nostrand Co.

Sicher, Lydia
    1955   "Education for freedom." The American Journal of Individual Psychology 11 (2).

8

APPLICATION OF HORIZONTAL METHODS TO CHILDREARING

"What went wrong? I thought I understood the principles." This is a common response of even the brightest students—many of whom are parents and teachers—when placed in simulated real-life situations in which they attempt to communicate with unfamiliar responses. What they must realize is that a workable transition from the understanding of a theory to its effective application is usually not easily or quickly accomplished. This requires much effort and time in practice as we work to overcome such things as sliding back into old behaviors or giving in to the pressures of a child who behaves vertically. Time and practice provide us the chance to approximate more closely new behaviors which are more effective in training a child to acquire traits that will enable him, as an adult, to respond horizontally with his fellows.

This chapter includes many real-life situations that can help you put theory into practice and thereby bridge the usual gap between the two. A rather detailed description is given of each situation, followed by suggested recommendations for change. Each case ends with a discussion.

The recommendations discussed are, of course, not the only ones possible; there may be many effective alternative actions for any particular problem. View them instead as patterns or guides that can help if followed. After you have a workable knowledge of the principles for understanding people and for rearing children, read a few of the cases, think through what you feel should be done in the following situations, and compare your ideas with the written suggestions. You may also wish to see if your rationale for your alternatives is consistent with your objectives in childrearing.

Practicing different responses in situations where the problem is simulated is often a vitally important step in learning. For example, a father who desires to stop his six-year-old son from whining may ask his wife to act as his son. He then practices communicating with her as if she were his son, as he works at perfecting his ability to relate effectively.

There are many advantages to simulation. First, the person desiring change can get immediate feedback on how he is doing from those assisting him. Second, he can practice with a minimum of risk to his relationship with the person with whom he desires to improve interaction. Third, his emotions will tend to interfere less with his learning in a simulated situation than in a real one. Fourth, he can build confidence in his ability to function differently so that when he does respond in the real situation, the other person will sense his confidence and be less willing to test him.

The crucial step, of course, is the application of the principles to actual life situations, which must be done with common sense, persistence, and consistency. It is usually best to choose only one or two things to work on at one time. Success tends to result in still more success. Working first on those situations in which you feel reasonably confident you will succeed is usually the best course. As you conquer somewhat simple problems, you will gain the confidence and skill that will enable you to work through those that are more complex.

Be kind to yourself. Discouragement and feelings of failure are usually self-defeating. When you make a mistake or don't respond as effectively as you think you should have, use your energies to discover what you can learn from your experience rather than spend time brooding in useless guilt and self-recrimination.

Once you decide to change behavior, it is often helpful to determine the frequency of the behavior before you begin your program to change it. If you measure the frequency of behavior *before, during,* and at the *end* of your correction program, you can determine the effectiveness of your efforts.

Suppose you decide to work on diminishing your child's screaming. In order to determine your effectiveness, you will want to establish what is called the child's *baseline rate.* This is the frequency at which the child screams over a period of time (a week or ten days) before you work to diminish it. A method you can use to achieve this is to make one mark on a daily observation sheet each time the child

Misbehavior Tally Sheet

Child _Reed_   Misbehavior in focus _screaming_

Jan 1-M	T	W	Th	F	S	Sun	Jan 8-M	T	W	Th	F	S	Sun
卌 卌 卌	/// 卌 卌 卌	卌 卌 卌 卌	卌 卌 卌 /	卌 卌 卌 卌	卌 卌 卌 卌 //	卌 卌 卌 卌 ///	卌 卌 卌	卌 卌 卌 //	卌 卌 卌 卌	卌 卌 卌 /	卌 卌 卌 卌	卌 卌 卌 卌	卌 卌 ////
Jan 15-M													
卌 卌 卌 卌 卌													

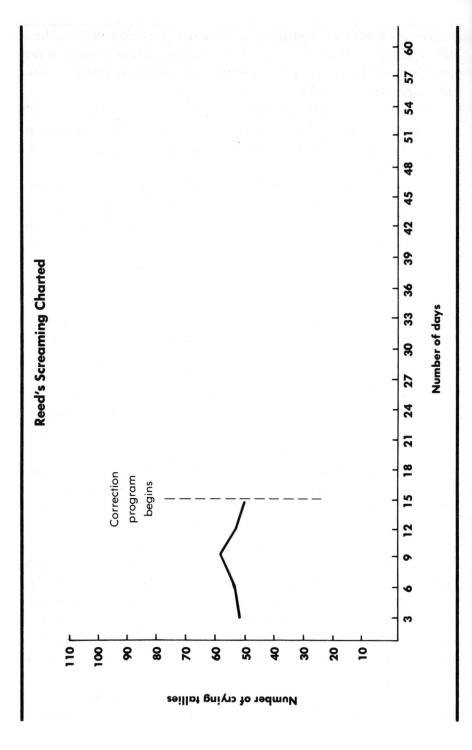

Reed's Screaming Charted

Correction program begins

Number of crying tallies

Number of days

begins to scream and another mark for about every three minutes he is still screaming. Thus, if the child screams for fifteen minutes at one time, he would have six tallies for the one screaming episode. Your tally sheet might look like the chart on page 91.

Usually one or two weeks of observation will provide a stable baseline rate of the child's screaming misbehavior. The frequency of the child's screaming should be graphed as shown on page 92 to help you determine when you have a stable baseline rate.

After you have charted the baseline of the child, you may then begin your program for changing his misbehavior. For example, you may have decided to walk into another room when the child screams and/or tell him to take his screaming to another room when it is not practical for you to leave.

Continue tallying the frequency of the child's screaming and charting the graph every three days for a period of a month or two. His frequency of screaming may sharply increase and then gradually or sharply decrease. As you count his misbehavior and graph it, you can better determine the progress of your correction program.

It is important to identify precisely the behavior you decide to change in order to effectively chart your progress. Being precise will enable you to deal specifically and concretely with the situation. It will assist you in establishing goals that will be achievable. "When we are in the supermarket, the child screams, tells me I'm stupid, and kicks me in the shins whenever I tell him he can't have a candy bar" is an example of precise identification of a child's misbehavior. "The child seems upset and hostile whenever we go to the supermarket" is an example of an ambiguous and less helpful description.

Tallying and charting progress can be helpful in many different relationships in which you wish to change behavior. For example, suppose that after reading this book you discover you are belittling your spouse in public and decide that you want to stop. By keeping a little black book with you at all times, you can place in it a tally mark each time you or your spouse discover you are being critical. You can then chart these tallies, as in the case of the child's screaming, and have a graphic picture of your progress.

In some of the following cases, recommendations for changing behavior are given which tend to be very workable if nothing is physically wrong with the child. If there is a chance that his problems are physical in origin, you may want to consult your physician before you proceed to change his behavior. You will want to keep this in mind as you analyze these situations and decide what is most appropriate for your circumstances.

TRAINING TO LOVE

THE SITUATION

Andrea is concerned about rearing her daughter Diane so that she will be capable of a healthy and profound love for other people. Andrea is from a broken home where her father and mother quarrelled constantly and were so involved with their own problems that they had little time and energy to give her the love and affection she needed. As a result Andrea has had difficulty in trusting and loving; but through the love, kindness, and respect shown to her by her husband, Bill, she is gradually learning to trust and to love. She wants her daughter to learn these traits while she is little.

RECOMMENDATION

One of the most important requirements in helping Diane learn to love is contact comfort. Andrea and Bill should hold, cuddle, and kiss her often, and always with genuine warmth. Touching and stroking can also help Diane learn to accept and give affection. Andrea and Bill should generally initiate their contact comfort when Diane is quiet and happy rather than when she is crying.

DISCUSSION

The above suggestions provide for only a beginning, but a very important beginning, in teaching Diane how to love. She is most impressionable as an infant, and her early experiences of her parents' physical affection will tend to stay with her and help her learn to love. She will tend to have a basic trust in people that she will communicate to them. They will feel it and will tend to respond in the same manner.

As she grows, her parents will find it necessary to augment contact comfort with such behavior as positive, horizontal conversation and recognition for her individual efforts. This will help her to progress toward a healthy affection for her fellowmen. But contact comfort is a powerful beginning.

One word about Andrea. She may find it difficult to give contact comfort freely. However, with wise, understanding responses from Bill and patience, perseverance, and practice on her part, she will learn. She must be careful not to be jealous of Bill's attention to Diane. Bill will wisely not neglect Andrea. Also she must learn and apply the techniques and skills discussed throughout this book that will enable her to keep from becoming enslaved to Diane's unreasonable demands. As she receives responses from Bill and structures her life so that she is relatively free from the undue, vertical demands of other people, Andrea will continue to develop her capacity to love. This will enable her to give her love to Diane as a free gift and in the process become a model of loving behavior.

Note: Concepts you may want to review are life-style, pp. 48-50; modeling, pp. 53-54; bonding, pp. 52-53; practice, pp. 54-55.

A QUESTION OF FEEDING SCHEDULES

THE SITUATION

Deborah is eight months pregnant with her first child. She and her husband, Dale, have been considering whether to feed their newborn on demand or on a schedule. They have read much on the subject, talked to friends and even several family doctors, but they come away from each discussion more confused.

They are concerned about rearing their child to respect other people; and if a particular feeding practice will make a difference, they want to use it.

RECOMMENDATION

Deborah and Dale can set up a feeding schedule and then follow it through. They will probably want to consult their pediatrician first.

DISCUSSION

The first obligation of the infant is to fit into a family's schedule. It is in such an environment that he begins, even though only a few days old, to learn to respect the rights of his mother and other members of the family. As he learns that his mother will not come running to feed him on demand, he will easily generalize that others besides his mother do not exist merely to respond to his every beck and call. He thereby will learn that all men have their own needs and interests. He comes to understand when he is most impressionable to respect the rights of others.

Another advantage of feeding the infant on a schedule is that it teaches him a degree of self-discipline, a prerequisite for successful and effective living with other people.

A third major benefit is that the biological processes of the body seem to be best served by a somewhat fixed rhythm of eating, eliminating, and sleeping.

Note: Concepts you may want to review are communal interest, pp. 47-48; modeling, pp. 53-54; practice, pp. 54-55.

GENESIS FOR SPOILING

THE SITUATION

Ted had been with the family only a few short weeks. He was large for his age and couldn't seem to get enough to eat. Almost from the time his bottle left his lips, and always within two hours from the time he was fed, he pulled the corners of his mouth down and sobbed as if his heart would break. While he sobbed, he beat random patterns in the air with his hands and feet. During this time all members of his family cuddled and rocked and walked the floor with him. Picking him up and cuddling him seemed to have little effect. He would continue to cry.

This went on for about one week until his parents strengthened his formula. He immediately quieted down the first day and returned to smiling and cooing. But the second day after being fed and played with, he cried and screamed when he was put down. His mother and father, feeling something was wrong again, picked him up, whereupon he quickly quieted down and commenced to smile and coo. This was repeated over a period of several days.

Ted's parents became frustrated with him, for although they sensed he was all right, he cried so hard and long that they felt something must be wrong. Sometimes they waited a half hour, and a few times a full hour, before they picked him up, not being able to stand his misery any longer and feeling sorry for him and somewhat guilty. He sobbed a few times and then quickly became his charming little self again.

Ted's parents have been wondering what to do with him, for they feel uneasy about what has been happening.

RECOMMENDATION

Ted's mother and father can set up rather rigid schedules for feeding and playing with their baby and follow these regardless of Ted's protests. For example, they can feed him at 6:00 a.m., 10:00 a.m., 2:00 p.m., 6:00 p.m., and 9:00 p.m. Playtime may be for about ten or fifteen minutes prior to his feeding at 10:00 a.m., 2:00 p.m., and 6:00 p.m., and at other unscheduled times when he is being quiet in his crib or playpen. After he has been fed and properly burped, and after his playtime, his mother and father can leave him to sleep or play by himself regardless of his crying protests. This strategy assumes of course that there is nothing physically wrong with him.

DISCUSSION

Ted's situation is a rather classical example of how a small infant can learn to influence his parents with the power of his cries and screams. His behavior, which began when he was truly hungry, taught him that his cries and screams would bring his mother and father to him. It was not a conscious endeavor with him. But it worked, so he used it.

It is important for Ted's parents to no longer pay off his cries, regardless of how hard he sobs. They might still want to go to him, but if they do, they will only stimulate him to cry longer and louder for future payoff—the attention, affection, and concern of his parents.

In order not to pay off Ted's crying behavior, his father and mother, once they put Ted down, must not return to him until he is quiet and peaceful.

It is more than likely than many an adult tyrant has begun his tyrannical life style in infancy under circumstances similar to Ted's. Such things as severe colic, an early operation, rheumatic fever, or severe respiratory infections have triggered crying behavior that was responded to by concerned, responsible parents. And this is as it should be, in most cases. However, the difficulty occurs when the physical illness is over, yet the infant or child continues to cry in order to keep receiving attention from his parents. If a child stops crying immediately upon being picked up and is soon contented and happy and shows no discomfort, his parents can be reasonably certain that his crying is an attempt to get them involved in giving him attention and is not a result of severe physical discomfort.

Parents must wisely refrain from obeying their first impulses to rescue a child when he has set a pattern of crying to get their attention. They should, however, redouble their efforts to recognize him, play with him, and talk with him when he is playing quietly, being peaceful, or exhibiting other types of horizontal behavior. Such an expression of interest, concern, and love the child will naturally trust, for it has not been manipulated. It is a free gift.

Note: A concept you may want to review is payoff, pp. 42-44, 53.

A CHILD WHO HOLDS HIS BREATH

THE SITUATION

Harry, a second child, is a delight most of the time. He is energetic, playful, and almost always smiles. But there is one thing he does that panics his parents. When Mary, his mother, does not get his food as fast as he would like, he lets out a scream and holds his breath until he turns red, then purple. Mary panics with fright. She grabs him, shakes him, blows in his face, and when he starts to breathe in great gulps of air, she holds him close and rocks him. Both Mary and Alex, his father, anxiously note that he starts to hold his breath when toys are taken from him, when he is lifted from his bath, and at many other times.

RECOMMENDATION

To diminish and stop Harry's misbehavior, Mary should immediately walk into another room as soon as Harry begins to scream and stay there without looking around the side of the door frame, even though he holds his breath. This action, of course, assumes that the child is in no real danger. She may return when he has quieted down and then say in a calm voice, "I see you are ready to eat quietly." If he screams a second time, she says, "It sounds like you are more interested in doing other things than eating." Then she takes him out of his highchair and places him gently on the floor and continues her housework (thus using the principle of logical consequences). He is not fed again until the next regularly scheduled feeding time, regardless of his tears.

It is suggested that Alex and Mary ignore Harry's breath holding when he is taken from his bath. This they can do by taking him out with no emotion, looking elsewhere than at him, wrapping him warmly and placing him in his crib. There he stays until he quiets down.

As with other disciplinary cases, Mary and Alex should get involved with Harry when he smiles and happily plays.

DISCUSSION

Holding his breath is a powerful device Harry is perfecting to get special attention and service. By frightening his parents he is able to get them to do his bidding. The more Mary and Alex respond by feeding him faster, or by giving him back his toys when he holds his breath, the more he will use his scare tactics in these and other situations. When his parents respond emotionally with behaviors such as concerned shaking, blowing, and cuddling, he receives tremendous payoff and is stimulated to continue to hold his breath in the future.

Being successful in holding his breath, he will tend to generalize this success to other power techniques such as yelling, screaming, and being sick to achieve his misguided purposes. He may then see himself as one who can best belong by being powerful. These illogical efforts work to lessen his innate potential to relate successfully with his fellowman.

Note: Concepts you may want to review are life-style, pp. 48-50; payoff, pp. 42-44; logical consequences, p. 86; personality traits, pp. 55-56.

A CASE OF CONTINUAL CRYING

THE SITUATION

Allen and Marjorie are young parents of six-month-old Allen Jr. They are both conscientious parents who vowed during their courtship that they would do all in their power to rear children who could relate well with others. Marjorie works hard to see that Allen's needs are met. She checks his diaper several times each hour and changes it if he is the least bit damp. She spends much time each day rocking, playing, and talking to him.

What concerns them is that in spite of all they are doing for their little son, it never seems enough. Marjorie can hardly leave his crib before he is sobbing. If she goes to him when he is crying and does not pick him up immediately, he rolls over on his stomach, doubles up his knees, rests his head on his hands and arms, and intensifies his sobbing until his entire body is quivering and shaking. Not being able to take it any longer, Marjorie picks him up. His sobbing quickly subsides between gasps, and he soon begins to smile and coo and continues to do so as long as Mother is holding him.

Marjorie finds most of her time completely taken up with Allen Jr. In spite of her great love for him, she finds at times that she feels not only pity for him, but anger and resentment. It is as if she no longer has any time for herself, her husband, or anyone else.

Allen and Marjorie have taken him to their pediatrician, who could find nothing physically wrong with the infant.

RECOMMENDATION

Neither Marjorie nor Allen should pick up their child or even approach his crib when he is crying for their attention. As long as they continue to go to him when he cries and sobs, he will continue such behavior. This allows him to achieve his goal—to get their attention and fondling. He will continue to cry as long as Marjorie and Allen enable him to achieve his purposes with it.

They should redouble their efforts to go to him when he is playing quietly. Talking to him, cuddling him, and smiling at him will be payoff for his constructive behavior. He will tend to exhibit more of it to the extent that Allen and Marjorie pay him off at such times.

DISCUSSION

It is vitally important that Marjorie and Allen discipline themselves to pay off Allen Jr.'s positive behaviors and not to pay off his crying, if they are to achieve the promises they made to each other prior to their marriage. For if Allen Jr. continues to bring people to him with his crying and sobbing, he may develop the attitude that he has a right to demand the servitude of others. He may become a junior tyrant, enslaving others to his self-centered demands. He may believe that life is wholly a matter of taking, not one of giving as well.

Not only will Allen Jr. tend to develop a tyrannical attitude toward other people, but as he cries and sobs to get his own way he will inevitably experience the feelings associated with such behavior.

As a result his whole life will tend to be replete with habitual frustration and misery. He may develop feelings of inadequacy and inferiority concerning his ability to cope successfully, which will be relieved only by feelings of superiority as he gets others to obey his crying demands.

Marjorie is especially vulnerable to Allen's crying, for she is the eldest of five children and has experienced the burden of much responsibility. When her parents went out at night, she was left in charge. If they returned to find things not as they should have been, she was criticized. Hence she has spent much of her life trying to see that everything goes smoothly about her.

Marjorie will need to acquire courage and strong discipline in order to respond effectively to Allen Jr., for the ghost of past criticism rides her shoulder, whispering in her ear when things are not right, "You are to blame. Do something now." Marjorie must look to the future and say to herself, "I am not going to him now when he cries, for I want him to grow up with character traits that will enable him to relate well with his fellowmen. I will go to him when he is quiet and thus pay off his cooperative behavior."

Note: Concepts you may want to review are payoff, pp. 42-44; life-style, pp. 48-50; holism, pp. 50-52.

TRAINING TO RESPECT PROPERTY
THE SITUATION

Cary is a handsome little boy with warm brown eyes and thick, dark hair. He is seven months old and has just learned to crawl. At first his mother and father were delighted with his efforts to move about on his own, but now they sometimes wish he were less mobile. He is always getting into mischief. If he is not pulling on the drapes, he is tipping over plants and figurines. His mother feels that her whole day is spent getting after him. If he seemed to be learning, his mother would feel that her efforts were worthwhile, but it appears that he is getting worse rather than better.

Cary's mother's friends tell her to baby proof the house by putting away and out of reach every item he might damage. Others suggest that there is really nothing she can do, because kids will be kids. But none of these suggestions seems right to her. She wants to train Cary to respect the property of others, and she feels this is the time to start.

RECOMMENDATION

Cary's parents can start by putting all figurines and vases out of Cary's reach. This will leave just the drapes and house plants that Cary can still touch, push, and grab. Whenever he pulls on the drapes or grabs and pushes at plants, his parents are to say, "No. No," one time. If he continues, they should immediately pick him up and at the same time say, "No. No," once more, and place him in his playpen. They should leave him there for ten minutes and then take him out. (While he is in the playpen, he is to be completely ignored.)

If he returns immediately to his mischievous behavior, his parents should repeat the same correction process, but this time leave him in his playpen for twenty minutes instead of ten, regardless of his protests.

DISCUSSION

Cary's parents are wise in wanting to train him at such an early age to respect the property of others. If they wait until later when he has had much experience in being disrespectful of other people's property, he will be much harder to train. With early training, they will avoid much heartache.

It is suggested that the mother and father remove figurines and vases and concentrate on training Cary to leave the drapes and plants alone because it facilitates learning. They have only so much energy; and by conserving and focusing it on just these two areas, they increase their chances for success. Such a strategy enables parents to be consistent. Also, by not trying to teach Cary too much at one time, they diminish the possibilities that he will become confused; they also increase his chances for learning.

The vases and figurines are replaced one by one as Cary learns to leave them alone. And if Cary's parents provide him with many interesting and stimulating objects (i.e., cloth picture book, plastic objects of varying shapes and colors), they will tend to keep him occupied in constructive ways.

Note: A concept you may want to review is logical consequences, p. 86.

BIRTH OF MASOCHISM

THE SITUATION

Nine-month-old Marsha was determined to get at her father's schoolbooks. Marsha, a wiry infant with a toothless grin and winning ways, had just learned to walk. Any drawer or door she could open in an attempt to discover strange new things to play with was an object of her attention. Of special interest were her father's schoolbooks, which were stored on shelves behind doors that opened easily.

The family was living in university housing at this time. It was a small two-bedroom apartment, containing just a little over five hundred square feet of floor space. The floors themselves consisted of concrete covered with asphalt tile, but they were so hard that they seemed to have no covering at all.

One day Marsha was determined to get into Father's books. She opened the doors and began to pull them out one at a time. Her father went to her, replaced the books, closed the doors, and said, "No, Marsha, you are not to get into Daddy's books." He picked her up and removed her from the area, placing her in the next room. Marsha immediately returned to the bookcase, opened a door, and continued as before. This time Father tied the doorknobs together so that it was impossible for her to get at the books.

Marsha quickly tried again. When she discovered the doors would not open as before, she began to scream. This continued for several minutes, Marsha looking over occasionally at Father with a pleading look in her eyes. Father remained where he was.

It was at this point that Marsha left the bookcase and toddled over directly in front of Father. Dropping down and resting her weight on both hands, her seat high in the air, she began to pound her head on the floor.

RECOMMENDATION

Father should avert his eyes from Marsha, say nothing, get up, and move quietly into the next room. He is not to look back at his daughter, regardless of his feelings.

DISCUSSION

It is at such a relatively early age that children first learn to mutilate themselves. The individual who, as a teenager, has set a pattern of purposely cutting himself probably first began such behavior at a very early age with responses similar to Marsha's.

104

When Marsha dropped to the floor and began to pound her head on the concrete floor, her father became extremely anxious. He had visions of her damaging brain cells and ruining herself for life. He thought that the least he could do was put his hand between her head and the concrete to cushion the blows. But he had heard that it was best to ignore such situations; so, gathering all the courage he could muster, he did walk into the next room.

The sequel to the story occurred one week later when the child's mother was home alone with her. She related it to her husband with a feeling of relief and tears of amusement. She had prevented Marsha from getting into the flour bin. Marsha screamed, went to the middle of the floor, dropped down on both hands, and started moving her head toward the concrete. In the middle of her downward motion she hesitated, struggled to her feet, and went over to the sofa. There she picked up a loose pillow and took it to the middle of the floor. She dropped it, fell on both hands, and very gently pounded her head into the pillow. This was the last time she attempted this behavior.

This case had a happy ending. But it could have been quite different if Marsha's father had picked her up, and cuddled her, and tried to soothe her when she first pounded her head on the concrete. If he had done this, or given her the books, it could have taught her a powerful, vicious, and bizarre technique for getting attention, defeating other people, and hurting them.

It is because parents and other people pay off such vertical behaviors with ever increasing concern, defeat, and hurt that children learn techniques of masochism. They become individuals who suffer self-inflicted pain in order to get others to panic over them and in bewilderment give in to any tyrannical demand that is made. An individual with masochistic traits is willing to force a place of belonging with his fellowmen even though he pays a painful price.

Note: Concepts you may want to review are vertical goals, pp. 16-23, 43; payoff, pp. 42-44, 53.

MAKING PREPARATIONS FOR TOILET TRAINING
THE SITUATION

Gordon and Jean are a young married couple living in a university housing complex. They have a new baby, Greg. Already they are becoming concerned about his future toilet training as it is a common topic for conversation among their friends in the complex. It seems to be a status symbol among the group to have their children trained early. Also, Jean has a sister whose little boy of four is still not trained, and it is driving his mother up the wall. Both Gordon and Jean have heard that boys are harder to train than girls. They are concerned and want to start preparing him immediately, if that is possible, so that he will be in a good position to learn fast.

RECOMMENDATION

Probably the best approach Gordon and Jean can take for preparing Greg is to prepare themselves. This they can do by not engaging in the vertical relationship with their friends in which an infant's bowel training is used for status.

A second important step is for them to make sure that Greg is changed often. As soon as he is wet or soiled, they should change him and show little or no emotion while doing so.

DISCUSSION

Many children have learned to use their elimination processes to tyrannize, to defeat, or to hurt their parents. Parents, who are usually more concerned about their children's being clean than their children are, may easily become victims. By not participating in the status game of My Child Was Trained Before Yours, Gordon and Jean will lessen the chances that Greg's toilet training will be tied to their own need for status and prestige. This will enable them to handle his training with the quiet calmness that is essential to his well-being.

If Greg's parents keep his diapers dry, he will become used to this comfort. When he comes of age to be trained, which is usually about eighteen months, he will soon realize that he can remain clean if he eliminates in a toilet or a potty, not in his diapers or pants.

Here is one word of caution to Greg's parents. They should change Greg's diapers quickly and with little or no emotional involvement. Otherwise he might learn to use wet and soiled diapers as a means of getting attention.

Note: Concepts you may want to review are self-esteem, pp. 46-47; bonding, pp. 52-53; vertical goals, pp. 16-23, 43.

A CHILD WHO IS DIFFICULT TO TOILET TRAIN

THE SITUATION

Two-year-old Dan is continually having bowel movements in his diaper or training pants. He also wets them. Mother finds herself scolding him, yelling at him, and spanking him. She sometimes gets so frustrated and angry that she sits him down with a bang on his potty chair.

It especially exasperates her when he says, "I'm all through, Mommy," then stands up from his chair and wets all over the floor. She often feels defeated.

Dan has a three-month-old baby brother for whom he shows much affection.

RECOMMENDATION

Dan's mother should concentrate her energies on being routinely consistent with him. She is to take him to the potty at regularly scheduled intervals throughout the day. She should focus her attention on whether she is being consistent and not on whether he has finished eliminating in the potty.

Her approach to him at these times should be calm and controlled. She must never raise her voice or spank him for not going in the potty. She should not make a fuss over Danny when she is changing his diaper, but rather change him in a matter-of-fact manner with little or no talking. She should give him no emotional response of any kind at this time.

It is also suggested that Dan's mother let him take a responsible part in helping her take care of the baby. Such things as holding the baby on his lap with his mother's assistance and holding his bottle are preferable to sending him out of the room to get a fresh diaper.

Both the mother and father should recognize Dan's efforts to be of help and to be independent by consistently paying off his constructive efforts.

DISCUSSION

It appears that Dan is receiving a good deal of attention from his mother in the form of scolding, yelling, and spanking. His mother's expressions of defeat are also forms of payoff for Dan because they reveal evidence of his power over her. His mother will be successful when she completely withdraws payoff for this kind of behavior. It will be helpful for his mother to focus her attention on responding in a calm and routine, consistent manner. To the extent that she is calm and consistent, she can take pleasure in knowing that she is being responsible. She cannot force Dan to be trained and should not feel that this is her responsibility. She can only structure the environment in such a way that he can best take advantage of it to train himself.

Keeping Dan close to her and the baby as she encourages him to assist her lessens the probability that he will feel threatened. When he is sent away to get a diaper and hears his mother cooing over the baby in the next room, he may readily feel that he has been sent out of the way so that his mother can love the baby. Her demonstrated affection for Dan while he is with the baby can help him *bond* to his baby brother the feelings of love that are aroused.

Dan's independence and self-reliance, stimulated by his parents' encouraging him to do such things as feed himself and get up and out out of his crib by himself, will help him have a good self-image. He will then respond more readily to toilet training.

Note: Concepts you may want to review are vertical goals, pp. 16-23, 43; payoff, pp. 42-44; practice, pp. 54-55; personality traits, pp. 55-56; belonging, pp. 45-46.

AN INCONSISTENCY IN TOILET TRAINING

THE SITUATION

Rachael and Bill, the parents of Morris and four older children, are beside themselves with frustration and anger. Morris was toilet trained at two, but for almost a year and a half he has been messing his pants. Rachael has tried many different things to restrain him, but nothing seems to work. He embarrasses them in public with his messiness and often at home when company comes. Rachael is resentful of having to clean up his "stinky messes." The older children tell him that he is a baby. However, much of the time they enjoy doing things for him, including those things that he can do for himself.

Alone with her thoughts, Rachael finds herself thinking about Morris and experiencing feelings of resentment, anger, hurt, embarrassment, and defeat. In fact, on occasion, she feels hate for him, and then experiences deep feelings of guilt. She is concerned that he will not be trained in time for school. Sometimes she imagines him as an adult still messing his pants. She worries continually about it.

RECOMMENDATION

First, Morris's problem should become a nontopic of conversation. Rachael and Bill should refer to it only when they have to deal directly with him, and then only briefly.

Second, since he is not trained, Morris should be kept in diapers until he demonstrates he can responsibly wear regular pants.

Third, Rachael and Bill will find it very helpful if they structure their environment in such a manner that Morris cannot embarrass them readily. For example, when company comes, they might have him go to his room until the company leaves. He is told before company comes, calmly and with few words and no hint of resentment, that other people do not like to smell messes. He should also be told that when he no longer messes his pants, they will be very happy to have him stay. A babysitter is brought in to sit with him when the family goes out into the community. He is told that boys who still mess their pants have to stay home, but that Mommy and Daddy would love to have him go with them when he decides to train himself not to mess.

Fourth, everyone in the family must work at not doing anything for Morris that he can do for himself. Each is to encourage him to dress himself, talk for himself, and do all those things that will make him feel that he is becoming a self-reliant boy.

Fifth, it is very important that his father, mother, brothers, and sisters cuddle him, smile at him, put their arms around him, and show him affection in other appropriate ways many times during the day when he is clean and behaving responsibly.

DISCUSSION

It seems apparent that Morris, by messing his pants, is achieving the goals of attention, power, and counterhurting. When other people talk about and fuss over his messing, he achieves payoff for his attention seeking. When they feel angry and defeated, he senses his power over them and also achieves payoff. When they feel hurt, embarrassed, and guilty, he feels that they are suffering as they have made him suffer, and he accomplishes his intent to counterhurt.

When Morris was two, soon after he was potty trained, Rachael took care of a baby for two months while the mother was sick. This took up most of her time, and she had little time for Morris. He apparently decided to be a baby again and regressed to messing in his pants. This powerful technique brought about the attention he wanted, as well as making his mother suffer as he felt she had made him suffer. Her payoff stimulated him to keep this behavior regardless of the physical discomfort to himself.

Morris's family members must stop paying off his disturbing behaviors. Also, as they stimulate him to become independent, he will think better of himself and will have less need to strike out at other people.

One must remember that the child does not consciously plot to get his parents' attention or to defeat or hurt them. His is a semi-conscious process. He tends to use tactics which enable him to have an emotional impact on those whom he loves.

If parents are to help a disturbing child, they must be *consistent*. The child must know for sure exactly what routine his parents will follow when he messes his pants.

Note: Concepts you may want to review are vertical goals, pp. 16-23, 43; payoff, pp. 42-44; logical consequences, p. 86; social linkage, pp. 44-45; bonding, pp. 52-53.

SEPARATION ANXIETY

THE SITUATION

Rob, the second child in a family of three, has an older brother, Andy, who is six and a younger sister, Cheryle, who is two. Rob's mother, Betty, a widow of two years, is very concerned about Rob. When she talks to other people about him, her chest gets tight and the tears fall.

Rob will not let Betty out of his sight. She has started him in a well-respected half-day nursery school, but when the time comes for him to get ready for school, he begins to cry and says he won't go. He refuses to get dressed, so Betty dresses him and fights with him the whole time. Rob then strikes out at his mother, screaming, "I hate you! I hate you!" By this time Betty is in tears. She takes him by the hand and starts for the door while Rob grabs a chair, then the doorknob, followed by the door frame as he desperately tries to hold back. By the time they arrive at nursery school, Betty is feeling intense emotions of pity, guilt, anger, and resentment. A scene similar to the one upon their leaving home is repeated at the school. Rob grabs the car door handle, lays on the ground as limp as a doll, and then grabs for any protruding object he can get hold of to retard his progress as Betty drags him screaming and yelling to the school. By this time Betty's cheeks are not only wet with tears, but flushed with embarrassment and guilt. She looks back after his teacher has taken him by the hand and sees his pathetic little figure struggling and kicking. Her ears ring with the screams. She feels torn up inside.

It is not just at nursery school that Rob acts in this manner; it is at almost any time that his mother attempts to leave him. Rob exhibits the same behavior when it is time for him to go to his Sunday School class. Whenever she attempts to go out for an evening with the Young Sociables, an organization for single people, she becomes the chair, the doorknob, and the door frame as Rob grabs frantically for her to get her to stay. She feels guilty anyway about going out; and when Rob responds this way, she is overwhelmed by guilt feelings and questions of doubt. At this point she tries reasoning with Rob, but he only cries and screams louder. Because of his behavior his mother has often changed her mind and decided not to leave him.

Lately Betty has been filled with rather continuous feelings of self-doubt, guilt about how terribly she feels she is treating Rob, and also deep resentment toward him because she feels trapped and enslaved.

RECOMMENDATION

Betty should tell Rob that she understands how hard it is for him to be apart from her, but he can learn to accept it and will become a person who will like himself better because of it. She must also explain that she is no longer going to talk to him about her going as she has in the past. She is to tell him that she will let him know when she is leaving, where she is going, who is staying with him (someone he knows) and when she will be back. She will say no more than this. Betty is then to leave regardless of his screams and yells and to do it without a backward glance.

With regard to his nursery school, Betty is not to get involved in a struggle to dress him. She is to say to Rob, "You get yourself dressed for nursery school, and I will help you tie your shoes if you want."

At first Rob will probably dawdle and not be dressed. Betty is never to remind him about his dressing. She is to say nothing. When it is time to leave she will pick him up and his clothes, even though he is half-dressed, carry both bundles to the car, and place them in the back. She may then say, "You can finish getting dressed in the car or at school. It's up to you."

Betty gives Rob the choice of walking to the car himself or of having Mother carry him if he hangs back. She says only once in a calm and gentle voice, "Would you like to walk or have me carry you?" If he does not answer, and does not move immediately, he has made his choice. Betty picks him up with no emotion and like a mechanical robot carries him to the car regardless of his frantic protestations. She does not pay off his vertical behaviors on the way to school.

When they arrive at school, Betty is to open the door and say, "Would you like to walk in by yourself or would you prefer to have me carry you?" Again, if he hesitates at all, Betty should pick him up and carry him with no emotion to his classroom. If he is still not dressed, she carries him with one arm and his clothes with the other and deposits them both with the teacher. She has previously contacted the teacher who has agreed to work cooperatively with her.

Betty must then immediately withdraw and return to the car, walking in a calm, confident manner and not looking back at struggling Rob.

She is to follow a similar pattern with Rob at Sunday School.

She should also be sure to pay off Rob's attempts to behave independently and horizontally.

DISCUSSION

Soon after Rob's father died, Rob was ill and had to spend three weeks in the hospital. The nurses babied him continually and Betty called him or visited him every day—even though they were fifty miles apart. At this time Betty was filled with loneliness and a sense of deep loss for her husband. Seeing little Rob alone in a big hospital, she often burst into tears in front of him and loved and cuddled him. Rob began, at this time, to cry and scream whenever it was time for his mother to leave. Often Betty talked the administrative staff into letting her stay longer as she attempted to calm him down with her continued presence, love, and physical affection. She continued to fight back the tears as she drove home, for she kept thinking about poor little Rob all alone in the big hospital.

It was in the above setting that Rob learned that he could have power over other people with his fear, cries, and screams. During this time he began to mold for himself a special place with other people. And, as he saw Andy's competence and Cheryle's cute charming ways, he chose to belong by using the unique, powerful behaviors that he learned in the hospital by manipulating the servitude of the nurses and a vulnerable, mourning mother.

Every time Betty hesitated to leave because of his tears, reasoned with him as he fought, or cried with frustration, Rob achieved payoff. As a result, he was able to reach his goal of forcing her to stay with him. Every time she felt pity for him or guilt as he screamed, "You don't love me," he achieved payoff. Mother's downcast eyes, tears, and hesitancy also paid him off. He perceived his emotional impact on her and realized his importance. This became his way of belonging, his way of having a unique place.

It may be helpful for Betty to search out a wise friend who can help her be firm with herself when she feels that she will begin to pay off Rob's tantrums. Such a friend can provide strength, support, and encouragement. Betty should, however, beware of the person who could undermine her resolve and make her even more vulnerable to Rob's manipulations.

It is also important for Betty to realize that time tends to heal, that her hurt over the loss of her husband will diminish and she will become stronger. As she builds a new life for herself, she will find her strength continuing to increase and will be more able to withstand Rob's assaults.

Looking to Rob's future will also help Betty to be firm with herself in not paying off his disturbing behavior. By projecting his behavior into the future, she may better understand how harmful to good relationships Rob's behavior will be if it continues. He will find misery as an adolescent with his peers, mother, brother, and sister, and with his associates in school, church, and elsewhere.

Betty should explain to Rob's nursery school teacher how she is trying to change his behavior. Most teachers will work cooperatively with parents who confide in them and seek their assistance.

Betty's not paying off Rob's tantrums will emancipate her from him. She will thereby feel freer and better able to give sincere payoff for his constructive acts. Her feelings of self-worth and interest in life will also increase.

It is important that Betty encourage Rob to do things on his own. As she communicates faith in him, he will gain greater self-confidence in his ability to be more independent and will be less afraid.

One word of caution. As with all children who have been successful in their misbehavior, Rob may get worse before he gets better. If he does this, it more than likely will be a sign that he is trying harder to get his mother to give him the old payoff. Betty must be especially firm at this time. If she gives in to his intensified crying and screaming, she will be training him to behave in an even worse manner.

By not paying off his fears, cries, screams, yells, and clutches to keep his mother in bondage to him, and by paying off his efforts to do things on his own, Betty will be making a responsible contribution to Rob's learning to respond horizontally. This responsible action will bring much happiness to Betty, Rob, and his brother and sister in the future.

Note: Concepts you may want to review are life-style, pp. 48-50; social linkage, pp. 44-45; vertical goals, pp. 16-23, 43; payoff, pp. 42-44; self-esteem, pp. 46-47; logical consequences, p. 86.

A CASE OF DAWDLING

THE SITUATION

Five-year-old Deanne is the youngest in a family of five, a charming little girl with the features of an elf. Every time her mother or father asks her to do anything, she ducks her head, grins, and looks up with a mischievous face and continues what she is doing. Though she is definitely exasperating, her parents find it very hard to get angry with her.

The thing that irritates her mother and father most is her protracted eating. She stirs her food and stabs at it, then turns on the edge

114

of her chair and tips it until her father believes she is going to fall over and break it. Eating time is one continual round of "Hurry up and eat. Turn around. Sit square in your chair. Eat it so you'll be a big girl."

She responds by grinning impishly, eating just a little faster, and then reverting to her former behavior.

RECOMMENDATION

Deanne's mother and father would probably find it very helpful if they would completely ignore Deanne's eating speed. Her dawdling should never be discussed in front of her. When her mother or father take their turn at doing the dishes, he or she should calmly remove all dishes, including dawdling Deanne's, and scrape the remains into the garbage. This, of course, is preceded by an agreement in the family council including all of the children and both parents that this is a reasonable response. It also shows respect for the time of the one whose turn it is to do the dishes.

DISCUSSION

Deanne's purpose in dawdling is to get attention from other people who give it to her by nagging her and telling her to hurry up. But this is an unconstructive way of belonging in the family. When her parents make her dawdling a nontopic of conversation and clear all the dishes from the table, including hers, they are withdrawing payoff and helping her to experience the logical consequences of her actions.

Note: Concepts you may want to review are life-style, pp. 48-50; payoff, pp. 42-44; logical consequences, p. 86.

CHANGING ROLES

THE SITUATION

Gwen, a sharp little girl of five, had acquired a vocabulary beyond her years. Her parents' eyes sparkled and their faces lit up as they described Gwen. They perceived her as being a good girl who tried to do what was right. She was obedient to her parents.

Three-year-old George was quite a different case, and their eyes were downcast and their faces tense as they described him. He was the child they were concerned about. He flushed articles of his own and his parents' clothing down the toilet. He wrote on walls with crayons. He ran out in the street. It seemed as though everyone were continually looking after and chasing after George.

One-year-old Sandy was the other child in the family. Her parents described her as cute, quiet, and without real problems.

The troubled parents of Gwen, George, and Sandy had come to get help in an attempt to change George's behavior. A discussion of the situation revealed that Gwen watched his every move and told her mother when he was doing something he shouldn't do. Her typical phrases were "Mommy, you better come quick. George is in the toilet again. Mother, George got a crayon and he's going to be naughty. Come quick. George has got one of your cuff links, Father." Gwen was continually tattling and George was continually misbehaving. Their mother, especially, was on the run throughout the day.

Further information about what was going on among the family members showed that, in typical fashion, George's behavior had real meaning only as he was considered within the context of the total family. (A so-called problem child can usually best be understood and his behavior most effectively changed when all individuals and their behaviors within the family or class are considered.) Gwen was an intelligent and good girl, but she was also good at George's expense. By continually tattling on him, she was able to demonstrate her goodness and George's badness. George, not believing he could compete with Gwen's goodness or Sandy's charming ways for the attention of his parents, chose instead to be good at being mischievous. And at this he became most skillful.

The parents were encouraged to change these patterns of vertical behavior by telling Gwen once that they were no longer going to pay attention to her tattling on George. Only when he was in real danger (ie., going out in the street) was she to come to them. Otherwise they were going to ignore her tattling. They were also to be careful not to pay off George's misbehavior, but instead use the principle of logical consequences. George was to clean off his crayon marks when he scribbled on the wall. His mother or father could work with him to get the job done, but they were to function only mechanically in order to give no payoff to his vertical behavior. He was to be denied crayons for a period of time after he used them improperly. His parents were to pay off George's attempts to be independent and useful by recognizing his constructive behaviors and encouraging him.

George's parents actually followed the above procedures and reported their progress. George was really coming out of it, and they were very happy with the progress they were making with him. Then the mother's face fell, and she said, "What is really worrying us now is that Gwen is becoming bad. She is getting hard to handle and is doing some of the very things that George used to do. It is as if George were becoming Gwen and Gwen were becoming George."

RECOMMENDATION

These parents should now respond to Gwen's misbehavior in the same way they had responded to George. They also should attempt to understand Gwen better by walking in her shoes.

The third suggestion is for them to redouble their efforts to help Gwen find a constructive place in the family by letting her help with tasks that interest her and that are helpful to the family without making another member look bad. Helping her mother plan a grocery list, prepare a meal, or arrange flowers can serve this purpose. Her parents are also to recognize her efforts to be helpful by saying such things as "It is appreciated, Gwen, that you helped plan the grocery list. Your ideas for arranging the flowers in the vase were most helpful."

DISCUSSION

This case demonstrates the assumption that an individual's behavior is part of a network of interbalancing relationships; and when behavior is changed within one part of the network, it upsets the balance and results in changes elsewhere within the system. Therefore, anyone— parent, teacher, or counselor—desiring to effect changes with one individual, if he is to act responsibly and efficiently, must look to others with whom that individual relates.

Since Gwen had found her place by disgracing George, it was only natural that her secure feelings of belonging were threatened when she discovered that her mother and father were no longer responding to her tattling. This was most disconcerting to her. Because the mother and father no longer paid off George's bad behavior but paid off his good behavior, his relationship with them became better. This was not only disconcerting, but extremely threatening to Gwen's place of belonging. Things were changing and Gwen felt confused and insecure.

To the extent that her mother and father understood the above, they were able to walk in Gwen's shoes. Gwen will gradually become secure within the new network of relationships as her parents pay off her constructive attempts to belong and refuse to pay off her attempts to belong by reverting to George's misbehavior.

If helped by her parents in this manner, Gwen will learn while very young that she can find a secure place of belonging with those people who are important to her without making anyone else appear less likeable. This great lesson will enable her to more readily relate to her fellows in a horizontal manner.

Note: Concepts you may want to review are agency, pp. 37-38; social linkage, pp. 44-45; holism, pp. 50-52; life-style, pp. 48-50; payoff, pp. 42-44; belonging, pp. 45-46.

THE DANGER OF DEFLECTING

THE SITUATION

Becky, a six-year-old with long curly hair and clear blue eyes, is a beautiful, only child who seems wise beyond her years. She almost continually tells her mother and father that she loves them. She is also physically demonstrative. Kisses and hugs are as common with her as the tremendous number of words that flow unendingly from her lips.

Lately her parents have become quite concerned about her because they have suddenly discovered that she tries to get them to forget requests they make of her by changing the subject and talking about other things or by smothering them with hugs and kisses. This happens when they ask her to pick up her clothes, help dry the dishes, or turn off the TV and get her work done. They find they usually forget their requests and do not hold her accountable for her responsibilities.

RECOMMENDATION

Her parents should remind Becky once to do her work. When she tries to change the subject, they must not talk with her. They must not respond at all when she hugs and kisses them. In other words, they must discipline themselves not to pay off her deflecting talk and affectionate, deflecting behavior. They must not allow themselves to be diverted from their purposes.

DISCUSSION

Many individuals learn to manipulate other people through their deflecting talk and affectionate physical behavior in order to avoid their responsibilities. If Becky were to continue this type of behavior, she could easily become an adult who would be of little constructive value to herself and her fellowman. Moreover, an individual who makes the most of deflecting behavior often acquires a contempt for the very people he is able to manipulate. He may even develop contempt for himself. In addition, he may also create resentment and division among those with whom he associates as he works to gain advantage over them with torrents of words and floods of physical affection.

Note: A concept you may want to review is payoff, pp. 42-44, 53.

A CHILD WHO BULLIES YOUNGER CHILDREN
THE SITUATION

Paul is all boy, athletic and aggressive. He gets along well with his younger sister much of the time, but too often his mother and father find him teasing or picking on little Olive.

Olive is a real charmer, with big brown eyes and a ready smile. If Paul is not pulling Olive's pigtails, he is taking something away from her—anything to annoy her.

One evening after Paul arrived home from school, Olive went crying to her mother with big tears rolling down her cheeks and said, "Mommy, Paul pulled my hair and it hurt." Mother yelled at Paul, "Paul, you leave your little baby sister alone. Don't you touch her again." But it wasn't five minutes later that Olive ran screaming in to her mother again and said, "Paul is chasing me!"

RECOMMENDATION

When she runs crying to them with complaints about how Paul is treating her, Olive's mother and father are to say, "Olive, that is between you and Paul. You go back and work it out with him." When she wails in response to the above, "He'll hit me. Don't you love me anymore?" Mother and Father are to respond, "It may be hard, but I'm sure you can work it out with him."

If, because of resentment that has been built up between Paul and Olive, their parents are afraid that Paul might actually hurt Olive physically, they should of course intervene. However, they are to do it by treating their two children as a group. They can use the following phrase to serve this purpose: "Olive and Paul, play peacefully together or play separately. It's up to you which you choose to do." If the children continue to have problems, they are to be sent to separate rooms to play until they can agree to come together and work out their problems peacefully or play quietly together.

DISCUSSION

Olive's parents are vulnerable to her attempts to get them to protect her. Whenever they go to her rescue, she receives payoff for being helpless and achieves special undue service from them at Paul's expense. Paul achieves payoff, even though it is negative, by getting his parents to focus their words and looks on him. Her parents' protectiveness stimulates Olive to have even more difficulty with Paul, for it is to her advantage to keep things stirred up. As her parents ally themselves with Olive, Paul feels they prefer her to him, and this makes him resentful of her. This also motivates him to strike out at her and hurt her as he feels she has hurt him. He may also try to hurt his parents as he feels they have hurt him.

Parents who try to settle their children's difficulties for them set themselves an impossible task. They can never be fair in the eyes of all their children as long as they take sides. Therefore, whenever children are picking on one another, teasing, quarrelling, or fighting, parents should stay out of the conflict completely or, when they get involved because of threatened danger, treat their children as a group and separate them. Parents should not burden themselves with the impossible task of discovering who is to blame and delivering punishment to the guilty child.

It takes two or more children to tease and quarrel. When this happens, each child is usually cooperating in his individual role to play out the scene in order to get some sort of payoff.

Parents are often amazed at how quickly children can resolve their differences when parental influence is withdrawn from their conflicts. This is because the original objects over which children quarrel are really not too important (i.e., a toy). But when parents involve themselves, the struggle becomes extremely important because then the children are maneuvering for their parents' preferred love. This preference is indicated by whom the parents protect and whom they punish.

Furthermore, when children work through their conflicts by themselves, they gain practice in developing skills for working through conflict that will assist them in their relationships outside the family. As a result they have a better chance of becoming adults who tend to be more effective in their relationships with other people. And as they become effective in working through conflict, they also find that they are freed from feelings of resentment. They also usually gain greater self-confidence, all of which stimulates in them greater ability to relate harmoniously with other people.

Note: Concepts you may want to review are social linkage, pp. 44-45; payoff, pp. 42-44; empathy, pp. 71-72; logical consequences, p. 86.

THE MARTYR ROLE
THE SITUATION

The only boy in a family of three, Henry has a very competent older sister who is ten and a younger one who is three.

It seems to the mother and father of this family that their opening phrase to Henry is always "What's the matter now?"

He comes home from school happily enough, walking down the block and playing and scuffling with his friends. But the minute he comes within sight of the house, he begins to drag his feet and his head sinks lower and lower between his shoulders. By the time he comes through the door, his chin is almost on his chest and his gait is down to a shuffle. His facial expression is so mournful that his parents are afraid he will burst into tears at any moment.

His usual response to the question "What is the matter now?" is that other people are picking on him or that someone has treated him unfairly. He describes his experiences in detail, with a pitiful tone of voice and a hangdog look of such proportions that his mother and father get angry just thinking about whoever has treated their son so poorly.

His father sometimes finds himself getting angry with Henry, for he wishes the boy would stand up for himself. But the predominating emotions his father and mother feel for him are those of pity and sorrow.

RECOMMENDATION

Henry's father and mother should no longer ask the question "What's wrong, Henry?" They must not show any concern for him in any way when he puts on his hangdog look. They are not to speak to or even look at him during these times. His parents are to busy themselves doing other things, perhaps in another room.

His father is to spend more time with Henry playing ball, swimming, and skiing, which they both enjoy. At such times, the father must remain uncritical. He is never to correct his boy's lack of skill unless the boy asks for assistance, and then he is to give it in a friendly, relaxed tone of voice. The primary objective is for the father and son to enjoy being with one another.

DISCUSSION

Henry had decided not to compete for his parents' attention with his competent older sister by trying to be competent. He had also rejected the notion of being as charming as his younger sister.

Henry appears to have learned to find a place for himself with his parents by playing the role of martyr. When his father and mother concentrate on him during his martyr attempts, they are paying off this behavior and stimulating him to continue expressing himself this way in the future. It is a powerful way for an individual to get attention and service from others and to also defeat them.

Henry's father and mother thought they were helping him to solve his problems by talking to him about his difficulties. His goal, however, was not to solve his problems, but to be special, to have a powerful place of belonging. If he were to solve his problems, he would no longer be able to achieve his goal and his parents might then lose interest in him. Therefore, his parents' efforts were doomed to failure.

122

Henry's father, a traveling businessman, was home very seldom and was rather demanding and critical of Henry. He demanded much from himself and expected much from his only son. This made Henry feel sorry for himself when he was very young; and as he expressed this in his dramatic martyred ways, he found himself suddenly the object of his parents' concern. He had discovered his own unique way of belonging. It was a safe role. He had no competition.

If Henry's father spends time with his son alone in a fun, uncritical way, he can help his son feel that he belongs. Henry feels, at times, overwhelmed by women and distant from his competent, critical father. It is very important that his father help him find his place in a constructive way. Henry's father is vitally important to him.

Note: Concepts you may want to review are life-style, pp. 48-50; social linkage, pp. 44-45; vertical goals, pp. 16-23, 43; payoff, pp. 42-44; belonging, pp. 45-46; warmth and respect, p. 71; self-esteem, pp. 46-47.

A CASE OF DIZZY SPELLS

THE SITUATION

Dean's family members were visiting relatives. He and an older cousin had been wrestling in a darkened room for some time. Suddenly the door flew open and nine-year-old Dean came staggering out with a strange look in his eyes and a look of consternation on his face. He said, "My head feels funny. Everything looks different. What's the matter." Everyone rushed to him and began to question him in a very emotional manner. "What do you mean your head feels funny? Here, let me look at you. You don't feel hot. Did you hurt yourself?" This procedure continued for some time until Dean's family left for home.

The following day Dean came into the room where his mother was sewing and complained again of his head feeling strange and different. She became upset and took him to their family doctor who checked Dean carefully and determined that there was nothing physically wrong with him.

Two or three days later Dean again complained of his head feeling as if it were going around and around, and his parents, especially his mother, questioned him closely, displaying a good deal of emotional concern. She tried to get him to describe his feelings in detail. Soon Dean was complaining about his head several times a day.

RECOMMENDATION

After first explaining to him what they feel is happening and how they are going to help him overcome it, Dean's parents must completely ignore their son's complaints about his head. When he comes complaining to his father while he is reading the paper, his father should not look up but reply very briefly in a disinterested way. Dean's mother is to follow the same procedure. She is not to look up from what she is doing or to show any interest whatsoever in Dean's complaint. If he hounds her with his complaints, she should walk into another room.

DISCUSSION

Dean's case is a rather common one. An individual experiences something in a random sort of way that has a tremendous emotional impact on other people. The results are so powerful in getting others to focus on him that he repeats the response again and again. So it is in the case of Dean. He was actually dizzy when he emerged from the darkened room where he had been tumbling over and over with his cousin. But his dizzy spells began occurring rather regularly because through them he was able to get a great amount of payoff from other people whenever he behaved in such a manner. With relatively very little effort, Dean can begin to use such behaviors to tyrannize his family. For example, he might soon express that he is having these strange feelings whenever he is asked to do something he does not want to do or when he is not able to get others to do what he wants.

It is vital that payoff be withdrawn immediately from Dean's unconstructive responses so that he will give them up and turn his energies to more constructive ways of belonging. His parents must be very careful to recognize with words and touch his responsible, cooperative efforts.

Dean's mother and father should expect their son's reports of strange feelings in his head to continue for some time, then gradually diminish. He experienced much success in having an emotional impact on others and he will not give up the behavior readily. In fact, he will

124

probably get worse before he gets better as he attempts to test his
parents with increased dizzy feelings in order to get them to respond
as they did previously.

Note: Concepts you may want to review are vertical goals, pp. 16-23, 43; payoff,
pp. 42-44, 53.

TAKING TIME FOR TRAINING
THE SITUATION

Connie, a cute and creative eight-year-old, had spent the morning
working through a plan that would help her earn money for a special
pair of sandals she wished to buy that were above her regular clothing
budget. Part of her plans included selling cold lemonade to the
hot and thirsty who passed by. She decided to include two of her
friends in her project, for they too were in need of extra money and
Connie felt it would be more fun to work with some other girls.

About four o'clock that same afternoon Connie entered her home
in an extremely disagreeable mood. No one could talk to her without
her snapping back. She was grumpy and cross. When her mother
asked her what was wrong, she responded in a high-pitched wail, "I
just hate Doreen. I'm never going to speak to her again."

"You sound pretty angry," her mother said.

Connie burst into tears. "I didn't get nearly as much money as I
thought I would, and it's all Doreen's fault."

Connie's mother responded, "I don't understand. Would you
describe in detail what happened."

Connie sobbed, "Me and Diane bought everything to go into
the lemonade, and Doreen didn't buy or bring anything. Then she
took a third of all we made. It's not fair."

Fighting to remain calm and to keep all trace of anger from her
voice and face, since she also felt the unfairness, her mother said,
"What did you say or do, Connie, when Doreen took it?"

"I didn't do anything."

"Did you say anything to her?"

"I just looked mad at her."

"Could that be one reason why you are so angry now, Connie?
Sometimes when we don't express our feelings to others they get
bigger and bigger inside. What do you think?"

"But she shouldn't have taken that money," Connie exclaimed. "It wasn't fair!"

Her mother continued to fold clothes and said in a friendly way, "Well, Connie, it has happened. What do you think you can do about it now?"

"I don't know."

"Usually it's never too late to work things out with other people. How would you feel about going to her now and telling her in a calm way just how you feel about what happened?"

Connie said nothing more. She sat around for another fifteen minutes seemingly in deep thought. All of a sudden she jumped up and flew out the door, running at top speed, banging it as she left.

She returned fifteen minutes later with Doreen. Each had her arm around the other.

Mother wisely said nothing about the quarrel at this time. Later on in the evening while she was reading and Connie was sitting close by, involved with her dolls, she said, "I see you worked things out with Doreen. Would you like to talk about it?"

"I told Doreen that I thought she was wrong for taking a third of all the money we made when she didn't give anything to make the lemonade. She got mad at me, but I continued talking to her and we finally decided that next time she would give all the lemonade. We're friends now."

"How did you feel inside, Connie, after you had told her what you felt and had reached a decision you both agreed to?" her mother asked.

"I liked her again, and I didn't feel bad anymore," Connie said, as she looked up from her play with a twinkle in her eye.

"I'm glad that you went to Doreen and told her how you felt and then stuck it out until you worked something through with her. You showed a lot of courage." Mother walked up to Connie as she was leaving and rested her hand lightly on her daughter's arm, then proceeded out of the room.

DISCUSSION

Connie's mother's primary efforts were to help her child understand her feelings and thus do something productive about them when in a conflict situation with another person.

It would have been easy for this mother, when Connie said she hated Doreen, to have said, "Now, Connie, you don't hate anybody. What would God think if he heard you speak like that?" She would have succeeded greatly in shutting off healthy communication and impeding the successful resolution of the conflict.

As it was, Connie's mother hit the nail on the head with her remark, "You sound pretty angry." This allowed Connie to feel free to burst forth with her emotions. This offers a general clue for parents to look for when they are trying to counsel a child effectively. If his emotions gush forth in parallel fashion to the words he uses, his parents can be fairly sure that they are understanding their child's feelings.

Mother's gentle comments also had the effect of enabling Connie to understand her own feelings, gain a clearer perception of what she was upset about, realize that action could be taken to resolve the problem, and increase her level of courage. Such a calm response is very helpful to the child when his major purpose is to sincerely resolve the conflict with which he is faced.

Note: Concepts you may want to review are empathy, pp. 71-72; warmth and respect, p. 71; genuineness, p. 71; modeling, pp. 53-54; payoff, pp. 42-44.

A PATTERN OF FUSSY NEGATIVISM

THE SITUATION

Flora, an eight-year-old only child, is forever (or so it seems to her mother) talking about things she does that are not quite right. The following is rather typical of their daily conversation.

"Mother, when I put my tooth brush back in the cup, it leaned over and touched yours."

"Flora, for heaven's sake I wish you would be more careful."

Fifteen minutes later: "Mother, I touched that dirty old rag with my clean hands. What shall I do now?"

"I wish you would watch more what you do. Go in and wash your hands."

Thirty minutes later: "You told me to be sure to rinse all the soap off my hands because they are getting all chappy. But I forgot. Mother, see how chappy my hands are."

"It seems you're right. I wish you would mind me better, Flora."

Ten minutes later: "See, Mother, I'm wearing my dirty blue dress."

"You take that off immediately before I paddle your bottom! Did you hear me? Take it off now. How many times do I have to tell you? You are not to wear dirty clothes."

Twenty minutes later: "Look, I got dirt in my sore that you said to keep clean."

"Must I follow you around all day to make sure you keep that cut clean? You'd better hope you don't get a staph infection."

"Yes, Mother."

Later: "Mother, you know my friend Colleen? Well, she has a very bad cold, and I got too close to her and she breathed all over me."

"I'm just going to have to keep you home," Mother shrieked in a high-pitched voice as the blood rushed to her face. "I'll be darned if I'm going to stay up with you during the night if you get a bad cold again for being so foolish."

"I only got close to her because she wanted me to see her new doll."

"You heard me."

"Yes, Mother."

Thirty minutes later: "Mother, I dropped the milk bottles and they broke all over the sidewalk."

"What am I going to do with you, Flora? Can't you do anything right?"

One hour later: "Mother, I put my hands on the toilet."

"I've told you time and time again to be careful when you go to the toilet. Now go back and wash your hands. Be sure to rinse them well. Hear now?"

"Yes, Mother."

Immediately following the above, Flora comes out of the bathroom with her hands still wet and bubbles of soap still clinging to them. "See, Mother, my hands are very chappy."

"No wonder. I told you to rinse them off. Now get back there and do what I told you." As Flora leaves, her mother yells, "Now get

128

that soap off, and be sure to dry them like I've told you a hundred times."

"Yes, Mother."

RECOMMENDATION

The mother should first recognize how she has been paying off Flora's vertical attempts to belong. Then she should explain briefly to her daughter that she is no longer going to pay attention to her fussy, negative comments, because she wants to help Flora overcome this destructive behavior. In this way she can help Flora learn to be happy and thus relate well with other people as well as her mother.

Flora's mother should not look at or listen to Flora's verbal or nonverbal communication regarding her negative exploits. Her mother must not respond emotionally to her in any way when Flora communicates in such a manner. It may be helpful for her mother to walk into another room or to concentrate on the activity in which she is engaged when Flora tries to involve her with such behavior.

DISCUSSION

Flora has learned to keep her mother busy with her and in her service by reporting to her all of her negative activity. Her payoff is her mother's continual response to her negative reports about herself. It is imperative that Flora's mother withdraw payoff by not responding in any way to her at such times. Otherwise, Flora will continue to believe that the way to belong is to be clumsy, unclean, and bad. Unless her mother withdraws payoff immediately, Flora's behavior will probably escalate as she gets older. She will tend to be more clumsy, more unclean, and more shocking with her reports about her bad behavior.

As her mother withdraws payoff for Flora's negative behavior, it is important that she initiate conversation with her daughter when she is behaving in a positive, constructive manner. This will help Flora to realize that she can belong by behaving horizontally and will eliminate her need to behave vertically.

Note: Concepts you may want to review are life-style, pp. 48-50; vertical goals, pp. 16-23, 43; payoff, pp. 42-44, 53.

PLANNING A FAMILY HOUSE
THE SITUATION

Richard, an architect, is the father of three boys and two girls, all under ten. He and his wife Sharon have decided to build a new home and have agreed with each other to pay close attention to the social, psychological, emotional, and esthetic needs of family members as they plan their home. They have been especially concerned of late about rearing their children to have those qualities and skills that will prepare them to live harmoniously with one another and their fellowmen. Both Richard and Sharon feel that any architectural change that would facilitate their childrearing objectives should be built into their home, even though such changes might be a departure from usual designs.

RECOMMENDATION

Richard and Sharon could benefit greatly from building into their home a nursery for the baby and a dormitory sleeping and living room for their older sons and one for their girls. Each child is to have his own bed, clothes closet, and chest of drawers, but each of these is located in an open area with those of the other children.

Richard and Sharon can also plan a quiet, thinking room lined with interesting objects such as books, maps, and pictures. Included in the room could be a long desk or writing area and comfortable easy chairs.

They can also build a time-out room. This is to be a small, well-lighted and ventilated, but rather sterile room. It is to have nothing in it that would be of interest to anyone. One sturdy chair would be sufficient. It should be somewhat soundproofed and have a door that can be locked from the outside.

DISCUSSION

A major advantage of dormitory style living for children is that it allows them to enjoy each other's company and also stimulates them to work through their problems with one another. Too many children are separated too much from their brothers and sisters and other people. Our modern society has too often attached status to physical structures that breed private lives. For example, we often find that it is prestigious to be able to afford one room for each child because this demonstrates our affluence.

Children sleeping and living together can experience many happy and joyful times that will remain as fond memories for the rest of their lives. Such experiences can add even more cement to strong bonds of brotherhood. As children reach out beyond the family, their memories will stimulate them to expect such experiences with others, and these experiences will tend to come true.

Another advantage of dormitory living is that it forces the children to deal with one another. When there are problems among them, they cannot flee to their private rooms and avoid or ignore those with whom they have had their disagreements. They are continually thrown together and therefore are stimulated to work through their difficulties. Such activities can make them more skillful in working through conflict with other people in a productive manner and will help prepare them for a life of equality and oneness.

Another distinct advantage of such living quarters is that if one of the children gets in trouble with someone outside of the home or does something he should not do, he will find it is most difficult to hide the fact from his brothers. They will have learned to read him well and his expressions will alert them to the fact that something is wrong. Dormitory living not only puts children in a position to be alert to the needs of one another, it also enables them to better influence each other to do that which is right and good for all concerned.

Each of the children has needs for privacy as well as social needs, however. The thinking or quiet room will help them meet those needs. Here each child can go to study; think about an exciting idea that is forming in his mind; think how to best work through a conflict situation with his brother, sister, or parent; or just experience the quietness of the room. A rule made for this room is that no one speaks above a whisper while there, except on special occasions.

The time-out room can be used in a similar, but somewhat different manner for the smaller children when they insist on moving in on the rights of others. The child who insists on throwing food at the table when he has been quietly told to either stop or leave the table can be taken to the time-out room. It is extremely valuable, when used correctly, for teaching a child the logical consequences of abusing the freedom he has by interfering with the rights of others. When that happens, his area of freedom is restricted until he can agree and demonstrate behaviorally that he can use his freedom responsibly.

No one should ever use the time-out room for revenge or as an excuse not to train a child. It is to be used for the purpose of maintaining order with the child who habitually interferes in a particular manner with other people's rights. The child is always given the choice of stopping his behavior or going to the time-out room before he is either sent or taken there. If he continues and refuses to stop, he is to be asked, "Would you like to go by yourself or would you like me to take you?" He is taken gently but firmly if he refuses to go by himself. The same principle of choice is used regardless of whether or not the door is locked. If the child is willing to stay in the room without its being locked, then of course it is best not to lock it. But if he insists on coming out before he has agreed to respect the rights of others, the door is locked. He decides at each step what happens to him—what the consequences will be.

One caution. Some children will more than likely use the time-out room as a vehicle for getting attention. They might do so by agreeing to be respectful, then quickly returning to their old behavior. They are then taken to the room again while all eyes focus on them. They then quickly repent while in the room, come out, and the process is repeated over and over.

In order to avoid this, parents can increase the time of each stay in the room. If the child begins again the same misbehavior soon after his return, he stays much longer the second time he is returned to the time-out room. When he says, "I'll stop, Daddy. Let me out," Dad responds firmly but kindly with "Son, you need more time to think over what you decide." For the same series of misbehavior, the time inside the time-out room is lengthened each time the child returns to the room.

The time-out room can be a great help to parents who are attempting to teach young children their obligations to respect the rights of other people. It enables them to respect the misbehaving child's rights as they provide choices along the way for him. Their action is not arbitrary.

Note: Concepts you may want to review are communal interest, pp. 47-48; social linkage, pp. 44-45; practice, pp. 54-55; logical consequences, p. 86.

STRENGTHENING THE FAMILY:
WISE USE OF FAMILY GET-TOGETHERS

THE SITUATION

Merrill and Marsha, parents of five children, have decided to have a special night each week for a family get-together. The primary objective, as they see it, is to help each member feel more a part of the family unit and to strengthen the bonds of affection that they feel for each other.

The parents are somewhat apprehensive for they have heard from a few other parents that children are not easily persuaded to cooperate, nor can the parents get them to do what they want for family occasions. Merrill and Marsha have decided to take a chance and go ahead with their plans. They are going to proceed by setting down some general guides for these family get-togethers. Other parents have told them that family evenings together are a most enjoyable experience.

RECOMMENDATION

The father of this family (or the mother in a single-parent family) can function as friendly consultant to the whole family unit and to the family member assigned to take charge for the week. This means that the one conducting for the week plans the program and takes charge for the evening, but makes his plans with the friendly guidance of his parents if it is needed. It is also suggested that each member of the family take turns in conducting the family get-togethers, if possible.

The parents can best demonstrate their sincere interest in the family by modeling behavior that their children can follow. They preserve this time with their family and refuse to let business or community affairs interfere. For example, if the family decides to meet together from seven to nine o'clock each Wednesday evening, the father and mother are always present.

The parents are to emphasize constructive, harmonious relationships rather than any particular tasks to be performed. Hence they are to concentrate their energies on being friendly, warm, affectionate, easy going, and relaxed with each member of the family rather than spurring family members forward to the accomplishment of a certain task. Merrill and Marsha are to very carefully guide those children who conduct so that their plans de-emphasize competitive situations and games. They should encourage plans that emphasize cooperative activities.

DISCUSSION

The parents' main objective is to strengthen the family by helping each member identify more specifically with it. This can be accomplished when each member contributes responsibly and experiences good relationships. The warmth and friendship he experiences will tend to become bonded to his thoughts for his family. As a result, when he thinks of them and home, his feelings will be characterized by warmth and love. Children will look forward with great anticipation to family get-togethers that are managed effectively. These provide them with experiences that can efficiently cement the bonds of brotherhood among family members and enhance their concern for each other's well-being.

If parents are always in attendance, they demonstrate what words cannot express: that they care for and are concerned about each member of the family. This each child will observe and appreciate. When parents are warm, friendly, and relaxed, they set an atmosphere that enables family members to participate within a context of love, free from criticism. The children will tend to model this behavior as they respond to one another in the family get-togethers.

It is also vitally important for the family to de-emphasize or eliminate completely situations and games that place members in win/lose relationships with each other. Competitive activities tend to breed discontent and division and are more often than not the antithesis of equality and harmony. A true feeling of brotherhood cannot exist when one person is forced to lose in order for another to win. The almost constant companions of competitive situations are anger, resentment, jealousy, fear, depression, and dislike or hate for self and others.

Cooperative efforts of the children may be guided into such activities as storytelling, entertaining one another individually and as a group with song and dance, remembering pleasant times, planning family outings, pulling candy, and constructing objects together.

A variation of the nuclear family get-together is the extended type. In the extended family associations married brothers and sisters can meet together with their parents and their own children over twelve

134

years of age once a month. It is planned for the same purposes as the nuclear family evening get-together and in much the same way. Some families find it convenient to meet together the first Sunday evening of each month, beginning at 8:00 p.m. When each nuclear family takes a turn at having the gathering in their home, they also arrange for the program—often an outside speaker—and a light refreshment. One hour is devoted to the more formal aspects of the evening, while the second hour is used for just chatting together and contacting by phone those who live too far to be in attendance. Through this activity many extended family members have been brought closer together.

Note: Concepts you may want to review are belonging, pp. 45-46; practice, pp. 54-55; warmth and respect, p. 71; genuineness, p. 71; modeling, pp. 53-54; personality traits, pp. 55-56.

TRAINING CHILDREN TO WORK COOPERATIVELY WITH OTHER PEOPLE: A FAMILY COUNCIL

THE SITUATION

Dave and Sheila would like to help their children learn the give-and-take skills required for people to successfully work through their difficulties. They would also like to train their children to take more responsibility for setting up the rules and regulations under which the family functions.

RECOMMENDATION

Dave and Sheila should implement their plans, referring to the following twenty-one guidelines for understanding and using the family council procedure:

- Introduce your family gradually to the idea of family council. They will have to learn how to use it.
- The family council is a problem-solving and rulemaking group in which situations are discussed and solutions sought. (It is different from family evening get-togethers, although some families hold a council before or after.)
- The council meets at a regular time each week, which is agreed upon by all members of the family and changed only upon their agreement.
- It is a group process during which each member participates in deci-

sion-making processes as much as his development will allow. As they participate in making decisions that affect themselves, children learn to use their creative power in responsible ways. By helping to implement decisions that they help make, children learn to be responsible members of the family or any other group.

- Some centralization of authority is needed for effective problem solving in order to coordinate the efforts of various family members and see that minority opinions are stated and respected. It is usually best if the father (or the mother if the family is a one-parent family) presides with each member taking a turn at conducting. This helps avoid problems that often result if one person becomes the boss.

- Attendance is voluntary, but all members must abide by the group's decision. Members usually learn that it is to their advantage to be in attendance so that they can voice their opinions.

- Each member is free to express his feelings and ideas and to evaluate the ideas of others. In the family council, children as well as parents present problems and offer solutions. Each child is stimulated to contribute his part.

- The approach is positive. As soon as a problem is presented, each member concentrates on solutions. He is not allowed to emphasize negative responses.

- A climate of openness is maintained in which individuals are free to state what is on their minds.

- Family members are allowed to experience the results of their decisions even when the decisions are poor ones. Because the council is a learning experience, errors will be committed. Some pain and discomfort, if handled positively, can be beneficial to learning. Poor decisions stand until the next meeting and are not discussed in between. "Bring it up at the next family council," is usually the best response to those who would change decisions during the week.

- Problems must be expected and allowed for. The first will be the hardest. If the experience is an entirely new one, children may be suspicious and may test their parents. It is far better, however, if parents firmly support the group's decision. Living with a poor decision for an entire week, knowing that they have the power to make changes at the next meeting, can be a great learning experience for the children.

- One vote per family member allows for a democratic approach. Parents may veto only when the decision is dangerous. However, it is best to work for unanimity. This tends to diminish the chances of cliques developing in the family.

- Only when each member feels a sense of belonging will there be a feeling of unity. Each member needs to feel confident that he is a respected member of the group.
- Each member must learn to be sensitive to others in the group. He can do so by listening carefully, trying to understand, drawing out any member who might be less active, and noticing how members react to each other.
- The successes of the group should be acknowledged. Children need to be aware of the family's progress.
- The limitation of the group should be delineated. This can be done with a description of what can be done and what the potentialities of the group are.
- Parents should recognize that they don't know all of the answers and that several heads are generally better than one.
- A summary of problems and solutions is often helpful and necessary. This can be done with a restatement of ideas, listing of accomplishments, listing of unsolved problems, review of factual data presented, and/or review of the process itself. This can take place at the end of the meeting or when discussion has become blocked or diversion has taken place.
- Common concerns and objectives should be recognized and emphasized. This helps the family members to be concerned about each individual's welfare and to achieve an atmosphere of harmony.
- If no decision can be reached, each member has the right to do what he feels is best until such time as a decision can be made. During this interim he must never impose his behavior on others.
- If any one member is preachy, autocratic, inflexible, cold, aloof, and quick-tempered, he will tend to destroy the harmonious atmosphere essential to the well-being of the family council.

DISCUSSION

Making a family council work successfully is one of the most challenging yet productive experiences that is available to members of the family. Through the wise use of the family council within an emotional context of trust and real affection, free from sarcasm, ridicule, and humiliation, each member can learn to be more responsible for the welfare of himself and other members. In the process he can learn those techniques and skills that will enable him to be a responsible, caring member of other groups.

If Dave and Sheila are examples of courteous, respectful, and affectionate behavior with one another and their children as the members struggle to set up rules for the family and solve their problems, their children will tend to adopt these same behaviors for themselves when they interact with one another and with groups. Such horizontal behaviors will bring them closer to their fellowman and stimulate positive relationships.

Note: Concepts you may want to review are practice, pp. 54-55; social linkage, pp. 44-45; communal interest, pp. 47-48; payoff, pp. 42-44; natural consequences, pp. 85-86; warmth and respect, p. 71; genuineness, p. 71; empathy, pp. 71-72; modeling, pp. 53-54; personality traits, pp. 55-56.

MAKING THE FAMILY COUNCIL WORK

THE SITUATION

Heber and Rachael sought advice through family counseling because they wanted to improve their skills in managing the family council more successfully. They felt they had been somewhat successful in these councils with their three sons and two daughters, but now find that they are at a loss for words and don't know quite how to proceed when the children bring into the discussions many extraneous ideas and get bogged down in telling how much they dislike something. The parents also have some difficulty getting discussions started, making them meaningful, and concluding them in a worthwhile, productive fashion.

They wish to take strong positive measures now to insure that their family councils will be productive and not degenerate into destructive and ever spiraling, conflict-habituated sessions.

RECOMMENDATION

Heber and Rachael need to learn procedures and accompanying phrases, such as the following, which will enable them to make their family councils more productive:

To identify and clarify the problem:

• How do we feel about . . . ?
• Would you like to talk about it?
• Please tell us more.
• What do you mean?
• Please describe in detail how it last happened.
• Let me see if I have an accurate picture of what you mean . . .

To encourage openness and participation:

• Mm hmm . . . (signifies close attention of listener).
• Would you care to talk about it?
• I get the feeling you were (upset, angry, hurt, sad).
• Yes, it's rough at times.
• Please go on.
• We haven't heard from *you.*
• How do you feel about it? We would like to know what you think.

To avoid digression:

• How does that relate to the problem?
• Are we getting off the track?
• I don't understand. Please help me to see how that relates to the problem we identified.
• Let us move back to the problem we were discussing. You were saying that . . .

To identify alternatives:

• How can we solve the problem of . . . ?
• How might we respond to help us feel better about . . . ?
• What do we feel we should do?
• What are the available possibilities open to us?
• Let me see if I understand; the alternatives available to us that we have mentioned are one: . . , two: . . , and three. . . . Do I have it right? Are there any we have left out?
• What are the advantages and disadvantages of each? Let us list them.

To achieve unanimity of decision and commitment:

- How many prefer the first alternative? (State the alternative.)
  How many prefer the second alternative?
  How many prefer the third alternative?
  It appears that all but two prefer the second alternative. How can we modify this alternative so that the two of you will be able to accept it?
- Are we all agreed, from now until . . . we will . . . ? (Wait until each person has said yes or nodded his head; then say, "Each one of us has committed himself to abide by this decision until . . .")

To summarize and make a progress statement:

- It appears to me that we have identified the problem of . . .
- We explored the following alternatives. . . . We selected . . . as being the one we could all best agree with after modifying it by . . .
- We have each agreed to work with this alternative until . . .
- Is this how the rest of you see what has happened here tonight?
- It appears to me that we have accomplished much tonight. We can feel good about our achievement.
- O.K. We'll meet next week at the same time. Thanks for your help. You made my job much easier.

There are times when disruptive elements within the family council will have to be dealt with and each member made aware of his responsibilities. The following phrases can assist in the accomplishment of this task:

- What is going on in our family council now?
- Is it helping or hindering what we want to accomplish?
- What is Randy getting out of pulling funny faces and talking out loud when others are talking?
- What do we do when he acts this way?
- Could this be what he is getting out of such actions?
- What are our responsibilities toward Randy?
- What can we do differently so that Randy will not want to behave this way in the future?
- Are we all agreed, from now on when Randy pulls faces and talks

out, that we will not look at him or giggle, but that we will keep focusing on what we are doing?

- What can we do with Randy when he is contributing horizontally so that he will want to continue to contribute and cooperate in this manner?

DISCUSSION

The above phrases can stimulate Heber and Rachael to give direction to their family council. They may prefer to modify or add to them as they gain experience and discover what works best for them.

The last set of questions for handling a disturbing child within the council can help parents to direct other children's thinking to the problems at hand without condemning or finding fault. This will help Randy's brothers and sisters to determine their responsibilities, if any, for his misbehavior. It will help them all to become more aware of how they can influence each other in positive, constructive ways.

The strategies and accompanying phrases are designed to assist the group members to be productive in their deliberations and deal effectively with disruptive elements without resorting to vertical techniques. The questions are also designed to maximize each individual's awareness of his responsibilities for making the family council work.

As Heber and Rachael's children grow up learning effective skills for productively working through problem situations with one another, they will be well prepared to stimulate cohesiveness and productivity with those group members with whom they associate.

Note: Concepts you may want to review are practice, pp. 54-55; social linkage, pp. 44-45; warmth and respect, p. 71; genuineness, p. 71; empathy, pp. 71-72; modeling, pp. 53-54; conflict resolution, pp. 78-79.

WORKING WITH IRREVERENT BEHAVIOR

THE SITUATION

Irvin, a three-year-old boy with sparkling eyes and a ready smile, never seems to be quiet for a moment during religious services. He runs up and down the aisles. He wiggles and worms around on the bench and on his father's lap. He lies down on the floor and crawls under the benches. No one sings louder than Irvin, if it can be called singing, but of this his father and mother are rather proud.

What concerns Irvin's parents is that when they try to quiet him by pulling him off the floor, getting him out from under the benches, or stopping him from running in the aisles, he screams, yells, and goes limp. It is most embarrassing. His father is afraid to be too firm because of Irvin's yelling. Though he talks to his son and coaxes him throughout the services, it does not seem to help.

RECOMMENDATION

Irvin's father can try the following procedures and evaluate how well they work. He should search out an unused room that will serve as a time-out room. This room should be devoid of anything that could interest Irvin. The father is then to say to his son that from now on he is going to tell him only once to be quiet or sit on his chair; then if he chooses to be unruly, he will be taken to another room. When Irvin agrees not to disturb the other people, he will be taken back into the meeting.

Irvin is to be taken to the time-out room as soon as he starts to misbehave. His father is not to wait until he becomes embarrassed by his child's behavior. This is to be done consistently and will enable the father to be less emotionally involved when he takes action. When Irvin reverts to his old misbehavior after being taken back into the meeting, he is immediately taken back to the time-out room. When he again says that he wants to return, his father says, "You seem to need more time to think about it, Irvin." They stay longer this time. The process is repeated and the time lengthened until Irvin demonstrates cooperative behavior that is respectful of the rights of others.

When Irvin is in the time-out room, his father is to become very uninterested in the child's actions. He does not talk to or relate to Irvin in any emotional way. His responses, when they are necessary, should be mechanical. He does not recognize Irvin's existence beyond what is absolutely necessary to facilitate the correction program. It is necessary that he relate to Irvin in this manner if he is to help his child learn to interact horizontally with other people.

DISCUSSION

The time-out room is used as a means of implementing logical consequences. The child learns that he does not have the right to interfere with the rights of other people who want to have a peaceful meeting. He also learns that when he abuses his freedom of attending such a meeting, his freedom will be restricted or expanded according to his agreements about and demonstrations of being a respectful and responsible person.

If Irvin's father is unemotionally involved with his child during his misbehavior, he will tend not to pay him off for it. If his father is affectionate and warm when Irvin is quiet in the meeting, Irvin will learn that it pays to be respectfully quiet.

Irvin's father's effective responses will enable him and other people to enjoy the child during the service. While they sit together, it is important that the father put his arm around Irvin, occasionally hug him, and pat his hand so that the principle of bonding can take effect. This means that Irvin's affectionate feelings for his father and the corollary feelings of security and love will become bonded to religious services. As he thinks of these meetings, he will recall the feelings of warmth and security which he felt for his father during past meetings.

This suggested procedure should help Irvin's father a good deal as he attempts to train the child to respect the rights of others and value his father's spiritual beliefs.

Note: Concepts you may want to review are payoff, pp. 42-44; logical consequences, p. 86; bonding, pp. 52-53.

TRAINING A MENTALLY RETARDED CHILD

THE SITUATION

Marty, a retarded boy of five, has an assessed intellectual age of three. He is friendly and charming much of the time, but several things he does drive his mother and father up the wall. When he is given permission to play in his own yard, he continually wanders off to his neighbor's. When he is given permission to play in the neighbor's yard, he is often found a block or two away. His mother finds herself running after him throughout the day.

He also screams and yells as he attempts to put his shirt and pants on while dressing. His parents try to help him, but they usually end up in a battle, and all three of them become frustrated and angry.

His mother and father are also concerned with Marty's passivity when other children pick on him. His little sister, Sandy, a normal three-year-old child, can take toys or food away from him and he will not fight to get them back. His typical response is to cry. Both of his parents react to such situations by scolding Sandy and either forcing her to give back what she has taken or taking the object from her and giving it to Marty themselves. They keep telling Marty to stand up for himself, but he seems to be doing it less and less.

Sandy is bossy and critical of Marty. She tells him what to do and corrects him whenever he says or does something wrong. She is often talking for him as well as interrupting him. As soon as Marty starts to tell his parents something, Sandy interrupts and finishes for him. She will also begin talking while Marty is talking and do it with such a loud voice and rapidity of words that her mother and father find themselves listening to her rather than to Marty.

The parents feel that now is the time to correct their children's disturbing behavior. They wonder if anything can be done for Marty because of his brain damage, but they are eager to stop Sandy's bossiness and criticism. They also would like to stop Marty's practice of running away and encourage him to stand up for himself.

RECOMMENDATION

Marty's and Sandy's parents must very carefully show Marty the boundaries in which he can play when he is allowed to play in his yard or the neighbor's yard. They should tell him that if he chooses to go outside these limits, his freedom will be restricted and he will have to play in his bedroom until he can agree to play within the boundaries set by his mother and father. He is also told that if he agrees and then goes out and runs away again, he will have to stay longer in his room the next time to give him more time to think about what he should do. His mother and father must then follow through in a consistent manner. The child must know without any doubts that his freedom will be restricted when he behaves irresponsibly with the freedom he is given.

With regard to his passivity, Marty's parents are not to make Sandy or any of Marty's playmates give back any food or toy they take from him, no matter how much he cries or how helpless and pitiful he looks at such times. They are to turn and involve themselves with other things.

When Marty starts to cry and scream during the dressing process, his mother and father are to leave the room immediately and say nothing to him. They are not to look in on him or say anything to him while he is throwing his tantrums. They may assist him only when he has quieted down.

To correct Sandy's interrupting behavior, her mother and father should first explain to her what they feel is wrong and how they are going to help her. They should then keep their eyes focused on Marty and discipline themselves not even to begin to turn in Sandy's direction when she takes over for him. The parents must keep their bodies unhesitatingly pointed in Marty's direction.

When Sandy starts to boss Marty or be critical of him, her mother and father should immediately leave the area where the children are playing, if possible. If that is impractical, they should treat Marty and Sandy as a group and tell them that if they are going to treat one another disrespectfully, their father and mother do not want to hear it. They can leave the area and play outside or in another part of the house. The parents must then follow through to see that their children either leave of their own free will or are taken by their hands and ushered elsewhere.

DISCUSSION

This case is rather typical of parents who conscientiously strive to help their handicapped children. Marty's parents felt they had to protect him from other children. They also felt they could not expect him to keep within the limits of his play area because of his intellectual deficiency. As a result, they found themselves chasing after Marty throughout the day and constantly defending him from other children. Marty achieved payoff for his running away and found no reason to change. He received much attention when his parents called and searched for him throughout the neighborhood. It was proof that he was important to them.

When his parents took Marty's part against Sandy and other children, he received additional proof that he was special. Each time that he cried and appeared helpless and his mother and father fought his battles for him, he learned that such behavior could be used to defeat his playmates, weaken his parents' resolve to respond equally to all participants, and make him an important, special person. Because he received consistent payoff, he had no reason to stand up for himself. However, if his parents withdraw, leaving him to suffer the consequences of his passive behavior with his friends, he will learn rather rapidly the value of defending himself.

His screams allowed him to actually defeat his parents in their desires to get him dressed quickly so that they could turn to other things. By using these powerful, vertical techniques, he was able to keep his parents' attention focused on him for long periods of time every morning. To stop his screaming behavior, it is important that his parents not interact with him in any way while he is screaming. When he learns that they will not go to him as long as he screams, his disturbing behavior will most likely quickly diminish.

Sandy has been learning at a rather young age to play the superior role. Her bossing and critical behaviors and her ability to maneuver the focus of her parents' attention from Marty to herself are demonstrations of her feeling superior. When her mother and father refuse to be deflected from Marty, they will stop paying off her interrupting behavior. Their refusal to interact with the children as long as Sandy is bossing and being critical of Marty will very likely result in Sandy's having no audience for her show of superiority. And with no audience, she will have no purpose in persisting.

Possibly the greatest difficulty in rearing a handicapped child is not the handicap itself so much as the pity that the child often elicits from concerned parents. Marty's mother's eyes filled with tears as she described her son. Because he could elicit feelings of sorrow and pity from her rather easily, he was able to make her vulnerable to his manipulations.

There is a fundamental similarity here to the story of Helen Keller and her ability to tyrannize family members who fed her every whim because of the pity they felt for her. It was not until her teacher Anne Sullivan set firm limits and expected much from her that she began developing into the beautiful person she became. *The Miracle Worker,* the story of Anne Sullivan and Helen Keller, is recommended as highly valuable reading.

Note: Concepts you may want to review are life-style, pp. 48-50; social linkage, pp. 44-45; holism, pp. 50-52; payoff, pp. 42-44; logical consequences, p. 86; practice, pp. 54-55.

RESPONSIBLE SUPERVISION

THE SITUATION

Connie, the mother of three small children, grew up in a neighborhood where a number of her friends and acquaintances spent a good deal of time on the town's streets vagrantly riding up and down. They had no supervision of any kind. She remembers how many of the boys got into trouble with the law and how many of the girls became promiscuous. She often looks at her own children and wonders what she can do to diminish the chances of this happening to them.

RECOMMENDATION

The best time to insure one's children against this type of vagrancy is to start responding to them in certain ways when they are very young. Specifically, Connie and her husband can begin now to use the principle of logical consequences when their children behave irresponsibly with the freedom they are given. For example, when a child has permission to play for one hour at his friend's house and stays two hours, his parents should help him to realize that he is not behaving responsibly and should not allow him to leave home again until he agrees to be more responsible next time. If he does not keep his word the next time, he should be kept home for a longer period of time. His parents should tell him gently but without equivocation, "I believe you need more time to think about coming home on time. Maybe after two days of thinking, you will be ready to come home as you should next time you go off to play."

Second, it is important that Connie and her husband know where, when, what, and with whom their children play. It is their rightful concern, and their children will become used to and expect reasonable supervision. This is not a supervision that is stifling; it is the kind that responsibly structures the environment of the child so that the choices of activities and friends that are available to him increase the probabilities of his rapid and efficient growth and development.

Third, and possibly most important, Connie and her husband must respond to one another and to their children in such a manner that the home atmosphere reflects courtesy, mutual respect, warmth, friendliness, and devotion. The home must be in general a safe harbor from the storms of life, where family members can find a relaxed atmosphere that gives them support and encouragement for renewed efforts to successfully cope with life's problems.

DISCUSSION

Many parents allow their young children unlimited freedom of movement in the neighorhood. This often seems just fine while they are small; but when they get older, these same parents often suddenly attempt to limit their children's activities in the communities. These attempts often create power struggles, bitterness, and vengeful activities on the part of the youth. These, of course, only make the problems worse. Children need to be trained while they are still very young to expect reasonable supervision of their activities.

Another advantage of early supervision is that it communicates to the child that his parents care enough to take the trouble to be concerned. It is a demonstration of love that children can believe, even though they may test its limits. Such testing is often their attempt to see if their parents care enough to remain firm. Children generally do not want their parents to give in when expectations are reasonable.

When parents create a home atmosphere that is peaceful and relaxed and full of affection, children will generally prefer to be there rather than on the streets.

Note: Concepts you may want to review are social linkage, pp. 44-45; practice, pp. 54-55; warmth and respect, p. 71; genuineness, p. 71; personality traits, pp. 55-56; logical consequences, p. 86; empathy, pp. 71-72.

BEGINNINGS OF HOMOSEXUALITY

THE SITUATION

This father is a robust, athletic male who demands much of himself and also of other people. He has a six-year-old son, Jed, whom he finds very difficult to understand. He tried to teach him to ride horses, but gave up since Jed just could not seem to get the hang of it. He was so busy crying that he would not listen to his father's directions. Jed's crying embarrassed his father; it made him disgusted to think that his son was such a boob. He also tried to teach Jed how to fly a kite, but Jed was afraid he would be pulled up in the air and began to cry. His father told him not to be such a cry baby and that only stupid little boys think such things.

Jed's father has never understood children's feelings. He was reared with no brothers and sisters near his age. He experienced no warmth or affection in his own family and finds it difficult to give or accept affection now. In fact when his son tries to sit on his lap or put his arms around him, his typical response is, "Don't be such a sissy," and he pushes him away.

His father believes the way to train a child is to point out all his mistakes so that the child will be aware of what to correct. This is done with sarcasm, anger, and even humiliating responses in order to motivate the child to do better. That was the way he was taught, and he believes it worked well with him.

The mother in this family is a sharp contrast to the father. She is a warm, quiet person who is most affectionate with Jed. She feels his father is too harsh with him and will often take the child in her arms and cuddle him after his father has been what she considers too demanding and critical. She feeds Jed goodies after he has had an especially rough time with his father. And all the while he is eating, she will coo to him and brush away his tears and fondle him. Increasingly Jed and his mother do things together. She encourages Jed to help with her flower arranging and cooking. They have great fun together drawing and painting as well as crocheting.

There are many little girls Jed's age in the neighborhood, and Mother encourages Jed to play with them since they do not play as roughly as boys. She has always been afraid that her children would get hurt and has constantly cautioned them to be careful. Since Jed is her only son, she is extremely cautious with him. She tells him how mean and vicious little boys can be and that he should be careful about playing with them. She finds fault with any of the boys Jed plays with or brings home. They in turn do not find Jed's home a welcome place and so they seldom visit him. Jed's mother feels more comfortable with the little girls he plays with, and they find themselves most welcome. Hence his companions are mostly girls rather than boys.

Jed's parents have always been somewhat distant from each other. His father's overinvolvement with community activities and his difficulty in giving and receiving affection have caused strain in the relationship from the beginning of the marriage. As children came, their mother found solace with them in her lonely hours. She found herself turning more and more to them in an attempt to achieve her goals to belong and feel worthwhile.

As time progressed, the father felt more and more isolated from his wife and children. He feels now that they are against him. Because he continues to experience feelings of alienation and loneliness in the home, he finds himself turning more and more to community activities.

Jed views his father as a giant of a man who will at any moment shower him with torrents of criticism, sarcasm, and ridicule. He feels his father is cold, distant, and hurtful. Around his father, Jed feels he is inadequate and worthless. Pain is the feeling that overwhelms Jed in the presence of his father. As a result he avoids his father whenever possible.

His parents have suddenly realized that Jed's body movements, voice inflections, play activities, and interests are more feminine than masculine. This was brought to their attention with impact when they both overheard a group of adults talking about Jed. One said to the others that Jed was growing up to be a little fairy. The group seemed to agree. Jed's mother and father moved quietly and rapidly away and soon found themselves talking with each other for the first time in a long time about their son. They decided to make changes.

RECOMMENDATION

- Jed's father must avoid critical words and critical nonverbal responses when relating with Jed.
- He should work to accept Jed the way he is at any given time.
- When Jed attempts to crawl in his lap, his father is to put one arm around him and let Jed sit with him even though it is difficult. He is not to move in on Jed but is to let Jed take the initiative and then work at responding more affectionately and uncritically in his interaction with him.
- He is to cut down on his community activities and make himself more quietly available to Jed by being around home more.
- He must also work at establishing a warm relationship with his wife, even if this requires professional help.
- Jed's mother must never look at Jed with sympathetic eyes or give him special affection and favors when she believes his father has

been too harsh with him. If she cannot tolerate what is going on, she should walk into another room. She should *never* interfere between father and son.

- She should not criticize Jed's male friends. She should encourage him to play with boys.
- She should not encourage him to do with her things that are considered feminine by his peers and would further confuse him as to his sexual identity.
- She can structure Jed's environment so that he will find it natural to play with boys. She should make it difficult for him to play with girls until he can easily identify with the male sex.
- She should never criticize her husband or the male sex to her son.
- She must also put her time and energies primarily to developing a better understanding and a closer, more affectionate and rewarding relationship with her husband.

DISCUSSION

Jed's situation is a rather classical example of how the child can become confused in his sex role. The harsh, cold, distant, and demanding father coupled with a warm, permissive, pampering, protective mother who undermines her husband's relationship with his son, stimulates the child to reject his masculine sex identity and to move more in the direction of feminine behavior. He rejects identifying with and learning male behaviors because the process is too painful. He identifies with and learns feminine behaviors because they are pleasant and include much payoff in the form of special involvement and attention.

The sexual urge itself is biological, but its expression, for the most part, is a learned response. The individual can learn to find sexual release that is personally satisfying with others of his same sex or with the opposite sex. It is primarily a matter of training that will determine how the child will express his sexual urges. Parents' behaviors with the child and with one another are crucial.

Most parents, like Jed's, want to train their children to accept their sexual identity. To do this, each parent must be respectful of and value both sexes. The father must value being a male and respect and value his wife's being a female. The mother must value being a woman and value and respect her husband's being a man. Fathers must teach their sons masculine behaviors within a context of warmth and affection in order for their sons to identify with their own sex. The same holds true for mothers teaching their daughters their sexual identity.

Many combinations of parental behaviors can disturb a child's sex role learning. Just as it is difficult for the son to identify with and learn from a cold, distant, critical, and demanding father whose behavior is criticized by his mother, it is difficult for a son to identify with a father who is weak, timid, passive, and the object of a mother's ridicule. It is difficult for little girls to learn their sex roles when their mother allows herself to be trampled on by their father or when she is cold, distant, and harshly critical of her husband and daughters. War between the sexes wherein derogatory generalized remarks or nonverbal responses are made about the sexes, such as "Men are vicious, cruel, and selfish" or "Women are not worth much," result only in intensified conflict for the children.

Parents who rear their boys to learn their necessary masculine behaviors and to value being males and who rear their girls to learn their necessary feminine behaviors and to like being females are helping their children to behave and relate responsibly in society.

Note: Concepts you may want to review are social linkage, pp. 44-45; life-style, pp. 48-50; self-esteem, pp. 46-47; modeling, pp. 53-54; bonding, pp. 52-53; personality traits, pp. 55-56; empathy, p. 71-72; warmth and respect, p. 71; genuineness, p. 71; practice, pp. 54-55; payoff, pp. 42-44, 53.

A PARENT'S MISDIRECTED ANGER

THE SITUATION

Ed was depressed and angry. He was a lawyer in a large firm and had felt for some time that one of his junior partners in the firm was out to discredit him before the senior members. As a result he was easily irritated at home.

One night he found himself getting annoyed with his seven-year-old daughter Eileen. The following is a sample of much of his conversation with her:

"Eileen, will you shut your mouth when you eat. I've told you a hundred times." He yelled, "Eileen, you get in here and clean out this bathtub. You left a ring an inch thick." He almost screamed, "You've been dawdling for two hours. You get to bed this instant or I'll skin you alive."

Eileen went crying to bed. Ed began to feel guilty, for he knew he had taken out his frustration on her. What should he do now?

DISCUSSION

Ed's behavior is not altogether uncommon. Most people have experienced feelings of anger for someone whom they could not, dared not, or did not know how to cope with and found themselves redirecting their anger against someone with whom they felt more secure. Those who are safer targets are often loved ones or those who are physically smaller. The child will be hurt by a parent and will go out and kick the cat. A teenager will be hurt at school by his peers and will return to his home and do something to hurt his parents. It is generally safer to hurt parents than to counterhurt peers, and so it was with Ed. Eileen was a safer target for his anger than his articulate lawyer-colleague, whom he did not know how to approach.

Ed thought over his behavior with Eileen and then went to her bedroom.

"Eileen, are you asleep?"

"No, Daddy."

"May I talk to you?"

Eileen's answer was to hold up her arms to her father. Ed covered the remaining distance quickly and hugged her to him.

"Honey, I'd like to talk to you about the way I've been acting the last few days. I've been very grumpy and have sounded very angry."

Eileen's response was to tighten her arms about his neck.

"Eileen, I want you to know that when I have sounded angry with you, most of the time it wasn't really because of you at all. You see, honey, I've had kind of a rough time at work and I come home angry. And this anger has sometimes just spilled over at you. I'm sorry, honey. I'll try not to let it happen tomorrow. O.K.? Am I forgiven?"

Eileen's response was to squeeze harder and say, "Please, Daddy, stay with me a little while."

Of course he stayed a while longer with his arms around his daughter as they shared some fun conversation.

Ed's going to his daughter and asking her forgiveness was therapeutic for both. First, it helped Eileen to understand the real cause of her father's anger. Children tend to grow up feeling worthless when they are the constant targets of misdirected hostility. Second, her father's admission that he had goofed gave her the courage to live more self-confidently. She realized that if someone as good as her father could make mistakes and still be good, then she also could make mistakes and still feel good about herself. It helped free her for further progression and development. Third, it brought father and daughter closer to each other because it fostered greater mutual love and respect. Fourth, it put things into clearer perspective for Ed. He realized how important his child was in his long-range plans and how relatively less important his problems were at work. Fifth, his child's love for him and ability to quickly forgive gave him greater strength and courage to work through his difficulties with his colleague.

Note: Concepts you may want to review are vertical goals, pp. 16-23, 43; warmth and respect, p. 71; genuineness, p. 71.

A PROBLEM OF RESPONSIBILITY

THE SITUATION

Twelve-year-old Robert has had his morning paper route for two months. During this time the relationship between Robert and his father has become strained.

Robert cannot seem to wake up on time. His father calls him six or seven times every morning before he will get up. (He is supposed to pick up his papers at 5:30.) Some mornings his father even pulls him out of bed. Then it is one continual round of "Hurry and get dressed. Have you eaten? Did you get your paper bag? Where is your jacket?" ad infinitum. By the time his son is gone his father is so upset he cannot go back to sleep.

A high percentage of the time Robert's father ends up driving his son along the route, for Robert is often so slow that he cannot complete his route by himself without being late for school. This frustrates his father because it often makes him late for work.

His father is also afraid that Robert is too slow in his collections. He has been after him time and again to get them collected, but Robert seems unconcerned.

154

What should Robert's father do to help his son become more dependable and responsible?

RECOMMENDATION

Robert's father can get his son an alarm clock, take it to him and say, "Son, I have been too involved with you and your paper route. So that it can become your own thing, here is an alarm clock for you. I will no longer wake you up nor take you by car on the route. It is your responsibility."

Regardless of his son's protestations, last-minute activities, or lateness for school and his collections, his father should not intervene or say anything about Robert's performance.

DISCUSSION

Robert's goals, which his father has been paying off beautifully, are to get attention and service. Through his irresponsible behavior, he has manipulated his father into treating him as if he were a prince. How many others have their own private chauffeur on paper routes!

If Robert's father withdraws this payoff, and lets his son experience the natural consequences of his behavior, he will learn to be more responsible. In this case, being late in the morning with his papers may make him late for school, and if his father does not come to his rescue, he will suffer those events applied by the school to latecomers. As Robert takes the responsibility for his paper route, his father will not feel used. This will enable them to relate more positively and harmoniously with each other.

Robert will probably put the pressure on when his father first withdraws. It is most essential at this time that his father be firm and not get drawn back into the old relationships. He must be firmly consistent with his own behavior. He must never call Robert to get up or take him by car to deliver his papers.

The above suggestions to the father for not being directly involved do not prevent him from encouraging his son. Such phrases as the following, when wisely used, can be most helpful: "It's rough, but you can do it. As you work harder, you'll get the money collected."

Learning that behaving irresponsibly is not a constructive way to belong to his fellows and learning to take pride in his own responsible accomplishments will make Robert feel more self-confident. As a result he will feel better toward himself and other people.

Note: Concepts you may want to review are payoff, pp. 42-44; natural consequences, pp. 85-86; empathy, pp. 71-72; warmth and respect, p. 71; self-esteem, pp. 46-47.

FATHER AND SON ESTRANGEMENT

THE SITUATION

Ed, known as Big Ed to his friends, is a two-hundred-twenty-five-pound, six-foot-four-inch mountain of energy. He even has a craggy, handsome face. He is a vice-president in a large corporation, holds a responsible position in his church, and is active in community service organizations. Because of all of these responsibilities, Ed is seldom home. He is critical and demanding of himself. He expects perfection and usually approaches it.

His seventeen-year-old son is a startling contrast to his father, and is of concern to him. Six feet and slender in build, he takes after his mother. He is also similar to her in temperament, being rather quiet although capable of outbursts of temper. He is not a sports enthusiast as was his father at his age. He prefers art and music instead. Not only does Ed, Jr., avoid running for school student body offices, he associates with just two or three friends rather than the large crowd his father feels he should gather around him if he is to be successful.

Ed, Jr., seldom talks to his father anymore. When he does, he does so in monosyllables and with averted eyes. This frustrates Ed and at times makes him angry with the boy. He feels that he could at least hold his head up like a man. Sometimes he speaks his thoughts, when he feels humiliated, angry, and hurt by his son's responses.

Ed feels he has given his son every opportunity and has gotten him out of many jams. He has paid Ed's traffic tickets and a fine for destroying tombstone heads in the local cemetery. His son's latest episode was being caught and charged with smoking marijuana. It took all of Big Ed's influence and skill to get the charges dropped. It was at this point that he and his wife decided to seek help.

Other children in the family include a daughter, fifteen, the apple of her father's eye. She is good-looking, athletic, popular, and academically oriented. Another daughter is thirteen and a second son is ten.

Ed would like to establish a closer relationship with his eldest son and have him keep out of trouble. It seems that the older his son gets the more jams his father has to get him out of.

RECOMMENDATION

First, Big Ed should become less involved in his community so that he can spend several nights home each week.

Second, he must never criticize his son.

Third, rather than concentrate on his son's skill or lack of it when he associates with him, Big Ed is to concentrate on nonskill activities, such as taking a walk with his son because Ed, Jr., likes this type of thing. He is to emphasize having a relaxing good time with his son. He is also to watch his talk ratio to make certain that he talks less than fifty percent of the time during these occasions.

Fourth, no more will he get his son out of jams. He may encourage and reassure him with phrases such as "I know it's hard, but you can work it through," but he is not to use his influence or affluence to intervene between his son and the natural consequences of his behavior.

Fifth, the young man's mother is never to show pity for Ed, Jr., when she feels that his father has been too harsh or unkind in not getting him out of his difficulties. It is best at this point for her not to discuss this with her husband as the negative pattern is too strong. Big Ed will need to become objectively critical about himself whenever he might fall back into vertical patterns with his son. Perhaps he can discuss his behaviors with a professional therapist or a trusted friend who can help him.

DISCUSSION

This is a rather typical example of an eldest child who, feeling he cannot meet great expectations, chooses a direction composed of paths that are free of competition with other family members, paths that also enable him to humiliate and counterhurt as he feels he has been hurt.

Ed, Jr., is probably a very discouraged young man, especially discouraged in believing he can be accepted by his father. His father's constant critical comments, coupled with his example of boundless energy and ever present good works, cause Ed, Jr., to feel terribly threatened. Big Ed's constant absence from the home may also have communicated to his son that other things are more important than he.

Because he has felt for so long that he cannot meet his father's expectations and therefore is not accepted by him, as evidenced by his continual critical comments, Ed, Jr., feels an ever present and intense hurt. Being hurt, he strikes back by humiliating his father, getting traffic tickets, smoking marijuana, and being unassertive when his father talks to him. His father's hurt and frustrations are payoff.

He also receives payoff from his mother when she sides with him when she feels his father is too harsh and demanding. Her responses compound her son's difficulties; as he appears more pathetic, she intervenes more often for him. As his father intervenes for his son in the community, his mother intervenes for him in the home. This provides him tremendous payoff.

As both parents withdraw payoff from their son's unconstructive behavior and allow him to experience natural consequences, it is important that they work to have an unthreatening (uncritical) warm relationship with him; otherwise he may feel abandoned.

By giving up many of his outside activities and being unobtrusively available if needed, Big Ed will be able to express his love for his son. And, as he disciplines himself to listen to rather than talk to his son, he can begin to build a closer relationship.

As his father works to never compare his son with his other children, Ed, Jr., will be further encouraged in his feelings of belonging.

By being accepted at home, developing an affectionate relationship with his father, and taking responsibility for his own behavior, Ed, Jr., will feel his self-esteem and respect for others grow. As a result he will develop a greater ability to relate positively with his fellowman.

Note: Concepts you may want to review are life-style, pp. 48-50; payoff, pp. 42-44; belonging, pp. 45-46; natural consequences, pp. 85-86; warmth and respect, p. 71; personality traits, p. 55-56; practice, pp. 54-55.

FATHER AND SON ALIENATION

THE SITUATION

This father and mother are deeply concerned about their thirteen-year-old son and have sought help. They describe their boy as being good in school, athletic, and a gentleman most of the time with other people. In the home, however, he is a terror. He has several younger sisters with whom he is constantly quarrelling and fighting. His father feels indignant about his son's hitting his sisters at times, and he has "whipped" him for such behavior.

During a family therapy session the father launched into a monologue about how women are not treated as respectfully in the world as they should be, but he is going to teach his son to respect them. He feels that he and his son are getting farther and farther apart emotionally. He loves his son and wants to get closer to him.

At this point in the therapy session the children expressed themselves. The girls explained that their brother beat up on them, and their eyes flashed with anger. The oldest girl struck a self-righteous pose, modeled to a lesser degree by her sisters. She also commented with a look of satisfaction that when their brother beat up on them they told their dad and then their brother really got it.

RECOMMENDATION

The father and mother should gather their children around them as soon as possible and inform them that from now on the children are going to have to work out their own difficulties. Their mother and father are not going to intervene in anyone's behalf in the future.

The father should also take time to hunt and fish with his son. Both enjoy these activities, but because of the father's community involvement, his participation in these activities has been minimal during the last four years. He should concentrate on having good, horizontal experiences with his son, free from any criticism.

DISCUSSION

These parents are very concerned about rearing their children in what they term "the right manner." The father has observed other men treat their women disrespectfully and has vowed that he is going to see to it that his son learns to respect womanhood.

His extreme concern, however, makes him vulnerable to the manipulations of his daughters, who have learned to make their older brother appear to be a vicious brute. Having their father defend them provides great payoff for their cries, screams, and paraded black and blue marks. The son also receives payoff, for he plays the notorious role of the child everybody is concerned about.

If the mother and father continue taking sides in their children's fights, everyone will still receive payoff and be stimulated to fight even more in the future. If the parents refrain from taking sides and if the father provides for increased, unthreatening, enjoyable association with his son, they will set the stage for better relationships for all members of the family. Such parental behavior stimulates children to accept responsibility for their acts and encourages them to relate more horizontally with one another.

Note: Concepts you may want to review are life-style, pp. 48-50; social linkage, pp. 44-45; belonging, pp. 45-46; payoff, pp. 42-44; natural consequences, pp. 85-86; bonding, pp. 52-53; warmth and respect, p. 71; genuineness, p. 71.

A TOO RESPONSIBLE MOTHER

THE SITUATION

Roberta and her husband were upset and concerned about their children. They felt they had provided them with a good home. They lived in a quiet neighborhood free from crime or drug problems and had always had enough money for food and clothing. However, they found that the older their children got, the more rebellious they tended to become. Because of this pattern, both parents felt they must be doing something that stimulated their children to rebel. But they had no idea what it could be. They were now asking for help in order to solve the problem.

Their oldest child was of special concern to them. She was harsh and critical of her parents. She continually corrected her mother and was skillful at doing this where it had its greatest impact, usually in front of company or out in public. She was disdainful of her father and ridiculed him unmercifully. At night she ran the streets saying she could not stand it at home.

Their second child, a boy, was an enigma to them. He was quiet and would agree with his mother verbally but still do what he wanted. His parents constantly criticized his clothes and hairstyles. The more they criticized, the more extreme his styles became. The more his mother talked to him, the less he responded to her. She often found herself speaking a monologue. In contrast, Roberta's talks with her daughter usually ended with her daughter shouting and crying and her mother responding in cold fury and afterwards crying alone.

Roberta was concerned about her children always "making the

house a mess." She would just get things in their proper places and someone would come along and disturb everything. She found herself constantly following after each child, even her husband, nagging and scolding in an effort to keep things as she felt they should be. The family had become so sloppy, according to Roberta, that she had made the living room off limits. It seemed that the harder she tried with her children, the worse things got. She and her husband were anxious for help.

RECOMMENDATION

Roberta's situation is rather typical of the highly demanding, perfectionistic and critical parent who expects much of herself and demands much of others. Such a parent, as in the case of Roberta, often gets the exact opposite of what she wants from her children.

In order for the parents to establish more horizontal relationships with their children so that they can help them behave and interact responsibly, they will find the following suggestions helpful:

- Both parents are to work at making their home a safe, warm place where their children want to be. This means that their mother will have to stop criticizing them. Both parents should focus on their children's strengths and assets and talk about them with their children.
- When Roberta is criticized in public by her daughter (i.e., when they are shopping), she should immediately walk away and refuse to continue shopping with her for that day. She should do this in a calm, somewhat disinterested manner.
- The father should not pay off his daughter's attempts to ridicule him. He is to continue what he is doing (i.e., reading the paper) without looking at her. He must show no sign of hurt.
- Roberta must never criticize or ridicule her husband.
- The father must work at having a closer relationship with his sons, especially with his oldest, by having masculine, fun experiences with them with the main objective being their enjoyment of each other, not their mastery of a particular skill.
- A family council should be held during which the family decides

how each member can relieve Roberta of the burden she feels regarding the upkeep of the home.

- In order for the parents to be encouraged to make the needed changes they should keep a record of their progress. Their awareness of the improvement and the better relationships with their children will pay off their efforts. For example, Roberta should make a tally mark every time she criticizes anyone in the family and then graph her progress each week (see page 91).

DISCUSSION

Roberta appears to be a key to the family difficulties. She dresses immaculately, with every hair of her head in place, and her makeup appears to have been applied by a professional. She sits with her back straight, head erect and tilted up. Her eyes appear to focus downward on those with whom she converses. She holds her legs closely together so that they form a perfect ninety-degree angle at the knees. Her general appearance is that of a forbidding statue of perfection that surveys, judges, and finds wanting everyone who comes within her view.

When she listens to her husband talk, she often turns her body from the waist up as if it were hinged there only and focuses on her husband just prior to correcting his story. He then turns red and ceases talking altogether or at varying times increases the speed with which he talks and sometimes stammers.

Roberta was the oldest of a large family and was expected by her parents to take care of her younger brothers and sisters. Whenever her parents left home to go out for entertainment or to take care of their religious or community responsibilities, they left her in charge. If anything went wrong while they were gone, such as the children's breaking a dish, spilling milk that had not been cleaned up, or leaving bread crumbs on the table after a snack, Roberta was chastised, regardless of the age of the offending child.

She grew to feel responsible for anything and everything her brothers and sisters did. She was almost constantly afraid that she would incur her parents' displeasure. This stimulated her to continually watch over her brothers and sisters to keep them from doing anything wrong when there was danger she would be blamed. She became bossy and critical.

She also learned that she could have a special, favored place with her parents by reporting to them the wrongdoings of others. By tattling to them, she was able to get their praise and at the same time protect herself by giving the report in such a manner that they would realize that she was not involved. She became quite skillful at painting a picture in which she appeared to be completely innocent and noble while the offending brother or sister appeared to be the very opposite.

Through such behavior, repeated over and over with the passage of years, Roberta learned by her own illogical reasoning that the way to belong and be worthwhile and at the same time protect herself from the displeasure of those in authority was to boss other people. If there were danger of her being implicated in wrongdoings, she would need only appear to be more superior and righteous than anyone else.

These were naturally the behaviors and attitudes she brought to her role as mother. Her great demands, high expectations, and extremely close supervision of her children communicated to them a lack of faith in their desires and abilities to grow up good and virtuous. Such things communicated a lack of trust, and the high demands resulted in discouragement. This caused her children to feel inferior, inadequate, and hurt. As a result they responded by striking out in hurtful ways, as indicated by the behavior of the eldest daughter, or withdrawing and refusing to battle overtly but doing their own thing covertly, as indicated in the behavior of the eldest son.

Roberta's desire to do what was best for her children, her ability to take responsibility, and her self-discipline enabled her to make swift changes once she had a clear picture of what was happening and a knowledge of the alternatives available to her.

It was also helpful for her to discover that she was listening to a ghostly monkey that was riding her back and whispering in her ear, "What will happen if your mother drops in on you unexpectedly? Will she criticize you for the way your house looks? Will she approve of what your children are doing?" By realizing how she was allowing this to burden herself and distort her relationships with members of her family, she was able to diminish its influence.

Roberta also confronted her mother several times in a warm, friendly, but firm manner, when she attempted to criticize the way her house looked or what her children were doing. Her mother was at first surprised and baffled by her confrontations; but as Roberta persisted with warmth and friendliness, her mother began to understand and backed off from criticizing her. A new, deeper, and more respectful relationship developed between mother and daughter that enabled Roberta to completely shake off her ghostly rider.

She also stopped criticizing her husband as she discovered through the intervention of other people when and how she was belittling him. Through simulation and practice she was able to develop more respectful relations with him. She learned to support him and to disagree in a respectful way without demeaning him. This enabled him to be held in greater esteem by his children, especially his sons.

As Roberta gained understanding of how the other family members felt when she was demanding and critical of them and as she learned how to let them be more responsible for themselves, she was relieved of a great burden. She became more relaxed and developed warm feelings toward other people. Home became a safe place for her.

Note: Concepts you may want to review are life-style, pp. 48-50; modeling, pp. 53-54; bonding, pp. 52-53; practice, pp. 54-55; payoff, pp. 42-44; personality traits, pp. 55-56; warmth and respect, p. 71.

DEVELOPMENT AND CORRECTION OF CRITICAL ATTITUDES

THE SITUATION

While in a meeting with local officials, Reed was told his children were found to be extremely critical of anyone in authority. Normally he would not have been too concerned; but there were two people in the group whom he uniquely respected (he himself did not usually have much respect for people in authority), and they reported specific comments his children had made. There were many, but those that stayed in his mind were "All leaders are in it for the money and power they get. The head of our town is a bigot."

Reed and his wife began to observe their children closely and were shocked to find how often they criticized someone. As a result they sought advice on how to help their children overcome this. The oldest son, especially, was continually finding fault with such things as officials' dress, speech patterns, talks, and private lives. The children were critical of not only school teachers, government and church officials, other adults in the neighborhood, but also their own parents.

When their children were critical of them, Reed and his wife usually got into a verbal battle with them and, with the oldest son, this usually ended in a shouting match.

Reed felt the atmosphere in his home was not as he would like it to be. He not only wanted to make it more harmonious, he also wanted to change his children's critical behavior.

RECOMMENDATION

Reed will find that it will help the situation a good deal if he concentrates his own critical comments on issues and topics, not people (he is also extremely critical of authority figures). When in doubt as to whether he should express criticism, he should refrain. He will also find charting his progress to be helpful (see Chapter 8).

Reed and his wife should not pay off their children when they are critical of other people. They can avoid this by continuing whatever they have been doing and not focusing on the critical child with words or looks even when they are the targets. They should explain to their children in the beginning what they are going to do and why.

Both parents will have to work at focusing on the assets and positive attributes of people in authority as well as on those of their own children. Both should agree to pay off their children when they speak about other people in positive ways.

DISCUSSION

Reed had been a rebellious second child who resented his older brother, whom he felt had been given special privileges. He got to drive at a younger age, stay up later at night, go out more, have a bigger allowance, and get bigger helpings of food. Reed had resented him and his parents, whom he felt had been unfair. He hated the words *but he is older* as he hated the fact that he was younger. He found he disliked anyone in authority whom he thought had special rights or who tried, or whom he thought might try, to boss him around.

Reed has discovered that his dislike for the rules and authority that had given his brother special privileges has generalized to rules and authorities in general. He has come to realize that he is modeling critical behavior for his children by being readily and harshly critical of people in local, state, and national government, in the neighborhood, and in the church. His criticism is focused not on issues or principles, but on the personalities whom he feels are trying to be superior to himself. His critical comments are not so much to constructively solve problems as they are to cut others down to size. He is locked in the phantom battles of the past and is modeling unconstructive critical behavior for his children. In trying to cut down others in authority he has been in fact refighting old battles between himself, his older brother, and his parents. Becoming aware of this has helped desensitize him so that he does not feel so angry himself with those holding positions of power.

Not only are Reed's children modeling his behavior, they are receiving payoff from both him and his wife whenever they use it. When they are critical of others who hold prestigious government or community positions, Reed tends to agree immediately with them and expand on their critical comments with his own. Even when they are critical of high religious leaders, which is taboo with Reed and his wife, telling their children in concerned, attendant emotional outbursts to stop such bad behavior is great payoff for them. Therefore, it is very important for Reed to stop his critical behavior and for both him and his wife to work at not paying off such responses from their children but work to pay off their constructive appraisals of other people.

Being a second child, Reed was basically fun-loving and not too demanding of his children. They had many good times together. Reed should continue to emphasize these fun relationships with his children.

Also, as Reed more actively participates in local government and accepts responsible positions in his local church, he will identify more with those in positions of authority and become more tolerant.

Note: Concepts you may want to review are communal interest, pp. 47-48; payoff, pp. 42-44; modeling, pp. 53-54; warmth and respect, p. 71; life-style, pp. 48-50; practice, pp. 54-55.

A CASE FOR COURAGE

THE SITUATION

It was sixteen-year-old Shane's first time away from home. He had gone to another state to work during the summer vacation. His work required him to spend long hours in water and mud moving rather heavy pieces of equipment. At other times he had to put on long-sleeved shirts, heavy gloves, and thick work pants as he followed a machine through the vast fields of pineapple, picking the ripe ones and placing them on the conveyor belt that dropped them into a produce truck. Shane's boss was known throughout the area as a reasonable man who treated his workers with respect.

During the first two weeks, Shane's letters and phone call to his parents were filled with excitement and pride over his accomplishments. However, after this time he began to complain about the long hours and heavy work. He wrote to his mother that sometimes he was too tired to eat supper when he returned to his bunk after a long, hard day. He told her over the phone that his muscles ached and cramped and that they were sore to the touch much of the time. She got the feeling that it would not take much for him to break down and cry when he talked to her.

After one discouraged letter and an emotional phone conversation, his mother told his father that they should go get him and bring him back home.

RECOMMENDATION

Shane's parents should not retrieve their son. They should let him stay where he is and finish his summer contract. Their letters and phone calls to him should reflect their understanding that it is hard for him, but they should also reflect their confidence in his ability to see a job through to its completion. They should not communicate sympathy or pity for him as this will undermine his efforts to be courageous.

DISCUSSION

It is usually difficult for all parents the first time their children leave home to work. It is especially hard when there is some distance between them and the work required is much harder than what the children have previously experienced.

Parents can best help and support their children when they empathize with their difficulties and cheer them on with words of encouragement indicating their faith in them. Empathy is different from sympathy. When a parent is empathetic, he understands; when he is sympathetic, he feels sorry for his child. Empathy tends to strengthen, sympathy to weaken.

If Shane's parents go to him for the purpose of rescuing him from his difficulties, they will communicate their lack of faith in his ability to cope. It could be devastating to his self-esteem and undermine his courage to come to grips with future difficult tasks.

The more encouraging behavior could consist of Shane's parents visiting him where he is working and there show interest and pride in his accomplishments as he takes them on a tour of the pineapple farm. This should help him feel good toward himself and closer to his parents as they thrill with him over his accomplishments. And as he successfully completes his summer's work experience, he will tend to see himself as one who can complete difficult tasks. His general stance toward life will be one of courage and optimism which are basic prerequisites for establishing horizontal relationships.

Note: Concepts you may want to review are self-esteem, pp. 46-47; natural consequences, pp. 85-86; empathy, pp. 71-72; payoff, pp. 42-44.

A CHILD-MOTHER
THE SITUATION

Pat, the youngest child in her own family, is a middle-aged mother of six children, three of whom are well into their teens. It seems to her that the older they get the more rebellious they become. They resent doing anything for her. For example, she will ask them to make her a soda while she is on the couch watching TV, and they will either refuse or do it grudgingly. When she asks them to do such things as to go downtown to get her candy, to fix her hair, adjust her slip, or clean up her bedroom, they often say, "Mother, why don't you ever do anything for yourself?"

She feels they are cruel to her. When she feels this way, she cries. The children will then usually do what she requests. Pat feels that this is not right of them; they should obey her before she cries.

Another concern Pat has is that the children do not keep to the time limits agreed upon for visiting friends or while on dates. Sometimes she forgets to follow through by insisting on their keeping to the limits. But when she does remember, her children usually give her such a hard time that she gives in. Quite often when Pat has continued to press the issue, her children have called her names. This makes her feel so bad that she usually says nothing more.

Pat wants to be an effective mother, but is often bewildered as to why her children are so rebellious. Her husband is away much of the time because of his work, and Pat must deal with the children, relying on her own resources.

RECOMMENDATION

- Pat should no longer request her children do anything for her of a personal nature that she can do for herself. For example, when she wants a soda while she is watching TV, rather than ask one of her children to get it for her, she should get it herself.

- Pat must practice not crying when her children do not respond to her requests. Rather than cry, she should ask in a calm voice such questions as "What are your feelings about it? What do you think is fair?"

- Pat should follow through each time with regard to those limits agreed upon for her children's visiting friends and dating. This means that she is aware each time the limits are overstepped and that she allows children to experience the reasonable consequences of such behavior.

DISCUSSION

Each one of us brings to his childrearing efforts a repertoire of behaviors we have learned in our family of origin. These behaviors either assist us or interfere with our efforts to be effective parents; so it is with Pat.

Being the youngest in her home of origin, Pat was treated by her parents as a special person. Her mother doted on her and gave her everything she wanted. Pat learned to belong by being helpless and dependent. Rather than get dressed herself, she was able, through her tears, to keep her mother dressing her even at the age of ten when she was quite capable of doing it herself. She learned to feel that she was a worthwhile and important person to the extent that she was able to get others to do her favors. Getting her busy mother to stop what she was doing and get her a dish of ice cream and cookies made her feel special. When her mother refused, Pat would cry, and her mother usually gave in.

Pat was rather automatically and unthinkingly using the same vertical behavior with her own children to gain a feeling of importance with them. But with them it was backfiring; it made them resentful. At times, the more resentful her children became of her undue service demands, the more demanding Pat became. She felt threatened in her need to have a secure place of belonging with her children. When they refused her requests, she tried harder in the only way she knew how to belong by demanding more and more service of them. A vicious spiraling effect often developed; the more her children refused, the more Pat demanded special service from them.

In order to break up the vicious spirals, it is important that Pat do more things for herself. This will lessen her children's resentment and increase their respect for her. Few enjoy being slaves to others. Her refusal to cry when things do not go her way and her efforts to understand her children's feelings at such times by asking appropriate questions will also increase her children's respect for her. Pat will learn new ways of belonging with her children that will be more satisfying to them and to her in the future.

As part of the undue service Pat was able to get from her own parents and older brothers and sisters, she was never made responsible for keeping to limits herself. Other people would always remind her, and she had not learned to discipline herself to abide by limits. By being irresponsible, she was able to get others to tell her what to do and thereby receive much payoff from them. She brought this same behavior with her to her own family.

If Pat is to train her children as she would like and if she is to gain their respect for her, she will have to work hard to keep them to the limits they agree upon. It will be helpful for her to chart her progress by making tally marks and graphing the results (see Chapter 8); this will give her the reinforcement she needs.

As Pat no longer requests undue service from her children, she will probably experience deep feelings of rootlessness. This is to be expected as she will be giving up old ways of belonging. There is usually a transition period of feeling lost before new ways become the familiar with known, looked-for results.

One thing Pat can do to help herself through this transition period is to structure fun times with her family. Another is to gain support and encouragement from her husband. A third might be to inform her children about what she is trying to change in her own behavior and to ask them to inform her when she is demanding undue service.

As Pat learns to have more respectful and equal interactions with other people, she will gain more respect for herself and more respect from them. Her ways will become more horizontal.

Note: Concepts you may want to review are life-style, pp. 48-50; belonging, pp. 45-46; social linkage, pp. 44-45; warmth and respect, p. 71; practice, pp. 54-55; payoff, pp. 42-44; logical consequences, p. 86.

THE PROMISCUOUS CHILD

THE SITUATION

Pam, a rather heavyset young lady in her middle teens, has one older and several younger brothers. Her father is an avid sportsman who spends much time in the hills with his sons. Her mother is meticulous about her own personal appearance and about the care of the house. She also holds down three church jobs and is usually involved in several community activities at one time, including those sponsored by two community service organizations in which she has membership.

Both parents were shocked and upset to discover, upon talking to school authorities, that they had solid information that Pam had had sexual relationships with several boys. At first the parents did not believe it; but as the evidence increased, they were forced to accept it as fact. Upon returning home, they confronted Pam with the evidence, and through tears and sobs she admitted it was true. At this point her father and mother were extremely anxious to know how to best proceed with their daughter.

RECOMMENDATION

The young lady who gives of herself freely in such sexual activities is actually allowing herself to be used by other people to her own disadvantage and is, thereby, entering vertical relationships. The objective then becomes to help her interact with others so that she can maintain her personal integrity.

- Pam's mother should give up all but one of her church jobs and community activities and spend more time with Pam, having enjoyable, fun times with her.
- She must refrain from any criticism of Pam expressed verbally or nonverbally.
- Pam's father should take Pam with him on hunting trips if she desires to go. He must work at showing her affection by listening attentively to her, putting his arm around her, and recognizing her contributions to the welfare of the family.
- He must never criticize Pam but rather emphasize her strengths and assets.
- Both the mother and father should never refer to her past sexual behavior in an attempt to humiliate her to get her to obey. They should, however, discuss with her things she and they can do to help her to be more happy in the home.
- Both parents are to actively work to help Pam feel more included in the family so that she feels loved and appreciated.
- Both parents should *consistently* follow through in giving Pam recognition for her constructive behaviors and expressing their affection for her. If they relapse into old behaviors of disinterest in her and Pam gets involved sexually again and they then redouble their efforts with her, they may give her the feeling that they will show their care and concern only when she misbehaves.

DISCUSSION

Pam's situation is representative of the not-too-uncommon occurrence of the child who has not found a satisfactory sense of belonging with either her mother or father and turns to her own peers, buying a form of acceptance at a high price to her own integrity.

Pam's father was too busy with his boys and their hunting expeditions to take much notice of Pam. In fact, he never really understood girls. He had come from a family of all boys and felt uncomfortable in the presence of girls. Because of these feelings, he avoided having very much to do with his daughter. Pam felt this and interpreted it to mean that something was wrong with her. She developed feelings of being unloved and unlovable and consequently resented her father while feeling a great need to be loved by him. The more she tried to gain his love, the more he seemed to rebuff her.

Pam's mother had a similar distant relationship with her daughter. Being somewhat a perfectionist herself in dress, looks, and endeavors, she was super critical of Pam. She felt distant from her husband, for much the same reason as Pam, and in her frustration hurled herself into church and community activities to find a way of belonging with other people. Because of her critical comments and excessive time spent away from the home, a wide gulf developed between her and Pam. In this relationship, too, Pam developed the feeling that she was unloved and unlovable, a sloppy large person whose mother could not stand to be with her.

She developed deep feelings of doubt, hurt, revenge, and loneliness. She doubted that she was a person who could be loved and felt a deep hurt that those she loved most did not love her. She felt semiconsciously that she wanted to hurt her parents as she felt they had hurt her. And she wanted to find companionship. Her goals became those of proving to herself that she was a lovable person, that she could get revenge, and that she could acquire companionship.

Pam's sexual activities were her attempts to achieve the above goals. By having boys fondle her, she proved, if even for a few moments, that there were things about her that were desirable. By getting involved in illicit sexual activities, she was able to hurt her parents deeply. And finally, she was able to secure a degree of belonging.

Pam's parents must help their daughter find her place with them so that she will not have to look for demeaning, dangerous ways to meet her needs to belong. Also, their nonreference to her sexual activities will withdraw payoff for the revenge goal.

It is imperative that parents take time with their young children to ensure that they have constructive ways of belonging with those whom they love. As a result, their children will feel very little or no need in later years to search outside the home for unconstructive and destructive substitutes.

Note: Concepts you may want to review are belonging, pp. 45-46; vertical goals, pp. 16-23, 43; self-esteem, pp. 46-47; bonding, pp. 52-53; payoff, pp. 42-44; life-style, pp. 48-50; warmth and respect, p. 71.

REASONS FOR SUICIDE

THE SITUATION

Sam is the eldest in a family of four. His father is a most successful professional man who has received national recognition for his many contributions. His mother is equally successful in her own right. All members of the family are academically oriented and have done extremely well in school. This has been fostered by the children's well-meaning parents, who have stressed the value of being the best academically in their school grades. Academic excellence was continually practiced and encouraged in the home by the parents structuring such things as spelling, math, and geography bees when the children were small. As they got older the game of who knows the most was commonly engaged in at breakfast, dinner, and supper. All of the children responded well to this academic training by being at the top of their grades almost every school year.

Yesterday Sam's parents were summoned to the university's hospital where he was attending school. They were stunned to learn that he had tried to commit suicide by taking a full bottle of sleeping tablets. He had been saved only by the quick action of a friend who visited him unexpectedly.

In their shock, grief, and bewilderment, Sam's parents went back over their experiences trying to recall what had happened to make him want to take his life. They also desperately wanted to know what they could do from this point on to best help Sam.

RECOMMENDATION

The action of the suicide is usually an attempt to lash out in deep anger against loved ones and, as in the case of Sam, to give up a life immersed in vertical relationships where he experienced the byproducts of insecurity, alienation, and hurt. Sam's parents will have to do a very definite about-face if they are to help him.

- They must never compare one child's knowledge with another's or any other person's.

- They must give up all of their competitive games among their children where one comes out a winner and the others are losers.
- They will have to learn and use words and phrases such as "But did you enjoy doing it? Is it what you would like to do? It makes me feel good to see you enjoying life. The important things are how it makes you feel and how it makes others feel. The important thing in life is to enjoy it."
- They will have to delete from their repertoire such phrases as "Make sure you're the best at whatever you do. You only came in second? Who was number one? Any job worth doing must be done better than anyone else could do it. Now you ought to be ashamed of yourself. Your younger sister knew the answer."
- They must talk to Sam openly about the pressures in the home when he was being reared and how they are going to work to change things.
- They must tell Sam that they accept and love him as he is. They are to work to demonstrate their love for and acceptance of him.
- They will have to accept the fact that he tried to commit suicide and rather than dwell on it in a negative way approach it from a posture of "What can be learned from this experience?" They will need to view the suicide attempt with a calm emotional attitude. This will probably have a calming effect on Sam.
- They will have to work to have relaxing enjoyable times with Sam when nothing is demanded of him and a skill is not required. He should never be criticized or corrected. The emphasis must be on their enjoyment of each other as people.

The above recommendations should apply to Sam's parents' relationships with all of their children.

DISCUSSION

There are too many Sams in our society. As technology demands more and more of people and as there is a greater stress among some for material wealth and its use to gain status, there is an ever-increasing number of casualties. Sam was such a casualty.

Parents who unwisely use competitive vertical techniques for motivating their children to succeed are running the terrible risk of fostering discouragement, disillusionment, hatred, hurt, and apathy among their children. Children reared in such an environment tend to grow up with the tendency to feel that all people are their potential enemies and they become alienated from their fellows, often structuring for themselves a perpetual battlefield or withdrawing into a surrogate womb where they give up relationships with other people.

Sam felt he was accepted by his parents only as long as he was the best. At his university the competition for good grades was more severe than anything he had experienced previously. Having struggled for many years to get on the top and stay there, he was a tired, worn-out old man at twenty. Not only was he tired, but underneath it all, he was sick with hurt, a hurt that was triggered by his belief that he was loved by those he loved most, his parents, only as long as he was on top. The conditional aspect of this love seared the deepest part of him.

Another aspect of Sam's competitive behavior was that he was in reality a ruthless competitor among his peers. This had a profound effect on his relationships with them, for it alienated him from them and their groups. This caused him only greater discouragement, for he saw evidence at every turn that he was indeed unloved. It was not long before he reached his point of complete despair.

Caught in his hopelessness, Sam could see no end to the struggle. His feelings of vulnerability to someone else's being better, his deep unrecognized hurt resulting from his belief that he was loved only for his outstanding academic achievements, and his subsequent alienation from his peers provided the impetus for his suicide attempt.

The suggested recommendations will function to help Sam feel that his parents really care, that he does not have to bring anything but himself to the relationship. He will come to believe that they love him for himself as he is now. And as they stress the enjoyment of doing things together with emphasis on their enjoyment of each other, they will be teaching him that man exists that he might be happy. All else is secondary. Theirs will become a true, horizontal relationship in action.

Usually it is best for the potential suicide and his family members to seek professional help in working through their difficulties.

Note: Concepts you may want to review are life-style, pp. 48-50; social linkage, pp. 44-45; holism, pp. 50-52; vertical goals, pp. 16-23, 43; belonging, pp. 45-46; warmth and respect, p. 71; empathy, pp. 71-72; genuineness, p. 71.

TRAFFIC LAWS AND THE CHILD

THE SITUATION

Ted is the only son of a well-respected law officer. His father and mother, who had waited many years for a child, finally adopted Ted when they were in their mid-thirties. They felt he was the cutest baby they had ever seen and spent many hours caring for him. They were cautious about his hygiene, still boiling his eating utensils and wearing face masks while holding and feeding him when he was three years of age.

As Ted has grown older, he has often gotten into trouble and been bailed out by his parents. Of special concern since he started driving is the number of times he has been stopped by his father's fellow law-enforcement officers for driving violations. Either Ted's glib tongue or the fact that his father is a policeman has made it possible for him to get off with only warnings.

Recently Ted ran his car into the back of another car, causing two hundred dollars damage. Ted's insurance has a hundred-dollar-deductible clause in it. His father's first impulse is to pay the one hundred dollars and talk to his colleagues so that they will go easy on his son, but this time he hesitates, for he feels uneasy about doing it.

RECOMMENDATION

It is fortunate that Ted's father feels uneasy about continuing to get his son out of trouble. The following actions can help him to help his son become a responsible community citizen.

- His father should tell Ted in a calm, kind way that the one hundred dollars is Ted's bill and that he is sure Ted can arrange to pay it off.
- He should talk to his colleagues and suggest to them that from now on they treat his son as they would anyone else.
- He must talk to Ted and tell him that he has realized that he has not been fair to Ted in the past by stepping in and paying his bills and clearing the way for him. He cares a good deal for him and wants him to learn the consequences of his own behavior. He will no longer go to his son's rescue. The discussion should end on a positive note. For example, he might assist Ted to identify several ways that he could earn one hundred dollars.

- He will want to redouble his efforts to take Ted to ball games and on fishing expeditions (Ted loves to do both).

DISCUSSION

Ted's behavior is rather predictable. Anytime parents do too much for their children, they are likely to rear individuals who expect other people to take the consequences for their irresponsible behavior.

Ted's parents had bailed him out of many situations—from fights with his friends to problems with his teachers. Not only had he not learned to take the consequences of his behavior, he had learned that by getting into trouble he could trigger much emotional involvement and protective reactions from his concerned parents. This was great payoff for his irresponsible behavior and stimulated him to behave the same way in the future.

For his parents to train him to respect the rights of others and to be more responsible for himself, it is important that they follow the first and second suggestions. Often when parents have a history of intervening for their children, the children take this as a token that they are loved. And when the parents stop intervening for them, they tend to believe that the parents no longer care for them as they once did. That is why suggestion number three is given. When Ted's parents no longer pay his debts and get him out of trouble with the law, it is important that they redouble their efforts to have friendly, constructive interactions with him so that he will know that his parents care during the transition period from irresponsible to more responsible behavior. Such an encouraging statement as "Yes, it's rough, Ted, but you can manage your affairs so that you get the one hundred dollars saved up" and an offer to help him come up with an acceptable plan can help Ted know that his parents care and that they have faith in his ability to work things through.

By means of such parental behaviors children learn the consequences of their own behavior and thereby learn to be more concerned about the rights of other people.

Note: Concepts you may want to review are vertical goals, pp. 16-23, 43; natural consequences, pp. 85-86; warmth and respect, p. 71; genuineness, p. 71; empathy, pp. 71-72; modeling, pp. 53-54.

A SON WITH LATE PAYMENTS

THE SITUATION

Larry talked his father into making a down payment on a car he bought with the promise that he would pay him back in six months. His father hesitated at the time because it sounded like a familiar refrain to him and reminded him of previous experiences with Larry and his bicycles. In these situations he usually paid the down payment and ended up paying for most of the installments. However, since Larry had a good job and was really a good boy, his father decided to give in.

Six months have now passed. Larry's father has not seen any part of his down payment and, because Larry pleaded extenuating circumstances, has paid for two of the installment payments. His father feels uneasy about this aspect of Larry's behavior, for another young man has just gotten into serious difficulty with the law over several unpaid installment loans. What is especially disconcerting is that his history is similar to Larry's; he too had a father who paid off his many unpaid bills.

RECOMMENDATION

If Larry is to learn not to take advantage of other people's generosity, his father will need to relate to him in a different manner. The following behaviors can be helpful.

- The father should have a friendly talk with his son and tell him that from now on he will have to be completely responsible for following through on his own financial arrangements. His father will no longer come to his rescue.
- The father should assist his son by helping him explore ways for improving his budgeting if he can do it with friendly feelings and if Larry requests his help.
- He should redouble his efforts to enjoy companionship with Larry in activities such as boating and horseback riding, both of which his son enjoys.

DISCUSSION

One of the serious pitfalls of affluent parents, especially those who experienced financial hardships as children, is the tendency to bail their children out of financial difficulties. It is easy for them to intervene when they see their children struggling and especially when the amount of money required seems so small to them. But it is such behavior that teaches children to take advantage of other people.

Parents who would teach their children financial integrity must first learn to hold themselves back from going to their children's rescue when they do not live up to their commitments. This is especially true of those children who have a history of defaulting on their responsibilities. In Larry's case it would be better for him to lose the car than for his father to come to his rescue again. Losing a bicycle or a car because of unwise financial planning or unwise monthly budgeting can do wonders for building character which enables a person to show respect for the obligations one has with others. This may be hard for the parent if he focuses on the financial loss involved. However, when he focuses on the need to build character, it becomes much easier to be resolute and firm in the face of the child who tries just about everything in order to make his parent feel guilty for not coming to his rescue.

It is easier for parents to teach their children to budget wisely when their children are still young. It is much easier not to give a seven-year-old child extra money beyond his allowance for a show ticket than it is not to pick up the car payments of a seventeen-year-old son who has learned great skill in putting pressure on the "old man," especially when the car may be repossessed.

Note: Concepts you may want to review are warmth and respect, p. 71; bonding, pp. 52-53; natural consequences, pp. 85-86.

SMOTHERING SUPERVISION

THE SITUATION

Vaughn was an older child in a large, competitive family. While growing up, he learned to be conscientious and to behave most responsibly in all he did. He found his place with other people by involving himself in many activities and doing each one of them better than any of his brothers and sisters. He also learned to belong by taking care of and closely supervising his younger siblings. In spite of all his efforts, however, he had deep feelings of insecurity.

As children came into his own family he worked to train them by supervising their every activity, criticizing their mistakes, and redoing for them those things they did not do well. He also spent much time preaching to them. He spent time each day telling them how important it was to be good and often referred to great spiritual men in the scriptures and compared their behavior to their own. Occasionally he compared his children's behavior to that of his brothers' and sisters' children.

In spite of Vaughn's efforts, he seemed to be losing each one of his children as they got old enough to be on their own. They became rebellious in their talk about religion and religious leaders and stopped going to meetings and activities. This was preceded by many verbal and occasional physical battles where Vaughn tried to impose his will.

Becoming more and more frustrated, Vaughn began to analyze the family situation. He discovered, among other things, that whenever his father visited the family, he, Vaughn, was concerned that his children make a good impression. He found himself being strict with them and, especially when his father visited, ordering them about and criticizing their poor behavior in front of his father. He also realized that his father was critical of the way he reared them. His father's typical comments included "You're not going to let them get away with that, are you, Vaughn? When you were little, you would never have done that. You know Bill's children? Well, they have all turned bad. I hope you know what your children are doing all the time. For Pete's sake, Vaughn, you'd better see your kids do better in school than that."

In his introspection he realized that whenever his father visited, he was tense and vulnerable to embarrassment by his children as he worked hard to make them be good in order to avoid his father's critical comments and to find favor with him. He also came to realize that when his father was not physically present he rode on Vaughn's shoulder as a ghost, whispering in his ear such things as "Now, Vaughn, you'd better do something about that quick. Make that kid shape up."

With this sudden realization Vaughn was engulfed by feelings of anger, fear, and bewilderment; his anger was directed toward himself and his father; his fear came when he was trying to decide how to handle his father; and he felt bewildered when he thought about how to deal with his children.

RECOMMENDATION

It is important that Vaughn talk through the problem with his father. He should tell him kindly, but with no equivocation, that from now on he is not to criticize the way he disciplines his own children. And if his father chooses to continue, Vaughn should respond immediately with such words as "Father, that is not your concern. Please let that be between me and (name the particular child involved)." After Vaughn has dealt firmly with his father, Vaughn should show forth increased love towards him so that he will not get the feeling that he is being rejected.

Second, it is important for Vaughn to start talking differently to himself. When his children misbehave, rather than thinking to himself, "What would Father think if he saw and heard that?" he should substitute the phrase, "What is best for my children?"

Third, Vaughn should concentrate his efforts on enjoying his children by having fun times with them devoid of critical comments.

Fourth, because he has been in many power struggles with his children, he should practice phrases that will enable him to sidestep such struggles. Such phrases as the following can be helpful in accomplishing this:

- You could be right.
- Yes, sometimes I goof too.
- Tell me more.
- Each one of us could see things a bit differently and each see a part of the truth.

Fifth, Vaughn could use the remainder of his energies to concentrate on setting a good example. He could work to influence his children by behaving as a courteous, respectful, courageous, and fun-loving father. He should do this with the realization that in the final analysis he cannot force his children to respect him and follow his ways. He can only try to live in such a manner that they will eventually desire to behave as he behaves because they respect him and trust him as a model.

182

DISCUSSION

The case of Vaughn is a rather typical case of the over-conscientious parent who is still trying desperately to win approval from his own parents. It is as though his children become his pawns as he attempts to gain his own parents' respect and prestige. Children sense such efforts and from deep feelings of resentment and anger will often lash out at those who would so use them. The resentment and anger springs from a knowledge, either at the conscious or semiconscious level, that their father is more concerned about his relationship with his father than he is about his relationship with them. They may develop concomitant feelings of inferiority and worthlessness, expect the worst of themselves, and then behave in such a fashion that they end up fulfilling their own prophecy and meet their own expectations.

The suggested recommendations are geared to help Vaughn rid himself of a heavy, unreasonable burden and relate to his children in a manner that communicates trust, faith, hope, and love. With such a change he will remove their reasons for resentment and augment the relationship with good times and positive expectations which his children will tend to meet. His interactions with them will cease being bitter, vertical relationships and will become horizontal and satisfying.

Note: Concepts you may want to review are life-style, pp. 48-50; social linkage, pp. 44-45; holism, pp. 50-52; warmth and respect, p. 71; empathy, pp. 71-72; bonding, pp. 52-53; modeling, pp. 53-54; self-esteem, pp. 46-47.

EXPANDING LIMITS FOR TEENAGERS

THE SITUATION

It was the rule in Stan's family that when he desired to go anywhere he had to phone or return home and clear it with one or the other of his parents. This did not seem to bother him when he was young, but he was now in his mid-teens and it caused some embarrassment for him in front of his friends. He also felt resentful because of his desire to be more independent, to have greater freedom to direct his own life.

RECOMMENDATION

The following suggested dialogue between Stan and his parents offers several points that can help both him and his parents relate in an openly respectful manner with each other.

Stan had just returned from going down to the local ice cream shop with one of his friends. He came through the outside door, slammed it shut, and stomped into the living room.

"What's wrong, Stan?" was his dad's immediate response as he looked up from the paper he was reading.

"I get so sick and tired of having to report to you every move I make."

"What do you mean?" Dad responded, setting aside his newspaper.

"I'm the only kid my age who has to check in with his parents to clear every move he makes."

"You sound pretty angry."

"I am angry, Dad. You don't know what it's like."

"How about talking about it?"

"What is there to tell? When the fellows want to go somewhere else and I say I don't know if I can go, I'll have to call home first, I get razzed." Stan slumped further into his chair, digging his hands deeper into his pockets. "Besides, I get the feeling you don't trust me."

"What can be done, then, Stan, to help you feel we trust you and to also help you avoid embarrassment with your friends?"

"I don't know."

"Please help me, Stan. Can you tell me some of the things you have thought about? We could discuss them and reach an agreement satisfactory to the three of us—you, your mother, and me."

"I really haven't thought much about it except I don't like the way things are." Stan threw down one of the younger children's toys he had picked up.

Dad ignored his angry response and shifted to a more relaxed position in his chair. "How about taking tonight and tomorrow to think about it, then the three of us can sit down tomorrow night and pool our thoughts. Should we do that?"

"Yeah!" was Stan's only reply as he marched off to bed.

"Good night, son," was his father's friendly parting response.

The next evening: "Well, Stan, what ideas for change have you come up with that you feel will save you embarrassment with your friends and help you to feel like we trust you more?"

"You won't like what I want."

"Try us."

"I don't want to have to report to you when I have permission to go one place and we get tired of being there and the fellows decide to go someplace else." Stan shot a challenging glance at his father and mother.

"We would feel uncomfortable about writing you a blank check so to speak. Is there any way we could hedge it up a bit so that you could have greater freedom within broader limits than you have had in the past?" His mother spoke the words in a friendly tone.

"What I hate is having to call you up in front of my friends. And I do feel like I deserve greater freedom. You know you can trust me. I have seldom come in later than the time we agreed upon, and only once or twice have gone places without your permission. How about just making it so that I don't have to check with you each time."

"Do you have something in mind?"

"Yeah! How about having an agreement that I can go to either Paul's, Gene's, Sandra's, the Tip Top Ice Cream Parlor, or the Teen Canteen without having to clear it with you before?"

"Every place you mention is a fine place, it seems to us. I can see no reason why we couldn't give approval to such a plan." The parents looked at each other and his mother nodded in agreement.

"However, it seems to me we would still have to agree to some general time limits when you go out," Stan's dad said in a thoughtful, considerate manner as he sat in a relaxed position, one leg across the other.

"That's no problem. Just so I don't have to tell the kids, 'I don't know. I'll have to ask my folks,' " Stan responded with obvious relief.

"Are we agreed then? Stan, there will be several places you can go without checking with us beforehand. But you will still inform us as to the approximate time you will be gone from home."

"Yeah. That's O.K. by me."

DISCUSSION

This situation is rather typical of conscientious parents who have properly supervised their children's activities but have not been as sensitive as they might to their growth and needs for greater independence. It takes sensitivity and a degree of artistic ability on the part of parents to expand limits at a pace that maintains the security and guidance their children need and at the same time allows them maximum freedom for directing their own lives responsibly. The dialogue demonstrates the parents' respectful interaction that stimulates their son to express himself freely and to take responsibility for his part in the discussion. It reflects horizontal behavior in action.

Note: Concepts you may want to review are empathy, pp. 71-72; warmth and respect, p. 71; genuineness, p. 71; conflict resolution, pp. 78-79.

A QUESTION OF INSECURITY
THE SITUATION
Seventeen-year-old Cindy had moved with her family from a somewhat protected environment to a large urban center. Cindy was at first shocked by the illicit sexual activity of her new associates. Then the initial shock gave way to doubts about her own standards as she discovered that those who engaged in such activities appeared to be just as happy as she and to be more popular.

RECOMMENDATION
Late one evening when she and her mother were alone, Cindy initiated the following dialogue.

"Mother, did you and Dad have sex before you were married?"

Mother, taking firm control of her first impulses of shock and anger, looked behind Cindy's words and responded, "I don't understand your question, Cindy. What are you concerned about?"

"I just don't know. I've always believed that I should be a virgin when I got married. Now I'm not so sure anymore."

Again her mother stilled herself as she fought the rising tide of emotion that threatened to burst out. She said in a relaxed tone, "You have some doubts now?"

"Yes."

"Would you like to talk about them?"

"You know Betty. Well, she has been going steady with her boyfriend for two years and they have been making out for one whole year."

"What do you mean making out, Cindy?"

"You know, Mother."

"You mean they have been necking, petting, or having sexual intercourse. Which is it? Words sometimes mean different things to different people." Her mother spoke in a gentle yet frank manner.

"You know, Mother. They have been having sexual intercourse." Cindy shifted uncomfortably in her chair.

"And what is troubling you about it, Cindy?"

"I don't know. It's hard to explain. But I thought that doing things like that before marriage would make people unhappy. Yet Betty seems happy and she is popular."

"Let me see if I understand. You believe, as you have been taught, that sexual immorality is wrong and that such activities will bring unhappiness. Is that right?"

"Well, partly, Mother."

"Are you also saying that you see no evidence for unhappiness in Betty's having sexual relations with her boyfriend?"

"Yes, that's it exactly," Cindy responded somewhat excitedly. "I expected misery, disease and all kinds of things to happen to those who were sexually involved before marriage, but I just don't see much evidence that that is so. In fact, I think some of the girls who pet and have sexual intercourse with their boyfriends are happier than I am. Many of them are certainly more popular. I just don't understand it."

"Some things are hard to understand, Cindy. Remember that things are not necessarily what they appear to be on the surface."

"You mean, Mother, that Betty and the others are not as happy as they seem to be?"

"Well, I was wondering about that," her mother spoke somewhat hesitantly.

"No, I don't buy that. Many of them are happy. I know that."

"Cindy, are you saying that you would like to be happier than you are?" Her mother looked up with an expression of gentle inquiry. There was a long pause, Cindy ducked her head, and her shoulders began to visibly shake.

"Sometimes it helps to talk about it," her mother said in a quiet voice as she moved over and put her arm around Cindy. Cindy began to sob uncontrollably. Her mother held her close and waited until the sobbing quieted.

"I have felt alone so very much of the time since we moved. I miss all my old friends."

"Moving is rough, especially at first, Cindy."

There was a long silence as she waited for Cindy to continue.

"I don't feel I really fit in. Everyone's values are so different from my own," Cindy said with an occasional catch in her voice.

"You feel all alone at times, Cindy?"

Cindy again began to cry in affirmation of her mother's question. Her mother waited for the crying to cease as she held her close.

"What can you do, Cindy, to help you feel less lonely?" her mother quietly asked after the crying had ceased.

"I don't know." Cindy kept her head buried in her mother's shoulder.

"Sometimes it helps not to place all your eggs in one basket. That way if the basket drops not all the eggs are broken. In other words as you concentrate on making friends with other girls, especially with those sharing your values, Betty's friendship and her activities will not be so important to you. What can you do to increase the number of people you have as friends?"

"I could go visit my old friends," was Cindy's quick reply.

"Yes, that could be helpful. What could you do about the situation at school?"

"I guess I could work at making friends with other girls even though they are not as popular as Betty."

"That seems like a reasonable solution, and with your personality I'm sure you can do it. Have we talked enough about the questions you had concerning morality and sex?"

"Well, it doesn't seem as important to me as it did, but I still wonder how people can be so happy doing it if it's so bad."

"Sometimes I've wondered the same thing, Cindy."

"You have?" Cindy gave her mother a look of astonishment.

"Yes, I have. Oh, not recently as much as before I was married to your father. I don't know how you'll answer this question for yourself, Cindy, but I would be happy to tell you how I've worked it through if you want me to."

"Yes, please tell me," was Cindy's urgent response.

"I guess the answers I have arrived at hinge primarily on two things; one I call the long-range view and the other I call faith. For most of us I think there is no question but that sexual activity can bring immediate pleasure. But I think the guidelines with regard to such activities must include answers to the following questions:

- What will such activity do to my feelings toward myself?
- What will it do to my feelings of loyalty and trust in others?
- What will it do to strengthen the love and loyalty found in my family?
- What will it do to my children, born or yet unborn?
- What will it do for the strengthening of society?
- What does history suggest is in store for those societies whose members generally engage in illicit sexual activity?

"The second major consideration I give is to what I interpret to be good spiritual, moral health. It seems to me that sexual immorality is next to murder and terribly destructive to society. I know professionals are divided about the consequences of illicit sex. Some even suggest it should take place. But I am cautious about trusting the advice of professionals when it can actually cause greater problems. Cindy, I don't know if this is helpful to you or not. I feel like I have rambled."

Cindy gave her mother a squeeze and said, drying her eyes, "Mother, you don't know how helpful you have been. Thanks for your ideas. I didn't know that you had thoughts like that about sex. Thanks for sharing them with me."

DISCUSSION

The question of sex should never be taken out of the interpersonal context in which it occurs. Sex is one more expression of interpersonal skill or lack of it. In Cindy's situation her overt question about sex masked her deeper feelings of loneliness and alienation, which were uncovered by a sensitive mother. The problem of sex then took on a more accurate picture as a foreground statement against a background of loneliness. Cindy's mother showed great skill in responding respectfully in a highly emotionally charged situation.

Note: Concepts you may want to review are empathy, pp. 71-72; warmth and respect, p. 71; genuineness, p. 71; personality traits, pp. 55-56; belonging, pp. 45-46.

A CHILD WHO IS BASHFUL AND HESITANT

THE SITUATION

Brad, whose father died while he was still young, lives at home with his mother, an older sister who is about nineteen, and a younger sister who is fifteen. All the women in the family are assertive and verbal.

The following is rather typical of conversation among these family members. The setting is Brad's home at dinnertime where his family is entertaining a guest.

"Well, Brad, it's nice to meet you again after all these years. Let me see, how old are you now?"

Brad ducked his head until his chin was almost on his chest and mumbled something that no one could hear.

"For heaven's sake, speak up, Brad," said his mother in an irritated tone.

"He's seventeen," said his older sister almost at the same time as Mother responded.

"Seventeen," said the guest in an obvious attempt to keep the conversation going. "You must be in your final year in high school."

Again Brad lowered his eyes, ducked his head even further, and mumbled.

"What was that?" said the guest, continuing his efforts.

"He is in grade twelve," his mother responded rather quickly.

"What subjects do you enjoy most?"

"He does best in math." His mother spoke in a rather loud voice and overrode Brad's obvious attempts to begin to speak. Brad lowered his eyes again.

"Is that right?" responded the guest, continuing his efforts to make contact with Brad.

Not waiting for Brad to answer, his mother said, "He's trying to get university entrance. We're all proud of Brad, aren't we girls?"

Brad looked as though he were about to crawl under the table.

"What things do you like doing the most? Do you have any hobbies that interest you?" The guest was beginning to feel frustrated.

"Well, I do enjoy . . ." Brad's voice trailed off into a mumble, and his younger sister began his sentence anew, finishing it for him.

"He enjoys stamp collecting, don't you, Brad."

"Would you care to show me your stamp collection? I've always had an interest in faraway places." The guest spoke with some relief, feeling he now had a way of possibly reaching Brad.

Brad spoke in a slow, rather hesitating manner, taking about fifteen seconds to say, "I'm—not—sure where—they . . ."

"Brad has an outstanding stamp collection, don't you, Brad?" His mother looked his way briefly and, not waiting for him to respond, looked back to the guest and continued, "He has an outstanding collection of stamps from Asian countries that he'll have to show you."

Brad's older sister brought back an album of stamps and handed them directly to the guest. His mother moved her chair closer to the guest, reached over to the album and began thumbing through the pages until she reached the section on Asia. She then turned to her son and said, "Come and show your stamps on India. I think they are most unique."

Brad slowly got up from his chair and walked hesitantly to the sofa where the guest sat. Then he sat down. If his movements had been timed by the guest from the moment Brad began to shift from his chair until the time he sat down on the sofa, the clock would have shown one hundred and twenty seconds.

Brad slowly moved his hands through the leaves in the album. He got to the middle then retraced his fingers back to the beginning again, fumbling with this page and that. His movements were slow and even.

"I do declare, Brad, Mother knows more about your own stamp collection than you do," responded his mother with much irritation and annoyance. She reached across, took the album from Brad's hands, and thumbed deftly to the section on India, then turned again to the guest. "Brad's a good boy, but sometimes he's kind of slow and doesn't speak for himself."

RECOMMENDATION

Brad's mother and both sisters must no longer talk for Brad. When he appears to be having a difficult time expressing himself, is hesitant, or his speech is trailing off into silence, they should sit quietly and patiently and allow him to pick up his conversation and finish it. They should also not finish things for him that he begins and with which he slowly and hesitantly proceeds. No matter how difficult it is for them, they must discipline themselves not to intervene and rescue him.

DISCUSSION

Brad has learned that he can get help from his sisters and mother by appearing helpless and dependent in his speech and actions. And his sisters, desiring to appear good and responsible before their mother, are quick to move in and rescue Brad. Their mother is also caught up in the web of Brad's manipulations of the family through her own desire to be a good mother. Her desire to compensate for the loss of Brad's father has made her sensitive and vulnerable to Brad's slow and hesitant behavior. All are paying off Brad's dependent behaviors by giving in to his manipulations and their own desire to be good. They also receive payoff as they take over for Brad.

The family relationships are, therefore, vertical. The mother and her daughters have an investment in keeping Brad helpless because in doing so they can run to his rescue and thereby feel responsible, good, and superior. Brad has found a place with the members of his family by being inferior and dependent.

If this behavior continues, these family members will pay a high price. Brad will be poorly prepared to make his own decisions to live effectively when he gets a little older. If he is to find true happiness, he must learn to think well of himself. This he cannot do as long as he maintains his present behavior, belonging by being inferior.

Also, Brad's sisters are being poorly prepared for marriage. Their relationship with him may tend to be their model for their relationships with their future husbands. They will experience much misery and unhappiness if they relate by talking and acting for and making decisions for their husbands.

It is not only important that Brad's mother and sisters not pay off his efforts to keep them in his service, but that they also provide him with opportunities to experiment and practice leadership behaviors in the family. His efforts here should never be criticized nor should anyone in the family step in and rescue him from his mistakes. Each should, however, be ready to give him consistent encouragement and reassurance for his horizontal efforts to belong.

Note: Concepts you may want to review are vertical goals, pp. 16-23, 43; payoff, pp. 42-44; warmth and respect, p. 71; life-style, pp. 48-50; self-esteem, pp. 46-47; holism, pp. 50-52.

A PATTERN OF DESTRUCTIVE BEHAVIOR

THE SITUATION

Doug is sixteen years old and a second child in a family of three. He has one older brother and a younger sister. The older brother is considered a brain at school and is believed to be just about perfect by his parents, so Doug feels. The younger sister is also sharp academically and is able to keep house about as well as her mother.

Doug gets poor grades in school even though his teachers say he has high ability. He is continually getting into trouble with his teachers. His father has helped him out of one difficulty after another. His most recent escapade was marking up headstones in the local cemetery with a group of his friends. He was brought to court and fined one hundred dollars. The judge gave him sixty days to pay the fine or be jailed for a week. One month has gone by and Doug has not saved up any money. The last few days he has been telling his father that he will go to jail if he does not pay the fine. His father is worried because he feels Doug will carry out his threat, and it would be most embarrassing to his good name in the community to have a son spend time in a jail.

RECOMMENDATION

As they search for ways to help their son become a more responsible person, Doug's parents will find the following suggestions helpful:

- They should let Doug keep the responsibility of paying off his fine or going to jail. His father may give him extra work so that he can pay it off, but Doug is to earn the money himself. His father must not pay the fine. He should handle the situation calmly and confidently.
- They must never compare Doug with his older brother or younger sister.
- They should never take sides with one child against another when they quarrel.
- They should refuse the alliance of either the older or younger child

when they are having difficulty with Doug and the other children step in on the parents' side.

- They must give Doug recognition for his unique skills, strengths, and assets.
- They should structure family activities so that all of the family members can enjoy them and be careful to make these free of competition.

DISCUSSION

Doug's parents have tried hard to rear him to be a good boy. They believe it is important to point out examples to their children to emulate. As a result they have used Doug's older brother as an example because he is a good student and is obedient. They have almost constantly referred to his brother as a person he should watch and imitate, saying such things as "If only you'd be more like Tom, you would enjoy school more. Why don't you ask Tom? He'll be glad to help you I'm sure. When Tom was your age, he was happy because he obeyed. Even your younger sister helps more than you do. Tom would never chase the streets and destroy the property of others."

Such phrases mean to Doug that he is not as good as, nor as acceptable as, his brother and sister. He feels that he is being continually judged and continually found wanting.

His hurt is deep and excruciating; he suffers greatly. He feels his parents are unfair. Engulfed with hurt and feeling that those he loves most are unfair, he seeks revenge by inflicting pain and suffering on his parents as he feels they have hurt him. His goal is not readily apparent to him, because it exists at a semiconscious level.

Not only is Doug seeking revenge, but he is discouraged. He feels that his parents expect him to do less well than his brother and sister. He in turn feels "If Mom and Dad think that is how I will behave, I guess that is the way it will be." He thus tends to meet their expectations.

It is important that Doug's parents not pay off his attempts by showing their feelings of hurt and guilt and rushing to his rescue. They should come to understand his hurt and work to help him feel that he is accepted and loved, that he has a secure place with them. While doing this, they should allow Doug to experience the reasonable consequences of his behavior so that he will learn to function more responsibly.

In order for Doug to be able to like himself and other people, it is important that his parents relate to him in a horizontal manner. They should never compare him with other people, even when others try to perpetuate comparisons.

Note: Concepts you may want to review are life-style, pp. 48-50; social linkage, pp. 44-45; vertical goals, pp. 16-23, 43; payoff, pp. 42-44; natural consequences, pp. 85-86; self-esteem, pp. 46-47; warmth and respect, p. 71; belonging, pp. 45-46.

COPING WITH DRUGS: A PROGRAM OF PREVENTION

THE SITUATION

Bill and Eva were still new parents when they made a pact to structure their home life so that their children would have no need or desire to turn to drugs. Their plans involved a total program for childrearing that they felt would bring their children and themselves what they hoped would be a maximum degree of happiness. Both parents were sensitive to the problems presented by drugs since each had relatives or friends who had been hooked.

RECOMMENDATION

Their plans included many ideas, but the following were those precipitated by their awareness of the drug culture:

- Eva agreed that she would work not to smother her sons. She would encourage them to make their own decisions and would support their efforts to develop a close relationship with Bill.
- Bill in turn agreed to encourage his daughters to develop a close relationship with Eva. He would also work to have a good relationship with them.
- They decided to refuse to give attention to a child when he attempted to appear good at the expense of another.
- They agreed to de-emphasize competition.
- They agreed to solve their differences themselves, refusing to allow their children to enter into their personal conflicts.
- They agreed that neither of them would ever use alcohol.
- They decided to de-emphasize the use of drugs for medicinal pur-

poses. Drugs prescribed for organic problems were to be used sparingly and were to be referred to only in clear cases of need.

- They decided that when symptoms occurred that are usually associated with interpersonal problems such as headaches, neck aches, and stomach problems, they would try to help their children solve their interpersonal problems unless there was good evidence that pain was organic in its genesis.
- Eva and Bill further agreed to emphasize the beauty in life, such as close, harmonious friendships and beautiful sunsets, so that their children would have no need to seek chemical thrills via the drug route in an attempt to compensate for a dreary life.

DISCUSSION

Bill and Eva were aware that among those people on drugs there seemed to be a high incidence of young men who had possessive, smothering mothers who often helped alienate them from their fathers. Many, both boys and girls, had poor relationships with their parents. Many also seemed to come from highly competitive families where they felt they belonged only to the degree that they out-performed the others.

Parents who used alcohol and pills for their troubled nerves and spirits rather than working through their difficulties in efficient ways served as models for a high percentage of young people on drugs.

It was with such an awareness of these patterns of destructive behavior that Bill and Eva constructed their program. They wanted to build more effective relationships, making the need for drugs nonexistent.

Note: Concepts you may want to review are warmth and respect, p. 71; bonding, pp. 52-53; communal interest, pp. 47-48; modeling, pp. 53-54; empathy, pp. 71-72.

A HOME WITHOUT AN ANCHOR

THE SITUATION

Les was orphaned when he was three years of age. He spent the next sixteen years in five different foster homes and grew up feeling unloved and unwanted, inadequate and inferior. He married a woman whom he felt was superior to him. They had four children, two girls and two boys.

Les and his wife experienced many difficulties in their relationships with each other. But what really troubled them was their children. As the children got older they became rebellious and vengeful. Each went against his parents' basic values and burdened them with cutting phrases such as "I hate you. I can't stand you. You're not a man, Dad."

RECOMMENDATION

Taking such steps as the following will prove helpful to Les as he tries to gain his wife's and children's respect and affection:

- He should search out and associate with his colleagues at work and in the community, those around whom he feels worthwhile and valued, who encourage and support him in his efforts and constructive contributions. This will help him to have the necessary courage to be firm at home.
- He should not give permission to his children to do something to which his wife has said no.
- He should think, "What is best for my children?" rather than, "Will they still like me?" when he makes a decision.
- Since he learned early to keep his feelings to himself and to communicate with many hinting and deflecting techniques to protect himself from being hurt, he will find it necessary to practice showing his feelings openly and honestly with his wife and children, communicating to them directly rather than indirectly.
- It is also vitally important, if he is to win the affection of other people, that he practice giving and accepting affection from his wife and children.

DISCUSSION

In this family's relationships there was very little firm and consistent discipline. The children could talk Les into and out of almost anything. When their mother tried to be firm and consistent, Les undermined her position by giving in to the children. He tried to buy their love through giving in to them. He was a man who had experienced so little love and so much hurt that his main goal was to be loved and accepted by pleasing his children.

His efforts, however, prevented him from having the very things he wanted most—the respect, affection and love of his wife and children. As he undermined his wife, he lost her respect. And as he gave in to his children's pressure because of his need to be loved and his desires to protect his children from the hurts and disappointments he had experienced, which really had little relationship to his children's experiences, he lost their respect and love. They wanted him to be firm and decisive; and when he was not, they were disappointed in him and also felt, though they could not put it into words, that he did not care enough about what happened to them to be firm.

They often tested him in an attempt to get him to show that he cared enough to be firm. One of his children tested him by coming in late at night after visiting with friends, partying, and dating. Another tested him by running with a wild crowd.

The home that exists without a male leader is a tragic experience for the children as well as the wife. It is imperative for children to feel secure and loved and to have an acceptable male model. A father who can be such a model exhibits the qualities of affection, self-esteem, self-confidence, fairness, consistency and firmness in discipline, emotional stability, emotional honesty, and concern about fulfilling his loved ones' needs.

When children feel secure in their parents' love, they tend to respect them, adopt their values as their own, and move horizontally with them. When children feel insecure because of inconsistent or little or no discipline, they tend to disrespect their parents, betray their values, and relate vertically against them.

Note: Concepts you may want to review are life-style, pp. 48-50; self-esteem, pp. 46-47; social linkage, pp. 44-45; holism, pp. 50-52; belonging, pp. 45-46; vertical goals, pp. 16-23, 43; warmth and respect, p. 71; genuineness, p. 71; practice, pp. 54-55; modeling, pp. 53-54.

PARENTS' VISITS TO MARRIED CHILDREN
THE SITUATION
The following dialogue is somewhat typical and therefore representative of the feelings expressed by parents who are somewhat upset by the actions of their new daughter- or son-in-law. This set of parents has sought help in solving their problem and have contacted a friend who is a family relations therapist.

"She seemed to be such a sweet thing before their marriage."

198

"What do you mean she seemed to be? What things have happened to cause you to change your mind?"

"Sometimes when we drop in to see them, she acts downright rude." The mother spoke eagerly with a trace of bitterness in her voice. "She'll come to the door and say, 'We have other plans.' Sometimes she will just stand in the doorway talking to us and won't invite us in. Can you believe it?"

"Do you phone first to see if it is all right if you drop in to visit them?"

"Heavens no. After all it is my son's home. Do you know, I guess I shouldn't be telling this but I will anyway, she came to the door one time at four o'clock in the afternoon with her hair all messed up and in her bath robe. She was rude. My son was home. Can you imagine? And in the middle of the day too." The mother lifted her nose slightly in the direction of the ceiling and ended her sentence with an audible "humph."

"How often do you visit them?"

The father, who had not said much up to this time, shifted uncomfortably in his chair and responded, "Three or four times a week."

The mother smoothed her dress with a gloved hand and picked up the conversation. "After all they live in the same town and are only a fifteen-minute drive away. I wish my son had more backbone. I've told him that he should do something about the way his wife treats us, but he doesn't seem to do anything about it."

DISCUSSION

This mother and father are making one of the traditional blunders. They are relating to their son and daughter-in-law in a vertical, superior fashion by insisting that they have rights to visit them unannounced and uninvited whenever they wish. The fruits of such behavior are those of anger and resentment, as expressed by the daughter-in-law.

In order to harvest the fruits of horizontal relationships, this mother and father will need to respect their children's rights. They can do this by realizing the importance of the sanctity of the newly established home.

The new husband and wife need time in privacy to develop,

strengthen, and make secure their new relationships. Specific things the mother and father can do to respect their children's rights when they visit are suggested in these phrases: "We love the two of you very much and would like to visit you occasionally, but not so often that we become pests. If we visit you so much that you feel we are intruding, please let us know and we will make our visits less frequent. We will always try to call you on the phone before we visit you. We would greatly appreciate it if you would tell us when you prefer that we not come over. We realize you could have other plans or other expectations and that, at times, it will not be convenient for you."

Such phrases as the above show respect and courtesy. And with such an attitude the mother and father will be welcome more times than not. The fruits of such behavior tend to be greater respect and love from married children and their desire to see their parents.

Note: Concepts you may want to review are warmth and respect, p. 71; empathy, pp. 71-72.

PRACTICE IN BEING CONSISTENT

Each of the following cases is presented with misbehavior occurring in series and each is rather typical of real-life situations. You may wish to practice correcting the behavior by selecting what you consider to be the best response for changing the misbehavior from the two alternatives given for each episode. You may then compare your selection with the suggested response that is found inverted at the end of the episode. The suggested alternatives should be considered as models, not as the only alternatives. In general these alternatives are probably more appropriate for parents initiating a particular plan of action. If children are familiar with the rules, their parents need give them only very brief explanations. Whenever parents take any action, they must be careful to be gentle as well as firm. There should be no harshness. Each child needs to feel that he is loved even if he is only semiconscious of this love. A child should never be made to feel that he is being rejected.

A FEARFUL CHILD

Three-year-old Sidney, who has a one-year-old sister, is fearful of almost everything that moves. He begins to scream when a butterfly

200

moves around on the lawn or when he sees a cat or dog down the block. His mother and father are continually running to him to see what he is frightened of, to comfort him, and to explain that there is nothing to be afraid of. This seems to be of little use, however, for he is getting worse.

EPISODE 1

The family was eating supper on the lawn. A butterfly flew across the lawn and Sidney began to scream. He ran to his mother with panic and tears in his eyes. To correct the misbehavior, his parents should:

—— a. Say with concern, "Sidney, it's only a butterfly." Give him a big hug.
—— b. Say quietly and calmly, "You'll be all right, Sidney. There is nothing to fear." Continue eating and talking. Do not pick up the child.

Answer: b

EPISODE 2

Sidney continued to cry. In fact he cried harder when he was ignored. To correct the misbehavior, his parents should:

—— a. Say quietly, "Would you like to stop crying, Sidney, or would you like to take your crying in the house?"
—— b. Take him up on their laps and cuddle him, for the little fellow is scared out of his wits.

Answer: a

EPISODE 3

Sidney began to cry harder. To correct the misbehavior, his parents should:

—— a. Take him into the house, return and have an enjoyable supper even though Sidney is looking out the window with tears in his eyes.
—— b. Give up in exasperation and spank him.

Answer: a

EPISODE 4

Sidney stopped crying and came out on the lawn again. He was there for five minutes when a dog crossed the street a block away. Sidney screamed and threw himself into his mother's lap. To correct the misbehavior, his parents should:

—— a. Cuddle him and try to quiet him down since there is more reason to be frightened of dogs.
—— b. Say nothing, but immediately take him into the house in a calm and gentle but firm manner. The parents return to their supper.

Answer: b

EPISODE 5

Sidney's mother and father tucked him into bed later that night. He was cooperative and calm. To correct his previous misbehavior, they should:

—— a. Say, "There is nothing to fear from butterflies, but it is understandable that you would be afraid of dogs."
—— b. Give him a hug and kiss and, while they hold him, say calmly, "Sidney, we know you had a rough night, but you will learn not to be afraid."

Answer: b

Note: Concepts you may want to review are vertical goals, pp. 16-23, 43; payoff, pp. 42-44; empathy, pp. 71-72; genuineness, p. 71; warmth and respect, p. 71; modeling, pp. 53-54; logical consequences, p. 86.

A CHILD WHO CLOWNS

It seems that wherever six-year-old Clare goes, other people laugh and point their fingers at him or get very upset. He is always clowning around or else doing something to shock people. He is the youngest of four children.

EPISODE 1

Halfway through supper, Clare took a spoonful of potatoes and smeared them all over his face. His older brothers and sisters began to laugh. To correct the misbehavior, the parents should:

—— a. Laugh with the rest since humor is important in rearing children.
—— b. Say quietly to all the children, "Would you care to settle down or would you prefer to leave the table?" (The other

children have previously agreed not to laugh at Clare and the parents have discussed this with him.)

EPISODE 2

Answer: b

Clare continued to put food on his face and giggle while Rick and Margaret continued to laugh at him. Keith and Karen became silent and stopped looking at Clare. To correct the misbehavior, the parents should:

—— a. Say, "Clare, Rick, and Margaret, please leave the table."
—— b. Say, "Clare, leave the table."

EPISODE 3

Answer: a

Rick and Margaret said almost together, "But we didn't do anything." To correct the misbehavior, the parents should:

—— a. Say, "We'll give you one more chance."
—— b. Say, "You are all in this together; please leave the table."

EPISODE 4

Answer: b

Margaret and Rick left the table. Clare said, "I'll be good." He stayed in his chair. To correct the misbehavior, the parents should:

—— a. Get up and gently but firmly remove him from the table.
—— b. Give him another chance as he promised to be better and he did it with that cute grin of his.

Answer: a

Note: Concepts you may want to review are life-style, pp. 48-50; social linkage, pp. 44-45; holism, pp. 50-52; vertical goals, pp. 16-23, 43; payoff, pp. 42-44; logical consequences, p. 86; warmth and respect, p. 71; personality traits, pp. 55-56.

AVOIDING HASSLES

Mother complains that Greg is a real sleepy head. It seems that every morning it's the same old routine. She calls him and shakes him several times to wake him up. He grunts and groans but doesn't get out of bed. His mother then goes in and practically stands him on his feet. She goes back to fixing breakfast. It seems to her that the same things happen at breakfast and while getting him off to school. She calls him several times for breakfast and has to keep telling him to hurry or he'll be late for school. She feels that she almost has to push him out the door.

EPISODE 1

As usual mother called to Greg and told him it was time to get up. He grunted "Yeah" but did not get up. To correct the misbehavior his mother should:

—— a. Call him again to pressure him to get up.
—— b. Not call him again, but later that day buy him an alarm clock so that getting up is his responsibility.

Answer: b

EPISODE 2

Mother finished preparing breakfast, then called in a loud voice, "Breakfast is ready, kids." They all came but Greg. To correct the misbehavior his mother should:

—— a. Call Greg and get him to answer so that Mother knows he has heard.
—— b. Sit down and eat with Father and the rest of the children and not call again.

Answer: b

EPISODE 3

When the family was almost finished eating, Greg came to the breakfast table and grumpily said, "How come you didn't tell me breakfast was ready?" To correct the misbehavior, his mother should:

—— a. Say gently, "I call only once for breakfast, Greg. It's your responsibility to hear me. If you choose not to listen for the call, it's your choice."
—— b. Say, "I did tell you. If you weren't so deaf you would have heard me."

Answer: a

EPISODE 4

Greg wolfed down his breakfast and then began to work on his stamp collection. He had only fifteen minutes to get to his school, which was six blocks from home. To correct the misbehavior his mother should:

—— a. Tell him that he is going to be late if he doesn't leave immediately. She should push him through the door if need be.

—— b. Say nothing. She is to let his getting to school on time be his responsibility.

Answer: b

EPISODE 5

Greg continued playing with his stamp collection. In fact, he brought it out in the kitchen where his mother was working. Ten minutes after school had started he looked at the clock and said, "Mother, school has been going for ten minutes. You have made me late." To correct the misbehavior, his mother should:

—— a. Say nothing. Continue sweeping the floor.

—— b. Hit him with the broom on the seat of his pants as he passes.

Answer: a

EPISODE 6

That night when Greg returned from school, he said to his mother, "I was thirty minutes late for school and had to stay in to make it up. It's all your fault, you old meany." To correct the misbehavior, his mother should:

—— a. Say, "Did the principal know that your teacher kept you after school?"

—— b. Say calmly, "Maybe you will learn not to be late."

Answer: b

Note: Concepts you may want to review are vertical goals, pp. 16-23, 43; payoff, pp. 42-44; natural consequences, pp. 85-86; warmth and respect, p. 71; personality traits, pp. 55-56.

CHILDREN WHO DON'T WANT TO GO TO BED

The parents in a particular family hate to see bedtime arrive because it is such a hassle. It seems as though it takes them two to three hours to get their children Sheryle and Harold to go to sleep. The parents are so exhausted in the evening that they have no energy left to enjoy each other's company. The children's bedtime is eight o'clock.

EPISODE 1

Father said, "It's time for bed, kids." Sheryle said, "I don't want to go to bed. I want to watch TV." Harold said, "Me too." To correct the misbehavior, their father should:

—— a. Say, "I'm not going to tell you again. Get to bed."
—— b. Say quietly but firmly, "Would you like to go by yourselves or do you want me to take you?"

Answer: b

EPISODE 2

Sheryle said, "I'm not going and you can't make me." Harold responded with "Me too." To correct the misbehavior, their father should:

—— a. Immediately get up and take each by a hand to their bedroom regardless of their resistance.
—— b. Tell them in a loud voice that they are being disrespectful and that he would appreciate it if they would go to bed.

Answer: a

EPISODE 3

Within five minutes of being placed in their bedroom, Sheryle and Harold came to the doorway and Sheryle shouted, "I'm thirsty; I want a drink." Harold kept yelling, "I'm hungry. I want something to eat." To correct the misbehavior, the parents should:

—— a. Go to them and say, "If you know what's good for you, you'll go to bed."
—— b. Say, "Would you like to be quiet or would you like the door shut?"

Answer: b

EPISODE 4

The children went back to bed, but within another five minutes they were yelling that mommy and daddy didn't love them. To correct the misbehavior, the parents should:

—— a. Go to their beds and tell them they are loved very much and that they should know this by now.
—— b. Go immediately to their door and shut it. Say nothing.

Answer: b

EPISODE 5

Almost immediately, one of the children threw the door open with so much force that it banged against the door stop. Sheryle yelled, "You old meanies." Harold said, "Yeah." To correct the misbehavior, the parents should:

—— a. Go immediately to the door, quietly shut it and lock it.
—— b. Stay where they are, but shout to the children that if they know what's good for them they'll settle down.

Answer: a

EPISODE 6

Sheryle and Harold began to pound and kick the door. To correct the misbehavior, the parents should:

—— a. Go to the door and say quietly, "Would you like to stop kicking the door or would you like to have the lights turned off from the master switch box?"
—— b. Rush quickly to the door, throw it open and give each a sound spanking.

Answer: a

EPISODE 7

The next morning at the breakfast table, Sheryle looked over at her mother and said with tears in her eyes, "Turning off our light wasn't fair, Mommy. You left us in the dark and it was scary." To correct the misbehavior, her mother should:

—— a. Say with a catch in her voice, "I know it's scary, honey, but what else are Mommy and Daddy to do?"
—— b. Say calmly, "Sheryle, you and Harold can choose to settle down at bedtime. Whenever you choose not to, you also choose to have the lights go off."

Answer: b

Note: Concepts you may want to review are vertical goals, pp. 16-23, 43; payoff, pp. 42-44; logical consequences, p. 86; warmth and respect, p. 71; personality traits, pp. 55-56.

A CHILD WHO WETS THE BED

Five-year-old Barry has an older brother, Larry, and a new baby sister. For the past four months Barry has been wetting the bed at night and his pants during the day, even though he had been completely trained at one time. His parents have taken him to a physician who has said that there is nothing organically wrong with him. They have also spent a good deal of time and effort trying to get Barry to go to the bathroom. They have even pleaded with him, but he is getting worse.

EPISODE I

Barry went into the kitchen where his mother was cooking breakfast and said, "See, Mommy, I'm all stinky again." To correct the misbehavior, his mother should:

—— a. Say again, "Barry, I can't understand what's wrong with you. You were so well trained at one time. When are you going to grow up?"
—— b. Change her behavior by continuing to scramble the eggs and by making bedwetting a nontopic of conversation. It is something Barry's mother does not discuss. Barry has been told he has two pair of pants to wear during the day.

Answer: b

EPISODE 2

At about ten o'clock while his mother was feeding the baby, Barry came and stood before them and wet. It ran down his legs and onto the carpet. To correct this misbehavior, his mother should:

—— a. Continue feeding the baby and say nothing to Barry. When the baby is finished and Barry is in the family room playing, she should quietly clean up the mess, then go to Barry and cut out paper horses with him for fifteen minutes.
—— b. Cry softly and tell Barry that he is making a mess of Mother's carpet.

Answer: a

EPISODE 3

At twelve Barry went to Mother and said, "My bottom stings." To correct the misbehavior, his mother should:

—— a. Say quietly, "Wet pants will make your bottom sting."
—— b. Say rather firmly, "That's what you get for being such a stinky boy."

Answer: a

EPISODE 4

Barry went to his bedroom and put on his second pair of pants. His

208

mother noticed that he wet them within thirty minutes. To correct the misbehavior, his mother should:

—— a. Say, "When are you going to listen to Mommy? Big boys don't wet their pants. They know better than to have stinky bottoms."

—— b. Say nothing about his wetting. Keep it a nontopic of conversation. Get Barry to help you dust. Give him recognition for his contribution by saying in a warm, excited voice, "Barry, you're such a big help. My, but you're growing up fast."

Answer: b

EPISODE 5

At bedtime Barry went to his mother and said, "Mommy, my bottom still hurts." To correct this misbehavior, his mother should:

—— a. Tell him that he is able to take care of the problem. (He has already been taught to apply medication to his sore bottom.) Talk about other things with Barry. His wetting is not mentioned.

—— b. Lift him up on her lap and apply medication. Say, "Barry, honey, if you'd just listen to Mother, you wouldn't have this problem."

Answer: a

EPISODE 6

Barry was playing in front of the TV and ready for bed when he wet his pants and thoroughly soaked his pajamas. To correct the misbehavior, his mother should:

—— a. Throw up her hands in frustration, get a wooden spoon, and spank Barry soundly before sending him to bed.

—— b. Say quietly, "It's time for bed, kids." When Barry says, "But Mommy, I'm all wet again," she should respond softly with, "I'm sure you can figure something out."

Answer: b

DISCUSSION

After the children are all in bed and the house has quieted down, Barry's mother and father can spend thirty minutes together planning three things each of them can do the next day to help Barry feel that he is worthwhile and that he can belong through behaving responsibly.

Note: Concepts you may want to review are life-style, pp. 48-50; social linkage, pp. 44-45; holism, pp. 50-52; vertical goals, pp. 16-23, 43; payoff, pp. 42-44; logical consequences, p. 86; belonging, pp. 45-46; warmth and respect, p. 71.

A CHILD WHO STEALS

EPISODE 1

While Pete's father was at work, a local store manager, whom the father does not care for, called and gruffly said that he had caught Pete, "that good-for-nothing son of yours, stealing and then destroying four model battery-powered cars." Pete is nine years old. To correct the misbehavior, Pete's father should:

——a. Say, "You old crowbait, if you treated the kids decently they wouldn't steal from you."

——b. Say, "I appreciate your calling me. I'll check into it as soon as I get home."

Answer: b

EPISODE 2

As soon as Pete's father arrived home he approached Pete. To correct the misbehavior, the father should:

——a. Take Pete into his bedroom away from his mother and the other children and say quietly, "Pete, I understand you took some things from Mr. Hardy's store without paying for them."

——b. Say in front of Pete's mother and the other children, "Hey, Pete, I understand you really made old Mr. Hardy mad today."

Answer: a

EPISODE 3

Pete turned red and began to cry. He said, "Well, all the other kids steal from Mr. Hardy. No one likes him." To correct the misbehavior, Pete's father should:

——a. Say, "Well, I can understand that. But, how come you let him catch you?"

——b. Say, "Pete, what do you think you can do to repay Mr. Hardy for the model cars and all the time and energy you have cost him?"

Answer: b

EPISODE 4

Pete began to cry harder. He then said, "I hate Mr. Hardy and I hate you too." To correct the misbehavior, the father should:

—— a. Say, "You ought to be ashamed of yourself talking to your dad like that."

—— b. Say nothing until he quiets down. Show no hurt in face or tone of voice. When he has quieted down say quietly, "Pete, what do you propose to do to make it up to Mr. Hardy?"

Answer: b

EPISODE 5

Pete began to cry again, but this time it was a quiet cry. He then began to sob and said, "I don't know what to do." To correct the misbehavior, his father should:

—— a. Say, "How about going to Mr. Hardy and telling him that you're sorry and that you want to make it up to him?"

—— b. Feel sorry for him because he is truly repentant. Tell him not to let it happen again.

Answer: a

EPISODE 6

Pete sobbed harder and said, "I am afraid to go to him. He's so mean." To correct the misbehavior, his father should:

—— a. Say, "I know it will be hard for you, son, but you can do it."

—— b. Remember that Mr. Hardy is a gruff old man and say, "Well, son, I think you have learned your lesson. Don't let it happen again."

Answer: a

EPISODE 7

Pete procrastinated. He did not go to Mr. Hardy. To correct the misbehavior, Pete's father should:

—— a. Forget it since the boy was really shook up. He has learned his lesson.

—— b. Say gently but firmly, "Pete, you have not yet met your obligation to Mr. Hardy. Until you do, you will not be able to play or watch TV. Your debt has top priority. Have Mr. Hardy call me when you have paid your debt to him."

Answer: b

Note: Concepts you may want to review are warmth and respect, p. 71; personality traits, pp. 55-56; communal interest, pp. 47-48; empathy, pp. 71-72; logical consequences, p. 86.

A CHILD WHO IS OVERACTIVE

It seems as though five-year-old Joey is always on the move. He won't sit in a chair for thirty seconds without hanging half off of it. He runs through the house, jumps on and off chairs, climbs on the back of the sofa, swings on the drapes, to name only a few. His parents have often told him how much they love him, showing their love with warm affection, and how they would like him to stop doing all of these annoying, destructive things. They have also spanked him as well as nagged, but nothing seems to work.

EPISODE 1

Joey's father walked into the living room and found Joey perched on the back of the sofa ready to jump off. To correct the misbehavior, his father should:

—— a. Grab him fast and give him a good swat on the seat.
—— b. Say calmly, "Joey, would you like to get off the sofa and settle down or would you like to leave the living room?"

Answer: b

EPISODE 2

Joey jumped down and began running through the house yelling. To stop the misbehavior, his parents should:

—— a. Take hold of him gently but firmly and say, "Joey, you have a choice. Stop running and yelling immediately, or you will have to take that behavior to the time-out room."
—— b. Yell after him to be quiet and give him a good swat the next time he passes by.

Answer: a

EPISODE 3

Joey continued to run as soon as he was let loose and began to yell louder. To correct the misbehavior, his parents should:

—— a. Sit him down and tell him that they love him very much but that all the noise upsets them.

—— b. Say nothing. Take hold of him and gently but confidently usher him to the time-out room.

Answer: b

EPISODE 4

After ten minutes of kicking the time-out door, Joey said, "Let me out; I'll be good." To correct the misbehavior, the parents should:

—— a. Not respond to him until he has quieted down for about five minutes, then let him out.

—— b. Let him out immediately before he changes his mind.

Answer: a

EPISODE 5

Ten minutes after Joey had come out of the time-out room he was jumping off one of the living room chairs. To correct the misbehavior, his parents should:

—— a. Take him immediately to the time-out room.

—— b. Tell him to get down immediately and give him a swat.

Answer: a

EPISODE 6

Joey said, "I'm ready to come out now." To correct the misbehavior, his parents should:

—— a. Let him out, but keep a watchful eye on him.

—— b. Say calmly, "You apparently need more time to think it over." He is left in the time-out room much longer. His parents should repeat the process each time he misbehaves.

Answer: b

Note: Concepts you may want to review are vertical goals, pp. 16-23, 43; payoff, pp. 42-44; logical consequences, p. 86; personality traits, pp. 55-56.

REFERENCES

Adler, Alfred
    1958   What Life Should Mean to You. New York: Capricorn Books.

Allred, G. Hugh
    1968   Mission for Mother: Guiding the Child. Salt Lake City: Bookcraft.

Ansbacher, Heinz L., and Rowena R. Ansbacher
    1956   The Individual Psychology of Alfred Adler. New York: Basic Books.

Beier, Ernst G.
    1966   The Silent Language of Psychotherapy. Chicago: Aldine Publishing Co.

Berenson, Bernard G., and Robert R. Carkhuff, eds.
    1967   Sources of Gain in Counseling and Psychotherapy. Chicago: Holt, Rinehart and Winston.

Bergin, Allen E., and Hans H. Strupp
    1972   Changing Frontiers in the Science of Psychotherapy. Chicago: Aldine Publishing Co.

Campbell, Susan Shafer
    1971   A comparison of the decision making of families with and without a drug abusing child. Masters thesis, Brigham Young University.

Cannon, Kenneth L.
    1968   What You Bring to Marriage. Provo, Utah: Brigham Young University Press.

Dinkmeyer, Don, and Gary D. McKay
    1973   Raising a Responsible Child. New York: Simon and Schuster.

Dreikurs, Rudolf
    1967   Psychology in the Classroom. New York: Harper and Row.

Dreikurs, Rudolf, et al.
    1957   Adlerian Family Counseling: A Manual for Counseling Centers. Eugene, Oregon: University of Oregon Press.

Dreikurs, Rudolf, and Vickie Soltz
    1964   Children: The Challenge. New York: Meredith Press.

Glasser, William
    1965   Reality Therapy: A New Approach to Psychiatry. New York: Harper and Row.

Klemer, Richard H.
    1965   Counseling in Marital and Sexual Problems: A Physician's Handbook. Baltimore: The Williams and Wilkins Co.

Ruesch, Jurgen
    1961   Therapeutic Communication. New York: W. W. Norton and Co.

Sicher, Lydia
    1955   "Education for freedom." The American Journal of Individual Psychology 11 (2).

Tharp, Roland G., and Ralph J. Wetzel
    1969   Behavior Modification in the Natural Environment. New York: Academic Press.

9
VERTICAL TRAITS AND METHODS

Among the many people who seek the advice of a professional therapist are those who have experienced rather severe punishment and hence exhibit the by-products of such experiences. The following simulated case is a rather typical example of a verbally aggressive person who had learned how to hate someone who had punished him in a rather brutal manner.

He shuffled into the room with downcast eyes. His fists opened and closed rhythmically as his intense hate burst forth in wave upon wave. He was a tall youth, about six feet two inches, slender and well into his seventeenth year. His face clearly reflected his intense negative emotions.

He first responded with suspicion to the interviewer but was soon candidly revealing the present objects of his hostility. Most adults were not to be trusted. All were caught up in their silly little rules, trying to get other people to obey them. His peers were stupid and friendly to him only for what they could selfishly get out of the relationship. He was willing to give a small amount of his trust only to other people who, like himself, were filled with resentment and anger.

"It's a stupid world."

"Everybody is out for what he can get."

"You have to do it to people before they do it to you."

"You really can't trust anybody."

"I hate teachers. Most of them just try to show you how big and important they are. Oh, some are O.K., but they're the exceptions."

"Church leaders are just like teachers. Most of them parade themselves and are puffed up with their own importance. They don't give a damn about people, really."

"Parents are stupid and don't know what's really going on. Oh, I guess some are all right, but I haven't seen any yet."

As he continued talking about parents, his eyes flashed and his facial muscles twitched. His whole body seemed to tense with over-powering hostile emotions that welled up inside of him and threatened to explode outward.

"And how about your parents?" was the quietly spoken catalyst.

"My parents? You've got to be kidding!" He exploded the words with a hatred that filled the whole room.

"I hated them both, especially my father. If I'd had a gun, many is the time I'd have killed him."

"I don't understand."

"He used to whip me and my brothers, but I was the oldest so I'd get it the hardest and the most."

"What do you mean?"

"He used to keep this long, thick leather strap, and when I'd get out of line, he'd get it and come after me as if he were crazy. He'd sometimes beat me until he was tired, the old S.O.B. If I'd had a gun some of those times I'd have killed him." He spat out the words between clenched teeth. Hate filled his eyes.

"But he stopped when I got bigger than he was and he knew I was getting ready to turn on him. I hate his guts."

The above is the fruit of severe punishment. The son is alienated from his father with a hatred that is not only directed toward himself but is free floating. It is free floating in the sense that it is ever there and ever ready to find an object for expression, be it other parents, teachers, community leaders, or peers.

Punishment is more often than not a vertical way of attempting to correct behavior. The goal of the person who punishes another person is typically that of counterhurting to get revenge (see pp. 20-22, 43).

Punishment refers to correction that is intended to make the one being corrected feel small, insignificant, worthless, bad, or evil. It involves blaming, shaming, belittling, demeaning, ridiculing and hurting. Punishment may be inflicted through verbal, nonverbal, physical methods, or a combination of them.

Listed below are some of the more common and sometimes not so common ways people have of inflicting punishment on one another.

- Ridiculing
- Scolding
- Yelling
- Screaming
- Threatening
- Rejecting
- Scaring
- Neglecting
- Lying
- Leaving
- Slapping
- Hitting
- Spanking
- Beating
- Whipping
- Hiding
- Gouging
- Poking
- Twisting
- Bending
- Pulling
- Kicking
- Slamming down
- Cutting
- Burning

- Refusing to notice
- Refusing to speak to
- Ignoring one person while playing up to others
- Withholding expressions of affection
- Withholding privileges
- Withholding food
- Withholding sleep
- Embarrassing someone in front of others
- Bringing up the past
- Labeling someone negatively
- Washing out someone's mouth with soap
- Locking someone outside

- Taking away money
- Loading a person with work
- Using foul language
- Being sarcastic

There are many fruits of punishment. One, the person giving the punishment often drives a wedge between himself and the one he is punishing. This is clearly demonstrated in the case of the seventeen-year-old boy. The boy's hatred of punishment had generalized to his father, the one doing the punishing, sometimes referred to as the punishing agent. He did not separate his father from the pain inflicted by the leather belt (the process of bonding had very definitely taken place). A chasm had developed between them filled with torrents of hate from the boy.

Second, the one receiving punishment will often, in his anger and resentment, look upon his relationship with the one doing the punishing as a game in which his whole purpose becomes that of outwitting him and getting revenge. This is often played without regard to costs. Some youths are willing to ruin their lives in order to see their parents, the punishing agents, suffer as they feel they have suffered. Promiscuous sex and drugs serve these children especially well as they attempt to counterhurt.

Third, the hostility generated by punishment often becomes free floating, as in the case cited above, and is directed toward those not responsible for the punishment. It is as if the individual loses all sense of discrimination and views all people as existing or potential punishing agents. He develops a basic distrust of other people because of such feelings. He often displays a reserve or belligerence which tends to make his ideas about others come true; for as he is reserved or belligerent, others tend to respond to him in the same way. He thus becomes his own self-fulfilling prophet, influencing other people's behavior in such a manner that they meet his expectations. He thereby sets off and continually stimulates a vicious circle of negative relationships.

Fourth, those who act as punishing agents serve as models for those being punished. The trait that those who are punished learn is to punish other people when they are in disagreement with them, especially those whom they feel are weaker and inferior. The learning law of modeling (see pp. 53-54) explains much of the quarrelling, fighting, and wars found in families, neighborhoods, nations, and between nations. As long as parents use punishment as a major technique for changing their children's behavior, it may be safely predicted that fighting and warring will continue. When they become adults, these children will tend to punish other people in the same way that their parents punished them.

There may be times when punishment is justified as the most appropriate response to a specific situation. Many specialists in human behavior are using forms of punishment to stop such things as hiccuping. Many parents have used some punishment and have reared their children successfully. However, these results do not invalidate the overwhelming body of evidence that suggests the serious side effects of punishment. The specialist or parent who decides to use punishment should use it only if he has a full awareness of the problems involved and if he responsibly controls its negative by-products.

Eliminating punishment from your repertoire of childrearing techniques does not mean an end to discipline. A child needs discipline as he needs water and food, for it is through discipline that a parent expresses his deep love and concern for him as he trains him to move effectively in the societies of man. What it does mean is the removal of a technique with demonstrated negative by-products and substitution of more effective, positive techniques, such as natural and logical consequences as described in the previous chapter.

Giving rewards is another approach to controlling the behavior of others that is common in a vertical relationship. The giving of rewards most often occurs in the situation where a bigger, stronger, or more intelligent individual tries to control the behavior of another by giving him something he wants which bears no relationship to the behavior other than that it reinforces it. An example of this is the parent who gives his children candy bars when they sit through supper without quarrelling.

The list on page 220 shows desirable behaviors and some rather common ways in which they are reinforced.

Giving rewards is a powerful technique for changing behavior. But there are by-products associated with rewards that must be taken

220

into account, even though they are not as well demonstrated or as well known as they are in the case of punishment.

Rewards can be given only, as indicated before, by someone in a position superior to that of the one receiving the reward. He judges the person, and if he meets with approval he is given the reward. Such a practice perpetuates the vertical relationship. It serves as a model for future relationships that are more appropriate to an autocratic than to an equalitarian society. This can also train recipients of rewards to form relationships merely for what material objects they can gain. In other words, the reward approach may foster the materialistic, dehumanizing problems found in contemporary society where, too often, the focus is on "What can I get from others?" rather than "What can I contribute?"

Using rewards may teach people to indulge themselves. For example, the child who is given candy and food for appropriate behavior may learn to give food a unique and special priority in his system of values. Food becomes an end in itself rather than a means to provide energy for worthwhile work and service. Obesity is often a by-product of such a value system.

Desirable Behavior/Reward

Desirable Behavior	Reward
wet in the potty	marshmallow
was quiet in the grocery store	candy bar
ate all of a meal	balloon
spoke kindly all day	toy bear
has a dry bed	marble
washed face	piece of candy
brushed teeth	piece of colored paper
took out the garbage	piece of cake
cleaned up room	ten cents
kissed Mother	building block
told the truth	beads
was quiet for three hours	milk shake
finished a puzzle	star
learned a new word	five cents
walked quietly in the house	pencil

The individual learns to focus inward on himself instead of outward on other people. The acquisition of goods and things—material objects—becomes the symbol of his worth. And, as he frantically accumulates his baubles, he loses perspective of what is truly of value —the welfare of each member of his society.

Another problem often caused by the reward system is that rewards tend to rob the individual of the opportunity to experience the joy of freely giving. For example, suppose you have a neighbor who is sick and in need of assistance. You give your time and effort willingly and are made happy by the fact that he becomes well, in part, because of your ministrations. How then would you feel if he offered you a check for twenty-five dollars, saying, "Here is payment for helping me out when I needed help."

So it is with our children when we reward them with material objects for being good and cooperative. They are robbed of the joy that results from their making a worthwhile contribution, and resentment often takes over.

The rewards approach is of course justified in some cases. However, it must be used with great care by those who are aware of its possible by-products. Even though not much is known about the by-products, common sense dicates that the wholesale and indiscriminate use of rewards in home, school, and church may produce a generation committed to doing things for wrong reasons. As it is with the young lady who acquires dozens of badges and certificates indicating her worth to herself yet freely gives of her sexual favors still believing she is a good person, so it will be with a generation trained to perform for baubles and candy.

REFERENCES

Allinsmith, B. B.
   1954   "Parental discipline and children's aggression in two social classes." Dissertation Abstracts 14:708.

Allred, G. Hugh
   1968   Mission for Mother: Guiding the Child. Salt Lake City: Bookcraft.

Azrin, H. H.
   1969   "Suggested effects of punishment," in R. W. Lundin, Personality: A Behavioral Analysis. London: The Macmillan Co., Collier-Macmillan Ltd.

222

Bandura, Albert, and Richard H. Walters
  1959   Adolescent Aggression. New York: Ronald Press.
  1963   Social Learning and Personality Development. New York: Holt, Rinehart and Winston.

Dreikurs, Rudolf
  1958   "The cultural implications of reward and punishment." The International Journal of Social Psychiatry 4 (3) (Winter).

Evans, Richard I.
  1968   B. F. Skinner: The Man and His Ideas. New York: E. P. Dutton and Co.

Hollenberg, Eleanor H., and Margaret S. Sperry
  1951   "Some antecedents of aggression and effects in doll play." Personality 1:32-43.

Madsen, Clifford K., and Charles H. Madsen, Jr.
  1972   Parents Children Discipline. Boston: Allyn and Bacon.

Marshall, H. R.
  1961   "Relations between home experiences and children's use of language in play interactions with peers." Psychology Monograph 75 (5).

Sears, Robert R., et al.
  1953   "Some child rearing antecedents of aggression and dependency in young children." Genetic Psychological Monographs 47:135-234.

Thornock, Carol Lou
  1972   A single subject strategy study: reducing assertive behavior in a child utilizing the mother as mediator. Masters thesis, Brigham Young University, Provo, Utah.

Whiting, John W. M., and Irvin L. Child
  1953   Child Training and Personality: A Cross Cultural Study. New Haven, Connecticut: Yale University Press.

Wright, G. O.
  1954   "Projection and displacement: a cross-cultural study of folktale aggression." Journal of Abnormal and Social Psychology 49:523-528.

FOUR

APPLICATION: ACHIEVING HORIZONTAL INTERACTION WITH MY SPOUSE

10

MAN
AND
WOMAN

The close intimacy that usually occurs in the marriage relationship can result in fulfillment and joy, satisfaction and contentment, or degradation and suffering. The marriages in our families, communities, states, and countries are prime examples of this, particularly—and sadly—of the latter case. Any intimate relationship tends to amplify both vertical as well as horizontal elements of interaction, but in the marriage relationship in particular there is too often a strong tendency for the individual to work vertically against his partner. This can happen for several reasons, some of the most basic being the necessity for couples to budget their money and time; the importance of their helping each other fulfill sexual needs; the necessity for them to rear their children in a manner that is satisfactory to both of them; the importance of both of them being able to accept and enjoy each other's family, friends, and interests.

The following simulated situations present several basic principles for relating horizontally which are essential to healthy, satisfying interaction of husband and wife. These principles, if practiced consistently, can be most valuable to a couple who want honest, open interaction and an equalitarian relationship.

A PROBLEM OF LOYALTY

THE SITUATION

Laura has been married less than a year. She has four sisters who have been married longer than she. Her mother and all five girls live in the same town and often get together. Laura has sensed from the time she was a little girl that her mother and father do not have a close relationship. This has been further impressed on her during these visits when her mother often talks critically of her husband as well as men in general. Her critical views are echoed by all of her married daughters except Laura. Laura loves her mother and sisters very much, but often finds herself upset when she is with them. She also finds herself becoming more critical of her husband as time passes, in spite of her vows to herself that she will not be influenced by their critical attitudes.

The following dialogue is rather typical of their conversation about men:

"Well, you know your father. He is just like most men. He doesn't know the value of a dollar," said Laura's mother.

The oldest daughter picked up the cue, "Yes, I can't get over how my man can't seem to budget either. If it weren't for me, we'd be thousands of dollars in debt."

The second daughter nodded her head in agreement with all that was being said. The third daughter, right on cue, excitedly proclaimed, "You'll never believe what my husband did yesterday. He is so stupid sometimes that I can hardly believe it. He bought a new suit that was out of style before he even tried it on. I told him he should have taken me with him."

Their mother looked over at her third daughter with a wise, all-knowing look of agreement. "Men," she sighed.

She then turned her gaze on Laura and said in a somewhat tired tone of voice, "Laura, when is that husband of yours going to get a nose job? He would look so much better."

Laura, even though she knew something like this was coming, felt unprepared to respond as all eyes turned her way. She felt the pressure and wanted to run screaming from the house, but instead answered lamely, "Oh, I don't know. I don't think his nose is all that bad." She saw her first and third sisters look over at their mother with a smile, their expressions seeming to say, "Poor, naive Laura; her bubble will burst." Laura's feelings alternated between wanting to fall through the floor and wanting to lash out at all of them.

Her mother continued after returning the look to her other daughters, "Yes, Laura, when you consider he has such a craggy face I guess his nose isn't too bad. But then again it would make his eyes seem not so narrow." She smothered a chuckle as her eyes swept around the room inviting her daughters to join in on the joke, which they did.

"Mother, I don't think that is fair," Laura responded rather heatedly, "My husband can't help how he looks."

"Of course he can't, my dear," Mother reached over and patted Laura's hand.

DISCUSSION

Laura is caught between the love for her husband and the tremendous pressure forced upon her by her mother and sisters. She feels that if she does not agree she will be alienated from them. She loves her mother and sisters very much, for in spite of this fault they have been good to her and are usually enjoyable to be around. But she feels uncomfortable and disloyal to her husband when she listens to their critical comments and in her fear says nothing or reacts defensively. She feels that she is caught in a terrible dilemma and does not know what to do; but she must do something and do it quick, for she is becoming ever more critical of her husband. After the conversation with her mother about her husband's nose and eyes, Laura, looking at her husband later that evening, wished that his nose were not as large and his eyes not so close together so that she would not have to suffer her mother's criticism. She felt herself becoming angry with him for putting her in an awkward position by having such a nose and eyes. When she discovered she was thinking this way, she shook her head hard as if to shake away the words and looks of her mother, but they remained, subtly haunting her and driving a barrier between her and her spontaneous expression of love for her husband.

It will take a great amount of courage and strength for Laura to change the situation with her family. It may be helpful for her to approach the task with the knowledge that she cannot control their behavior but that she can control her own. She will find the following suggestions very helpful as she attempts to do this:

- She should frankly and openly tell her mother and sisters that she does not feel they should criticize her father, her husband, or anyone else who is not in the group at the time.
- If they disagree with her and suggest that she is too sensitive and that they will continue, she should then tell them that being critical is

their prerogative, but from now on whenever they start criticizing her father or one of the husbands she is going to leave the group for that day.

- As she is being firm in refusing to participate in such behavior, she should redouble her efforts to be friendly to her mother and sisters so that they will not feel she is rejecting them.

- She may go through a period of time when she feels alone and isolated from her family. But by turning to her understanding husband, she can gain the necessary strength to follow through with firmness and love.

As Laura works to change her responses to the unhealthy family situation, she can expect many different and skillfully applied pressures to bring her into line with the rest. She may be laughed at, ridiculed, and treated with sarcasm. Her sisters may ally with their mother against her. She may be treated as naive and inexperienced. Her past problems and faults may be thrown at her in an attempt to get her to doubt herself so that her resolve to be firm will be weakened. They may even threaten her with rejection if she does not conform.

Through all of this, Laura should realize that time is on her side. If she is continually persistent in walking out when they begin criticizing the male loved ones, and if she continues to express her love and affection for her mother and sisters, she will more than likely win their love and friendship. This of course assumes that she does not act superior to or better than her mother and sisters. Her attitude should be "I love you, but I will not be with you when you criticize our husbands. You can do what you want, but my behavior will always be the same. I will remove myself at such times."

Laura can redouble her efforts to show her love and concern for her family by such things as always returning to the next gathering of her sisters and mother, greeting each with warmth and friendliness, remembering their birth dates and anniversaries, dropping in on them and inviting them to her home, and focusing on the positive characteristics of each and talking to them about these.

All of the above call for Laura to have faith that things can change and to have courage and perseverance. And as mentioned before, the support of a wise, understanding husband who can re-assure and encourage Laura in her efforts to initiate a more horizontal relationship among her loved ones will be a great help.

Note: Concepts you may want to review are life-style, pp. 48-50; social linkage, pp. 44-45; communal interest, pp. 47-48; self-esteem, pp. 46-47; agency, pp. 37-38; logical consequences, p. 86; vertical goals, pp. 16-23, 43; payoff, pp. 42-44; model-ing, pp. 53-54; warmth and respect, p. 71; personality traits, pp. 55-56.

THE SPOILED HUSBAND

THE SITUATION

The following phrases are typical of Saul's interaction with his wife. It is seldom that he says anything to her of a different nature.

"Run my bath water. Be sure not to get it too hot."

"Come in and run some more hot water for me. You got it too cold."

"You didn't lay out my pajamas. Will you hurry and lay them out for me! I'm all dried and ready for them and you forgot to put them out. Do you want me to catch cold?"

"Get my shirt. Here, do up the top button."

"Get my pants."

"Where are my socks? You forgot to lay them out for me again."

"Here, tie my shoes for me. It's hard for me to bend down."

"This egg is cooked too hard. Cook me another one. Oh, if you're going to act like that you can forget it. I'll go without breakfast. Don't blame me if I get sick this morning and can't work."

"I had a real lousy day at work. I felt bad this morning when I arrived at work and it upset my whole day. If I'd had my egg. . . . Get me my slippers."

The above phrases were expressed with whines, sighs, commands and shouts. Close observation would have revealed Saul's lower lip frequently stuck out, his eyelids often half closed, and at times his face flushed and even red. On occasion he stamped his right foot when his wife did not respond fast enough to his directives.

His wife wore a haggard expression and felt chronic fatigue. She described herself as feeling as though she were a wrung-out sponge that was still being squeezed, but had not a drop left to give.

DISCUSSION

Saul was reared by a mother who felt alone and alienated from her husband. In her loneliness she turned all her attention to Saul and they developed a special relationship that excluded all others. In this relationship Saul learned he could keep his mother busy with him and get her to respond to his every wish by whining, crying, shouting, screaming, stamping his foot, throwing himself on the floor, and drumming his heels into the floorboards. He grew up with the belief that he was special and different from everyone else and that a loved one would demonstrate love by responding to his every desire and obeying his every command. He had thus learned to belong, and he brought the same expectations and behaviors to his marriage relationship.

His wife was first attracted to him because of his seeming helplessness and his apparent need to be taken care of. This also fit into her life-style, for she had grown up in a family where she had belonged by taking care of her younger brothers and sisters. This made her feel worthwhile, important, valuable, and superior.

But with Saul she got more than she bargained for. He had learned to be a tyrant and was too demanding, skillful, and powerful for her. She knew how to cope with him only by giving in. On the few occasions when she tried to resist his unreasonable demands, she found herself with feelings of guilt and unworthiness following his outbursts of crying and phrases of "You don't care for me any more. All you care about is yourself. I might as well just go out and kill myself. You never did respect the man of the house."

Saul's goals were to belong through getting undue service, achieving power over his wife, and counterhurting her as he felt she hurt him when she did not give in to his demands. He also put her in a double bind when he demanded that she take care of him yet resented her making him feel as though he were a little boy. This lowered his self-esteem. He blamed her for this, not consciously, but in a semiconscious way. And in his resentment and hurt he lashed out to hurt her, illogically demanding more service and shouting cruel words in her direction. His wife could not satisfy him, for he resented her when she gave him service and also when she did not. With the use of such a strategy he was able to keep her off balance and maintain his power over her and as a result find his place as a tyrant in his home.

His wife's strategy for coping with him consisted of her being too tired to carry out his demands. While this allowed her not to give in to him it also let her avoid taking the responsibility for her actions. Rather than saying, "I don't want to do it for you because your demands for service are unreasonable," she was able to say, "I'm just too tired to do it for you. If I were well I would do it." With such a response she got her way and at the same time avoided much of his wrath, for how could he attack a fatigued wife? She was not consciously aware of what she was doing. It worked, so she used it.

To change this vertical interaction which causes both people to be unhappy to a more horizontal one, it is important that they both discover the need for change. They can begin to do this by analyzing the fruits of their relationship. It would be helpful, for example, if Saul were to focus not only on his belief that his wife does love him when she waits on him, but also on his feelings of low self-esteem and his resentment toward her for doing things that make her appear superior and more capable than he. It would be helpful for his spouse to recognize her anger when Saul is tyrannizing her and to analyze her feelings toward herself and him when she does those things that she feels he forces her to do.

Once the couple has decided they are dissatisfied with their past interaction, they can make the second major step toward realizing a change, but this is only the second step in the process. It is vitally important that they be openly honest in their communication to themselves and to each other as they search for greater understanding concerning the problems they are facing and ways of relating which will result in greater mutual respect and satisfaction.

Saul will have to learn to accept other evidences of his wife's love and not expect her to show this by giving him undue service, which produces anger and resentment in both of them. He will also have to learn that he can be worthwhile by doing such constructive things as encouraging his wife to progress, giving his family economic security, being happy himself when he is around his wife, developing his talents, having children and rearing them to be productive and independent, and contributing to the welfare of his fellowmen outside the family. As he learns to look outward to other people by practicing more horizontal behavior, his initial doubts, frustrations, and fears of leaving familiar behavior behind and standing in strange territory will give way to happiness. This will happen as the strange but more constructive behaviors become the familiar ones with the passage of time.

If Saul's wife is to find happiness and is to learn to like herself and Saul, she must maintain her integrity. This means she must communicate directly to Saul that he is demanding things of her he should be doing for himself when she feels that this is happening. She must then refrain from betraying herself by giving in to his unreasonable demands regardless of his manipulations. She can no longer resort to fatigue in order to escape him and honest communication. She must tell him gently, firmly, and directly what she thinks, feels, and is willing to do. This will take a great amount of courage, but she will find it necessary if she is to have peace of mind.

Saul and his wife will find it helpful for them to sit down together and list on paper in detail those services that each of them can reasonably be expected to provide. They can then commit themselves not to demand more of one another than what is agreed upon unless both agree to it and make the change in writing on the contract.

As Saul's wife experiences relief when he backs off from his demands, she will have to be firm with herself. Her first impulse will be to move in and give him more service because in the past she found her value by being superior and by doing things for other people that they could do for themselves.

Rather than giving her husband undue service, she can help him and herself by expressing her love through supporting him with encouragement, warmth, and affection when he attempts to relate more constructively.

Accomplishing the above will take much practice, hard work, and patience, but the joy and happiness that more horizontal, respectful interaction will bring will be well worth the efforts and time involved.

Note: Concepts you may want to review are vertical goals, pp. 16-23, 43; payoff, pp. 42-44; life-style, pp. 48-50; social linkage, pp. 44-45; self-esteem, pp. 46-47; agency, pp. 37-38; communal interest, pp. 47-48; conflict resolution, pp. 78-79; warmth and respect, p. 71; practice, pp. 54-55.

A PROBLEM OF LONELINESS

THE SITUATION

"There is so much to do," Peggy sighed when her husband told her he was going on a three-day rock-collecting trip while he was on vacation.

As her husband began his preparations for his trip, Peggy talked with him less and less and pulled the corners of her mouth down more. She often sighed, her chest heaving up and down. Her movements became slower; and as she said goodbye to her husband, she kissed him on the cheek, averted her eyes from his, and said in a barely audible whisper, "Well, I hope *you* have fun."

As soon as her husband had left, Peggy began scrubbing the walls of their home. After she was finished with the walls, she shampooed each carpet. She then went into the kitchen, removed each dish, cleaned and then varnished each shelf. About noon of the second day, she went into the yard. She mowed the lawn, cut back all the bushes and trees, dug out all the weeds, and then transplanted two rather large shrubs.

When she had completed all of this, it was the evening of the third day, the time her husband was expected to return home. Peggy began to feel faint. She noticed that her heart was beginning to thump rather loudly as it often did when she had done too much. She became frightened and went immediately to bed for she knew her heart was acting up again. When her husband returned he found Peggy in bed. "What's wrong, Peggy?" he exclaimed with a worried look.

Peggy looked away from him and stared at the wall. "I overdid it and my heart is giving out. I think you had better call our doctor and have him take a cardiograph," she said in a whisper interspersed with sighs. Her hand fluttered to her bosom and she clutched her nightgown.

"Have you been overdoing it *again,* Peggy?" her husband asked, feeling guilty and not knowing why.

Peggy continued to look at the wall as she responded, "I just did my regular spring cleaning and the yard work."

"But, I told you I would help you when I got back!" He almost shouted the words.

"I know, but it had to be done when I did it and I knew you

would rather go collect your old rocks than help me," she said between clenched teeth as she turned to him with her eyes flashing. "Now you better call our doctor immediately," she said loudly, then gasped, clutched her nightgown again directly over her heart, and fell back down on her pillow.

As her husband turned away, he muttered, "I told you I would help you when I returned." As he left, he felt the old familiar feeling of a deep sense of guilt well up inside. If he had been asked at this time what he was feeling, he would not have been able to identify it, for he had never analyzed it. All he knew was that he felt miserable and that he was a no-good person. It seemed to him that he was feeling more of these feelings as time went on. Picking up the phone, he quickly dialed the doctor's number. When the doctor came on the line, Peggy's husband felt somewhat embarrassed as he said, "Doc, you better come quick. Peggy is having another one of her heart spells." He said *spells* because their doctor had been to their home many times before and had always found Peggy's heart to be strong and healthy. He did not consciously think through why he used the term *spell* rather than attack, nor why he felt embarrassed when he heard the doctor's voice on the telephone.

Within fifteen minutes their doctor arrived and took a heart reading. After a few minutes he looked up at Peggy and said, "Peggy, I just can't find anything wrong with your heart. It is beating with a strong, regular beat."

Peggy looked disappointed and then somewhat angry and became uncommunicative. Her husband looked relieved.

As soon as the doctor left, Peggy jumped out of bed and said in a loud angry voice, "Doctors are all alike. They are a bunch of quacks." She then quickly got dressed and began to iron a large basket of clothes.

Her husband's relief turned to fear and an increased feeling of guilt. "Now, Peggy, you must take it easy. What if you do have a heart condition? You might bring on a fatal attack." By this time he was wringing his hands.

Peggy tossed her head as she said in a clear, loud, commanding voice, "You get away from me and leave me alone." She abruptly shifted her position so that her back was to him. She muttered in a low whiney voice, loud enough for him to hear, "No one gives a damn what happens to me, no one."

Feelings of guilt, pity, anger toward himself and toward Peggy, and defeat welled up inside her husband, and he left the room feeling as if he were a bad boy.

DISCUSSION

Peggy was born the middle child in a large family. As she grew up, she discovered that her otherwise busy parents would drop everything and focus their attention and concern on her when she was sick. When she felt lonely and inadequate around competent older brothers and sisters and two charming younger sisters, she used headaches and stomachaches as ways of belonging. She did not do this consciously, but her illnesses worked, so she used them.

Peggy developed strong feelings of resentment toward her brothers and sisters, for she felt her parents preferred them over her. After she was married, she found herself becoming resentful of her husband's family, his work, and his hobby of rock collecting. She began to resent anything that took him away from her, including his community activities.

Peggy brought to her marriage great skill in getting other people to pay off her illnesses. Through being sick, she was able to achieve her goal of getting *power* over her husband. Through increasing her heart palpitations when he did not do what she wanted—leaving her to go rock hunting—she was able to *hurt* him as she felt he had hurt her. Through hinting and other more outright means, she communicated that if only he had stayed with her and helped her, she would not have become ill.

When the doctor said that her heartbeat was normal, she snatched victory from defeat by saying that the doctor was a quack, hinting that she really did have a bad heart and getting up out of bed and working hard. This frightened her husband. He tried to get her to go back to bed, but she refused, turning a cold shoulder to him. He felt defeated, guilty, and hurt. She was thereby able to retain her power over him and at the same time make him feel bad. She wanted him to suffer as she had suffered in her loneliness while he was away from her and in feeling that he did not love her as much as he loved to collect rocks.

As he showed his guilt by his facial expressions and his eagerness to do her bidding, he paid off her bossy, vengeful behavior. As a result he encouraged her in her use of such techniques.

Both Peggy and her husband were miserable. Peggy's triumphs over her husband were not really satisfying her. She felt she was becoming estranged from him. He felt confused, angry, and increasingly resentful toward Peggy whom he said he loved but did not understand. Both wanted to change.

In order for Peggy and her husband to achieve greater understanding and more respectful relationships, it would be helpful for Peggy to (1) recall her childhood and gain an understanding of those unconstructive and destructive techniques she learned to use and realize which ones she is using in her relationships with her husband; (2) learn how such techniques are actually driving a wedge between her and her husband; and (3) express her feelings of being unloved, lonely, and hurt directly to her husband rather than hinting about them.

Peggy's husband can best help the relationship by (1) remaining calm when she uses sickness to achieve her useless goals; he does not have to pay her off by getting excited or by giving in to her unreasonable demands; (2) understanding her basic feelings of insecurity with regard to his love for her; and (3) expressing his love for her several times each day through words and touch, giving it as a free gift when she is not hinting for it.

When a person feels that he is loved, he also feels loveable. On the other hand, if he feels unloved, he tends to use useless or destructive techniques that push loved ones away from him. It is up to Peggy and her husband to work hard to break up the vicious circle in which they find themselves if they are to find happiness as a unified family. As Peggy comes to feel that she is really loved and as she learns to replace her tyrannical behavior over her husband with that which is more worthwhile, she will more than likely become more beautiful to him as well as more loveable.

Note: Concepts you may want to review are vertical goals, pp. 16-23, 43; payoff,

BEING TOO RESPONSIBLE

THE SITUATION

Ross was a tall, self-confident young man, the eldest in his family. He held many responsible positions in his community, church, and profession. He was a bundle of energy and left many of his colleagues rather breathless at the amount of work he took on and completed. He was well satisfied with his life generally, but was somewhat concerned for his wife when he took the time to think about her. This was not too often because he was so busy.

His main concern was that she was listless and apathetic. Ross at first dismissed this since his wife had been pregnant twice within a five-year period. However, he became more concerned as time went on because she seemed to be getting worse rather than better. Ross took her to their family doctor, but he could discover nothing physically wrong with her. He then took her to a specialist who suggested that her fatigue and apathy were probably a result of problems between herself and people important to her.

Upon hearing the doctor's words, Ross was at first indignant and loudly protested, "Such an idea is ridiculous." When they got in the car to return home, his wife turned to him and said in a quiet, intense manner, "I think he may have something." She paused and her hand shook as she clutched Ross' coat sleeve, looked at him in a pleading way, and said, "Ross, please, for me, let's go to a marriage counselor."

Her words smashed into him. He felt as though he had been hit by a freight train. "But darling we have a good marriage. We go to church all the time. We have two lovely children and I have a good income. You're just tired. You'll feel better tomorrow." Ross patted her hand and began to put the keys of the car into the ignition.

She grabbed his arm and turned to him with moist eyes, "Please, Ross, listen to me. For some time I've felt that there has been something very wrong about our marriage. I love you very much, but sometimes I feel angry, resentful, and hurt. I know it's probably just me, but please help me to find out what's wrong." She broke off the conversation by burying her face in her hands. Her shoulders began to shake and she sobbed as Ross took her into his arms.

"Well, if you think it will help, you can go to a marriage counselor. I don't know how often I can go with you since I'm terribly busy, and I'll probably have to sit with the children part of the time. You know how hard it is to get a baby-sitter." Ross's response was bewildered, dazed, and somewhat frightened, bewildered and dazed because he was faced with the unknown, which he seldom confronted in his well-ordered world, and frightened because, though he could not put his feelings into words at this time, he felt a threat to his relationship with his wife. In addition he felt a threat to his status with his colleagues at work and in the community and church if they were to discover that he and his wife were getting marriage counseling.

His wife continued to cry for some time. Then she turned to Ross and said quietly and intensely, "Thank you, Ross. Thank you."

DISCUSSION

Ross and his wife did go for marriage counseling. Ross was hesitant, skeptical, and defensive at first; but because he wanted to please his wife, whom he loved greatly, he attended the initial sessions. He then became involved as he discovered new things about himself and his wife and practiced changing his behavior to help bring her greater happiness.

Their counselor discovered in talking to the couple and having them simulate real-life and home situations that something was indeed very wrong between Ross and his wife, in spite of the fact that both were basically good people who had the best of intentions. Ross was entirely too responsible. He felt responsible for everything that went on around him and felt obligated to step in to correct or change anything that he felt was wrong or inefficient. It was with this behavior that he had learned to belong in his own family. He was also ever ready to express his opinion and to insist on having things his way. He was as critical of his wife as he was of himself.

After coming home from work, Ross would often say to his wife in an impatient, almost angry voice, "For heaven's sake, this house is in a clutter. Can't you keep things picked up?"

"I see you didn't clean out the corners when you mopped the

kitchen floor. That's a place where germs will collect. They must be kept clean."

"What! Haven't you made the beds yet?"

His wife's responses to his critical comments were defensive, consisting primarily of such phrases as "But Ross, I've been so busy," or "You just don't understand," given in a soft, almost whining tone of voice.

Simulation of their home behavior with one another in the counseling sessions helped Ross discover that he often criticized his wife when she cooked. For example, she would be frying chicken and Ross would leap from his chair and rush to the stove, almost knocking his wife aside as he took the fork she was holding from her hand. Immediately he would say, "You're going to burn the chicken. Your heat is way too high. Here, let me do it." He would then take over and finish cooking the meat. As a result his wife would wander listlessly into their bedroom and lie down.

Ross would even rearrange such things as his wife's cooking utensils. "Now I'm sure you'll find it more convenient for you if you keep your knives, forks, and spoons on this side of the stove" was his rather pompous proclamation as he changed them for her.

He also chose the clothes she bought and wore. When she had the temerity to buy a new dress or new pair of shoes on her own without his approval, which was seldom, he became most critical. "That dress sags on you. I've seen better tailor work done by children. Those shoes will never last." She was bombarded with such comments whenever she wore her own choices. As a result she seldom wore them; and being resentful of Ross's choices, she seldom wore his. The few clothes she did like she wore over and over.

Ross's wife's listlessness and disinterest in living were caused by his constant criticism and his taking over her jobs. This left her with nothing to do that she could call her own. And because she had nothing of her own, her life had no meaning. As a result she suffered from low self-esteem and felt worthless. And being subject to her husband's constant criticism, she was deeply resentful of him.

Ross had to learn to stop his criticizing and allow his wife her rights in taking care of the home, which they both felt was proper. He agreed to stop rearranging her things and to stop taking over her cooking. He also agreed that he would no longer tell her what clothes to buy and that he would never criticize what she bought.

Putting the above into practice proved harder for Ross than his verbal commitment to do so. Many times he slipped and gave in to his first impulse, which was the old, familiar, critical and bossy behavior. But as he made great effort to practice horizontal behavior, partly by simulating more respectful relationships in the counseling sessions, he made rapid progress.

Ross's wife, feeling unsure of herself, believing she could never get him to understand, and attempting to avoid his criticism, had not been very open or honest with him. She would not tell him openly how she felt; and because of her resentment, she would sometimes hurt him by turning a cold shoulder as she felt he had hurt her. In order to avoid his criticism, she often pressured him into making decisions for her. In this way she could place the blame on Ross if the decision turned out to be a poor one. She did this when they went shopping for clothes; she would wring her hands and wait so long to make a decision concerning which dress to buy that Ross would finally step in and tell her what to do. Phrases she used that put the responsibility on Ross included:

"What do you think I should do? What do you think is the best buy? Which do you like the best?"

In the counseling sessions she learned that she must be responsible to herself and to Ross by telling him exactly how she felt when he criticized her or made decisions for her. After she discovered the reasons for her disinterest, resentment, and anger, she realized it was difficult for her to be honest with Ross about her feelings and to take more responsibility. Reasons for this included her fear of being defeated, initial doubts about her rights to control her own responsibilities, fear of being criticized for her decisions, and self-doubts about her value as a person.

As Ross supported his wife's attempts to be more assertive and to take more responsibility for herself by complimenting her in her efforts, never criticizing her work or decisions and never taking over her tasks for her in an attempt to do them better or to show her up, she began to be much happier. She took more of an interest in living and became much more responsive to Ross.

It was hard for Ross to pull back, because he had trained himself so well to take over. He felt useless at first. He was finally able however to direct this energy into a more constructive channel by using it to encourage and reassure his wife in her efforts to change. When she expressed her appreciation to Ross when he was respectful in his relationships with her, she gave him the feedback he needed in order to know that he was on the right track. This payoff motivated him to want to continue such horizontal behavior in the future.

Note: Concepts you may want to review are life-style, pp. 48-50; social linkage, pp. 44-45; holism, pp. 50-52; communal interest, pp. 47-48; warmth and respect, p. 71; empathy, pp. 71-72; self-esteem, pp. 46-47; practice, pp. 54-55.

RESPECT AND COURTESY IN CONVERSATION

THE SITUATION

Harold and his wife were visiting friends. They had recently returned from an extended fishing trip, and Harold was excitedly telling the group about his experiences.

"It was a beautiful place where we camped. Our tent was directly under a giant Austrian pine."

"It was a Douglas pine. It had short needles," his wife said in a firm tone for all to hear.

"Well anyway it was big," Harold exclaimed. "We set up camp and then . . ."

"You mean I set up camp while you went off and fished," his wife broke in.

Harold was quiet for a moment. "Well, I thought we were all finished. I can't help it if you would rather sweep out the tent floor than fish," he whined defensively.

"Anyway," he continued, "I flicked my fly out right where I wanted it to go. It landed next to a sunken log. And would you believe it, I caught a one-and-a-half pound rainbow trout with that first cast."

"It was a grayling and it weighed only one pound." She spoke the words quickly and sharply with just a hint of sarcasm.

"Well anyway, I caught a lot of fish that morning. I must have had ten in my bag by nine o'clock."

"No, you had only eight. Remember, I counted them."

Harold began to say something, hesitated, looked down at his hands, and said nothing. A careful observer would have noticed the back of his neck going red.

His wife picked up the conversation and spent the next fifteen minutes telling her version of the trip. Harold offered only one or two additional comments in a half-hearted manner.

DISCUSSION

Harold's wife was the oldest child in her family and had taken it upon herself to correct her younger brothers and sisters when they made mistakes. Her conscious goal was to help them grow and develop. Her not-so-conscious goal was to be superior to them and keep them dependent on her. She was moving vertically against them in an attempt to belong.

It was only natural that she should bring this same behavior to her marriage. It especially surfaced whenever Harold talked in groups. She was quick to point out his errors to him and to others as she demonstrated her superior memory and knowledge. It got so that he would say, "Why don't you tell it?" and she would. This way he avoided the embarrassment of her correcting him in public, and she played her familiar role of correcting him and then finishing his story.

This behavior made Harold feel small, insignificant, and worthless. He also became resentful toward his wife and would usually turn away from her when they returned home and were in bed.

In order to improve their relationships, it is important for Harold's wife to work at not correcting Harold's storytelling even when she knows he is wrong. They are his stories. This will diminish his resentment toward her and stimulate him to enjoy his associations with her and other people to a greater degree.

As this couple works to improve their interaction, Harold must let his wife know how it makes him feel when she corrects him. If he does this immediately, he will be able to do it more easily and with courtesy and warmth. If he waits until he becomes full of emotion, he will tend to be too hesitant, angry, anxious, and/or embarrassed to respond effectively.

Note: Concepts you may want to review are life-style, pp. 48-50; communal interest, pp. 47-48; warmth and respect, p. 71; empathy, pp. 71-72; self-esteem, pp. 46-47; practice, pp. 54-55.

KNOWING WHEN TO USE HUMOR

THE SITUATION

Marie's laugh was hollow. "I really don't know what I am doing here. Some days I feel things are all right and other days I feel I just don't know my husband Joe. Everybody seems to like him, but I don't know him. Maybe it's all in my head. He's a good provider and the life of any party we go to. I guess this will sound weird to you. He is a stranger to me."

Marie continued the interview, repeating the same refrain over and over. She seemed a lonely, confused, and at times even bitter young wife. It was agreed that both she and Joe would attend the next session.

Joe and Marie arrived punctually. Joe was thirty, maybe fifty, pounds overweight. His eyes twinkled mischievously as he shook the counselor's hand. The interview had not proceeded five minutes before Joe was busy making humorous comments. And it was not long before a pattern emerged. Whenever Marie would talk about things that were important to her or about feelings she had which were not happy ones, Joe would make light of them with a humorous statement or story and begin talking about other things. When Marie's jaw was set, he told a humorous story. When she was close to tears, he tried to kid her out of her mood.

DISCUSSION

Joe grew up in a family where he had learned to belong by getting attention with joking and clowning. He became proficient at keeping the attention of other people focused on him as he performed for them. His family members also had a pattern of ridiculing anyone who felt sad or angry. Such expressions were frightening to Joe, for they caused him to fear that he would be ridiculed if he exposed those feelings or accepted them in anyone else.

Because of the life-style Joe had built for himself, he had not learned how to relate authentically with his wife. His attempts to keep her attention and to deflect her from meaningful discussions through the use of humor prevented him from developing an honest, close relationship with her. Neither of them could reveal their real thoughts, feelings, and emotions to each other. As a result they were strangers involved in a vertical relationship.

In order for Joe and Marie to work toward more satisfactory interactions with each other, Joe must encourage Marie to express her real thoughts and feelings to him and avoid the impulse to deflect her from them. If Joe will listen carefully and be accepting, their relationship will become richer and more meaningful. Joe must also work to share his real feelings with Marie if he is to find their life together more rewarding. It will take hard work on his part and much practice, but the rewards will be well worth his efforts.

Note: Concepts you may want to review are vertical goals, pp. 16-23, 43; payoff, pp. 42-44; life-style, pp. 48-50; genuineness, p. 71; empathy, pp. 71-72; practice, pp. 54-55.

A PATTERN OF COUNTERHURTING BEHAVIOR

THE SITUATION

Cora's hands moved down the length of her body caressing the shimmering gown as she turned slowly before the mirrors. She tilted her head, and her eyes blazed back defiantly as she thrilled and then shuddered at her reflection. She hesitated momentarily, then drew her shoulders back and tossed her head as she said in a voice that seemed to boom across the exclusive showroom, "I'll take it."

A perceptive observer would have noticed Cora's head and shoulders fall slightly forward as she appeared to retreat from her own voice.

Cora paid by check. As she picked up the exquisitely packaged dress, she was filled with alternating feelings of triumph and remorse, feelings she could not understand.

She walked out and passed several stores, feeling somewhat lost but mostly lonely. She entered the first cosmetic store she came to and wandered slowly up and down the aisles. Her handbag fell slightly open; and as the clerks busied themselves with other customers, she deftly pushed several items into her handbag as her eyes gazed intently at items two shelves above where her hand was busy working. She continued to walk to the end of the aisle and brushed off a clerk's offer to assist her with, "I'm only looking." As she reached the sidewalk, she experienced again the feelings of triumph and remorse. They came upon her so strongly this time that she found herself almost running in an effort to keep them from overcoming her. Two blocks later she gained control of her emotions. She slowed her pace, quickly hailed a cab, and returned home.

Cora placed the cosmetics in her vanity and the dress on the bed. She looked at her watch. It was four o'clock. She thought to herself, I have an hour and a half. She felt fear grip her in its icy hands. It held her in an even tighter and colder grip with the passage of time. She began to pace the floor, clasping and unclasping her moist palms. She went to the package and placed it in the back of the closet. Five minutes later she took it out and placed it on the bed again. She sat down on the bed, her hands tightly holding the bedpost. She waited, her wet palms dampening the spread. The door slammed. "Where's supper? I've got an early meeting with the city commission, so I'll have to leave in thirty minutes," her husband's strong, assertive voice echoed throughout the quiet house.

Cora shuddered. Can't I ever do anything right, she thought as she got up from the bed and moved more quickly than necessary, following the sound of her husband's voice.

"I'm sorry, dear, but I was shopping. I forgot all about supper." She shifted her weight from one foot to the other as she looked at her husband with pleading eyes.

"For heaven's sake, Cora, is it really too much for a busy husband to expect his wife to have supper ready for him? If it isn't one thing it's another. Surely, with all the time you have, you can keep up with the everyday household chores. I've supplied you with a beautiful house and all the modern conveniences. Next thing I know you'll be wanting a maid." He turned on his heel and began to move toward the bathroom. He suddenly stopped and whirled his large body in her direction, all in one quick motion. "Did you say shopping?" His eyes blazed.

Cora looked away. "Yes," she said in a low, quavering voice.

"You know you have no money in your account. Every month you promise me you won't do this. It's most embarrassing for me to have to cover your bad checks. Can't you learn to be more responsible?" His voice rose to a crescendo.

Cora busied herself opening cans, her eyes concentrating on the movements of her hands.

Her husband moved into the bedroom and came out holding the top of the box in one hand and the bottom containing the dress in the other. "You must have paid a fortune for this. Where is the price tag?" he growled.

"Isn't it there?" she asked, her voice shaking.

"No, it isn't. How much?"

"I'm not sure. I can't remember—the tax and all . . ." Her voice trailed off to nothing as she fought for time.

"Oh come on. You're not a child. Quit acting like one. How much did you spend this afternoon?"

Her heart pounded as she told him. And, as he stood in front of her shaking his fist in the air and shouting at her stupidity, her fear was gradually replaced by feelings of resentment and anger, feelings which she held in check and controlled as always. No one looking at her would have guessed the anger raging inside. She then felt a quiet satisfaction as her husband reached the peak of his shouting and then helplessly shrugged his shoulders and stomped into their bedroom. He came out fifteen minutes later. He had shaved, showered, and changed his clothes. He walked rapidly past the kitchen, not glancing at the hastily prepared meal placed in haphazard fashion on the table. He reached the front door, opened it, and shouted back, "Don't wait up for me. I'll be late." The door slammed shut underscoring the word *late*.

Cora's fleeting feeling of satisfaction was replaced by fear and panic as she heard the door slam. She wanted to run after him and cling to him sobbing, "Don't leave me again. Please don't ever leave me again. I feel I have no one."

But she did not. She held tightly to the back of a kitchen chair. Her fingers were white under the pressure; her head swam. Finally she ran to the bathroom and vomited. She sat before the toilet as if in a dream and seemed to hear her husband's voice from out of the past.

"Now Cora, you have overspent your food allowance again. It

looks like I'll have to go shopping with you for awhile to make sure you keep within the budget I've set up."

"You'll have to go without me. I have a meeting."

"I'll be home late. Eat without me."

"No, I can't take you. I have another meeting I have to attend to."

"Don't be so stupid."

"Won't you ever learn?"

"Go by yourself."

"I have to meet my friends."

"I must go. My professional future depends on it. We'll go another time."

"This fork isn't clean."

"You paid too much. Don't you ever watch the sales?"

"Buying a larger package would save money."

"Stupid."

"I have to go."

"Think next time."

"Stupid."

"I won't be home."

The phrases seemed to swirl round and round in her head at an ever faster pace until the words were jumbled together. Cora slumped down. Her head touched her lap and her hands covered her face as she sobbed, "What am I to do?"

DISCUSSION

The phrases Cora seemed to hear her husband speaking were the actual words he had used over and over with her in the past. He was a demanding and ambitious man. He had found his place in his own family by being critical of his brothers and sisters and by doing things better than they. He also searched for his worth by involving himself in many different things at one time. These behaviors he brought to his marriage relationship with Cora. He was critical and demanding of her, which enabled him to maintain his sense of belonging by being more powerful than she. He lost himself in his drive to be the best in his profession and therefore had little time for Cora.

Cora's responses to his critical, demanding, and bossing behavior alternated between giving in and occasionally flaring up when she would angrily battle him verbally. She found she usually lost out and ended up feeling guilty and bad. With the passage of time she gradually held her feelings in, pushing them down so far that she oftentimes could not tell what she was feeling when she related to her husband. It was about this time that she began writing bad checks and stealing. If someone had asked Cora why she did these things, she could not have answered because she did not know. She had chosen an indirect way of communicating to her husband in order to achieve her goals, a way which kept her free from taking responsibility for her actions.

Her husband was a powerful man, fluent in speech and unbeatable in an argument. He had a biting and sarcastic tongue and was capable of deeply hurting others. Cora had decided because of past experience with him that a direct approach would be too painful. She, therefore, turned to indirect approaches, which also enabled her to gain a degree of power over her husband.

Cora felt deep anger and hurt as a result of her husband's constant criticism and bossing. She interpreted this to mean that he did not care for her. This feeling was supported by his putting his business and professional life before his relationship with her. As a result she felt unloved, alone, and deeply hurt.

Cora felt she could not go to her husband about these feelings. She sensed she could not discuss them clearly since they were confusing to her. And she might feel even worse if she tried. He might say, "Don't be silly" or "That's right, I don't love you."

She therefore chose in a semiconscious way to communicate indirectly to achieve her goals with him. These goals were to get him to pay attention to her and to hurt him as he had hurt her. By writing bad checks, she hurt him, for his prestige in the community was threatened. He gave her attention by reacting so strongly to her poor behavior, and gave her service by making good her checks. When she stole, she felt that she was tarnishing his good name in the community even if no one found out. It was her little secret revenge game. There was always the chance that someone would catch her, and this was exciting to her.

In order to replace their vertical relationships with horizontal ones, Cora and her husband need to follow a well-thought-out plan. They will want to follow these suggestions:

- Cora's husband should never boss or criticize her.
- He should schedule several times each week for spending time with her. He should refuse to let anything else interfere.
- He should express his affection for her several times each day in both verbal and nonverbal ways.
- He should respond quietly to her check writing and let her suffer the consequences by letting payment for her purchases be her responsibility.
- Cora should tell her husband when she feels unloved and alone. She should tell him specifically which of his behaviors influence her to feel this way.
- She should tell him when she feels hurt and refer specifically to behaviors that bring about this feeling.
- She should express her anger directly to him as she did when they were first married. This would lessen her need to strike back in unconscious ways (i.e., not fixing meals, over-spending).
- She should work to be more responsible in her role as housewife.
- She should get involved in a variety of activities with other people and thereby build up her feelings of self-worth and self-respect.

In order to accomplish the above, Cora will need to work hard to courageously meet the challenge to communicate directly with her husband. Her husband will need to discipline himself in order to keep from reverting to his old critical, bossy behavior. He will also have to work hard at directing more of his time and energy to Cora.

Note: Concepts you may want to review are vertical goals, pp. 16-23, 43; payoff, pp. 42-44; life-style, pp. 48-50; belonging, pp. 45-46; communal interest, pp. 47-48; warmth and respect, p. 71; empathy, pp. 71-72; natural consequences, pp. 85-86; practice, pp. 54-55.

ACHIEVING THE PERFECT MARRIAGE

THE SITUATION

Celeste was a beautiful, immaculate young wife and mother. It seemed that every hair on her head was always in place and she was perfectly groomed. She had expected much of herself and, generally, had been able to meet her expectations.

Ever since she had been a little girl, she had dreamed of having a perfect marriage. For Celeste this meant being married in a religious setting to a husband who always attended his religious services, including those specifically for men. He would also be appointed to responsible positions in his church and community. And he would see to it that other members of the family attended to their religious duties.

The troubles started during the honeymoon. The newlyweds were in a strange town but had located the nearest meetinghouse and, upon her insistence, her husband had phoned and found out the times of the various meetings. Their conversation one morning went something like this:

"Gary, you'd better hurry or you are going to miss your meeting."

"But Celeste, it's our honeymoon. I'd rather stay here with you."

"Gary, I'm surprised at you. Don't you remember the vows we took just three days ago?"

"Oh come on. Don't be that way. I'm sure the Lord won't mind if I miss my meeting today. This is a special Sunday for us."

"All the more reason for you to go." Celeste pushed herself out of bed and stood over her husband. "I'll be very disappointed in you if you don't go," she exclaimed in a brittle tone of voice as she tilted her nose slightly toward the ceiling and marched into the bathroom.

Gary went to his meeting thirty minutes late.

This initial interaction seemed to set the pattern. Celeste would prod her husband to go to his meetings, and he would resist, and then usually go. Later, however, he seemed to be going less and less. Celeste was driven by the fear that unless Gary assumed more of his spiritual responsibilities their marriage would not be approved by their families and friends. As a result she had resorted to many different techniques to get Gary to attend his meetings.

"Gary, isn't this a beautiful sunrise. You know the sun is rising at seven now." (His meeting starts at eight.)

"Gary, I've fixed ham and eggs for breakfast—your favorite. If you get up now you'll be able to enjoy them before you go to your meeting."

"I'll run the water for you while you shave so you won't be late for your meeting."

"You're staying home again! What will the children think?"

"If you loved me, you'd go to your meeting."

"My father always went to each one of his meetings. He loves his wife and children."

"My brothers always go to their meetings."

Celeste feels that she has tried every strategy she knows, but nothing seems to work to get Gary to his meetings.

She also wants very much to be proud of him when they are in public together. Much of the time she is proud, but sometimes she feels that he dresses too casually and is not as careful with his speech as he could be. This of course embarrasses Celeste. She tries to improve him by mothering him. The following pattern of behavior is now rather strongly set:

Just as they were entering their church house to attend a meeting, Celeste said, "Gary, your tie knot is too loose. The button on your collar is showing." She moved over and tightened his tie.

"There, that looks much better." She took his arm and hurried him into the meetinghouse, oblivious to Gary's flushed cheeks and the stares of others.

"I do wish you'd keep your shoes shined. A man with your potential must look his best." This she whispered in rather loud tones after they were seated and Gary had stretched out his feet.

Celeste reached over and buttoned the top button of his jacket and exclaimed while patting his arm, "There now, that looks much better."

After church, Gary and Celeste and some of their friends were talking about the events of the past week. During the conversation Gary said, "Don't he know that taxes have to be paid before that date?"

Celeste put on her best smile and said sweetly, "Gary, the word is *doesn't*, not *don't*." She did not notice the slight drop in his shoulders following her comment.

Later on, during the same conversation, Gary became enthusiastic about a particular topic being discussed and interjected, "But that don't make sense. Deductions is deductions and should be allowed."

Celeste smiled even more sweetly as she moved closer to Gary and looking up into his face said softly, "The correct words are *doesn't* and *are*."

Gary seemed to shrivel. He stopped talking and five minutes later said to Celeste in a gruff tone of voice, "Come on, let's go home." And as they walked down the stairs of the meetinghouse he said, "I'm sick of this place."

Fear rose in Celeste's throat and seemed to almost choke her as she walked down the stairs. She felt that she was stumbling all the way down, but an observer would have only noticed her straight back and sure steps, so completely was she in control of her outward self.

DISCUSSION

Celeste is her own worst enemy. Her desires to have a perfect marriage immediately and her direct and indirect attempts to mold Gary tend to prevent her from realizing the things she wants most. As she takes it upon herself to tell him to go to religious services, she is subtly communicating that she has judged him and found him wanting. She is also communicating that she is a superior, better person and must make sure that he does what she thinks is right. She compares him with her father and brothers. This further compounds her problems with Gary and pushes him farther from sharing their religious values with her.

Celeste's efforts include power tactics to get Gary to do what she wants. But as she tries to force the issue, he feels he must fight her to maintain his self-respect. She has placed him in a double bind. He cannot win, for if he gives in to her and goes to his meetings he loses because he has done it in response to her nagging. If he does not go to them in order to prove he is his own boss, he still loses because he really wants to go. Not only has Celeste used power, she has also tried to hurt Gary as she feels he has hurt her. Her comparing him with other people and using such phrases as "I'm disappointed in you" are all for the purpose of hurting him and getting him to respond as she would like him to.

Celeste further compounds her problems with Gary by correcting his dress and speech when they are on the meetinghouse grounds. This causes Gary to have a negative feeling towards religious services. The principle of bonding has definitely taken effect. The correction and criticism are bonded with the services as are the concomitant feelings of embarrassment, anger, and resentment. He therefore attempts to stay away from church.

If Celeste and Gary are to work themselves out of their destructive situations in which they find themselves, they must follow a step-by-step plan of action which both of them can feel good about.

It is Celeste's responsibility to no longer give Gary direct or indirect messages that tell him what she thinks are his spiritual responsibilities. She can do this by saying nothing and implying nothing through her facial expressions or in any other way about his going to his meetings. He knows how she feels, and he knows his spiritual responsibilities. If Celeste will say nothing, she will remove the double bind and free him so that he can go to his meetings because he wants to.

Second, she must work to *never* criticize him or correct him in public. She must apply this principle in their private lives as well, as long as Gary is not infringing on her rights.

Third, Celeste should work to respond to her husband with warmth and sincere affection, in public (if they both wish) as well as in private.

Fourth, when Gary decides to stay home from religious services, Celeste can of course still go if she wishes. If she should leave alone, it will be helpful if she bids Gary a warm goodbye and then returns with a warm hello with no hint of resentment because he did not go with her. In other words, she respects both her husband and herself by taking care of her responsibilities and allowing Gary the same right.

The above procedures may be hard for the people with Celeste's behavioral patterns, but it is only by letting a loved one loose, be it husband, child, or friend, that we can actually win his respect and love. As a result a far more nearly perfect marriage relationship can exist.

Gary's obligation in his relationship to his wife includes insisting that Celeste stop telling him to go to religious services and stop correcting and criticizing him in public so that he can be free to go to his meetings on his own. By not letting her criticize his behavior at these services, he will help destroy the negative feelings that he has felt for a long time whenever he thinks about or is at these religious meetings.

These suggested behavior changes will require that Gary and Celeste put forth a good deal of courageous, hard work. But the effort will result in their interacting more horizontally with each other. They will, in effect, put their religious beliefs into action.

Note: Concepts you may want to review are life-style, pp. 48-50; social linkage, pp. 44-45; communal interest, pp. 47-48; vertical goals, pp. 16-23, 43; self-esteem, pp. 46-47; warmth and respect, p. 71; empathy, pp. 71-72; bonding, pp. 52-53; practice, pp. 54-55.

LEARNING TO BE PATIENT IN INTIMATE RELATIONSHIPS

THE SITUATION

A young man in his middle twenties opened the door and made his way to the nearest chair. Although at first hesitant, he soon became more spontaneous in expressing himself.

"You see, it's like this: I've been married a whole month and things just are not what they should be for my wife."

"Please go on."

He continued a little hesitantly, "When we were going together, we both were eagerly looking forward to marriage. But now not much is happening for my wife."

"Are you suggesting your wife is somewhat disappointed in your sexual relations?"

"Yes. I can't understand it. We expected great things after marriage."

"That must be hard for you to take."

"It is. I never dreamed she would respond as she does. Oh, she says she enjoys our lovemaking, but it's not too fulfilling for her."

DISCUSSION

This young couple had made a rather common error in this very intimate and important relationship. They assumed that the wife could quickly and automatically respond sexually. Usually the husband can, but often the wife is different. Her arousal is more complex and takes longer than her husband's. Studies have shown that whereas the husband can be aroused in minutes, even seconds, it takes an experienced wife under rather ideal circumstances as much as twenty minutes to fully respond.

What are some of the guidelines couples can follow to improve their sexual relationships? First, young couples must realize that this relationship, if it is to be satisfying for both of them, takes patience, time, and understanding.

Second, the foundation of such a relationship is good relations between husband and wife in all other areas. It is difficult for a wife to give of herself spontaneously and freely if she is resentful and angry with her husband. Both must work to be respectful, courteous, loving with each other in all areas of their interaction so that they can give freely and without fear of being hurt in this most intimate of relationships.

Third, the husband must know what to expect from himself and from his wife, and she should know the same. For example, this requires that they work to be open in their communication to each other about what is pleasing to each of them and what is not. It also suggests that each should know something about men and women in general. Knowing that historically most men have been stimulated by the erotic and that most women have been stimulated by tenderness and romance is valuable knowledge. The husband, especially, should be aware of those things that tend to be pleasurable to his wife.

Fourth, both man and wife should be sensitive to those things that impede good sexual relationships. Unproductive and unresolved conflict; lack of privacy; fear of being ridiculed, hurt, dominated, or used; fear of losing oneself to another; fatigue; in-law problems; business difficulties; and lack of confidence in oneself or one's mate are among those things that most often hinder good sexual relationships.

Fifth, a courageous, confident approach encompassed by love, respect, sincerity, good humor, and understanding can do much to enable almost any couple to achieve exciting and fulfilling sexual relations.

As a man and wife begin their lovemaking, it is important that the wife communicate her desires to her husband. She may use both nonverbal and verbal signals to indicate her feelings. Those things that tend to please her usually include words of affection, appreciation, and love as well as caresses. Every woman is somewhat different, and it is extremely vital that each wife communicate her feelings to her husband so that he can be aware of them. A nonresponsive wife tends to have a clumsy husband. But a clumsy husband tends to have a noncommunicative wife.

Couples who want a more detailed, clinical discussion will find the writings of such authors as Masters and Johnson and Seymour Fisher to be helpful.

Historically, husbands have often used their wives for their own sexual gratification with little or no thought for the needs of their wives. The principles of unity and equality of course presuppose that the wife has as much right as the husband to meet her sexual needs. Woman was made to achieve the beautiful, mystifying, and renewing experience which is part of the great value of sexual relationships. The considerate and loving husband will be as concerned about filling her needs as he will be about filling his own.

The husband and wife who successfully love one another and who are able to express that love freely in sexual relationships which are satisfactory to both of them are cooperating in one of the greatest and most divine relationships available to man. They are brought closer spiritually through an act of love that can create new life.

Healthy sexual relationships may be used for many constructive purposes, the most obvious being to create new life. Second, they are used to cement the bonds of love between husband and wife, reassuring each that he or she is accepted and belongs. Third, they reaffirm to each that he or she is a worthwhile person. Fourth, they motivate the couple to continue sharing and cooperating. Cooperation in sexual relations is a reflection of the ability of the couple to cooperate in other aspects of their interactions. Fifth, good, healthy sexual relations make life more pleasurable. Sixth, they can encourage and console when a spouse feels discouraged and hurt. Seventh, they are wonderfully relaxing. Eighth, they produce a physical and emotional closeness that is difficult to duplicate in any other way.

A healthy sexual relationship will strengthen husband and wife relationships in general. Just as a good relationship in other areas makes the sexual relationship satisfactory, so does a healthy sexual relationship tend to improve all other aspects of the relationship between husband and wife.

A healthy sexual experience requires the wife and husband to lower all of their defenses and appear before one another completely open. There are no defense mechanisms to keep the other away. Each stands before his mate defenseless and vulnerable and experiences kindness, courtesy, and respect. As a result their trust in one another is strengthened.

In the vertical sexual relationship the primary concern is that of achieving personal sexual satisfaction with little or no regard for the spouse. One may use sex to defeat or hurt a spouse or to prove one's power and importance. In horizontal interaction the husband and wife are concerned about helping each other have a satisfactory experience. This results in a marriage relationship which is beautiful and strong.

Note: Concepts you may want to review are warmth and respect, p. 71; empathy, pp. 71-72; genuineness, p. 71; self-esteem, pp. 46-47; communal interest, pp. 47-48; bonding, pp. 52-53; practice, pp. 54-55.

A MISUNDERSTANDING

THE SITUATION

Barbara was a vivacious, married woman in her middle twenties. She was happily married, but was occasionally disturbed by her husband's behavior.

She said, "At times I get the feeling that all my husband thinks about when he sees me is that he wants to have sex. I will go up to give him an affectionate kiss and a hug; and before I know it, he is moving in on me physically. Sometimes all I want is an expression of his love, but I get the feeling that his mind is on one track. It is discouraging for me. It seems I could be anyone. Oh, I know that's not true even though I feel that way sometimes."

DISCUSSION

Further discussion with Barbara during a counseling session revealed that she and her husband appeared to have a fairly normal relationship. She was sexually responsive on most occasions and generally enjoyed her relationship with her husband except when she felt he was using her.

Barbara's husband came in with her for the next interview. His responses to her statements were as follows:

"But honey, I love you very much. It's just that whenever I kiss you or hug you, you arouse me and I then find I want you."

"I feel you don't love me when you act that way," Barbara said.

"Darling, I look at you and I get a warm feeling. Then I go to you to express my feelings of love and I become aroused. Every time I kiss, hug, or even touch you I become aroused."

"Are you saying that your feelings of love usually come first and that your physical feelings follow?" Barbara asked with surprise.

"That's it exactly. I love you so much, Barbara."

Barbara shifted her position and faced the counselor, "Are all men like that?"

"Generally, yes. His approach of love can easily and quickly arouse him as you respond with warmth and affection."

"Hmm. And all this time I thought he always had sex on his mind first." She reached over, took his hand, and smiled into his eyes.

They left the office hand in hand.

It is understandable that a wife who feels her husband's primary interest is physical would develop feelings of resentment. If a husband relates to his wife as an object or thing rather than as another human being of equal worth, he causes their relationship to become a vertical one. She becomes a thing to be used rather than a person whose total needs are met by a man who is respectful, loving, and considerate of her every need.

Note: Concepts you may want to review are warmth and respect, p. 71; empathy, pp. 71-72; genuineness, p. 71; self-esteem, pp. 46-47.

CHILDHOOD PROBLEMS IN ADULT RELATIONSHIPS
THE SITUATION

Doug's young wife was confused and somewhat frightened by his responses to her. She stated that after sexual intimacy Doug would turn away from her and avoid talking to her for sometimes up to a full day. He seemed to brood and resent her. She said that if she declined his advances, he became angry; and if she responded to him, he became angry. She was bewildered.

DISCUSSION

Doug was reared in a home where he was taught to avoid anything that was crude. The natural body processes of elimination were spoken of in low tones with a trace of disgust. Sex was seldom mentioned; but when it was, it was within a context of shame and distaste. Doug was caught in conflict himself. He had normal sexual urges;

but when he responded to them, his learned, negative attitudes toward sex engulfed him and he directed these toward his wife as well as toward himself. When he did not respond to them, he of course felt on-going sexual tension. His responses to his conflict put his wife in a double bind because she could not please him regardless of how she responded. If she did not respond to his sexual advances, he put pressure on her. When she did respond to him, he afterwards turned a cold shoulder to her.

The double bind is used by many powerful people to keep their close associates vulnerable to their manipulations. In Doug's case it was an interpersonal strategy isolated to the area of sex. His goal was not so much to keep his wife off-balance and in servitude to his demands as it was to stay in harmony with his learned attitudes regarding sex and at the same time find release from sexual tension. His situation was untenable.

Doug wanted to have a positive relationship with his wife that would be free of so much conflict, and he chose to work to overcome his past sexual training. This was accomplished in part by his achieving greater understanding of the techniques his mother used to train him. He recalled the words, tone of voice, and gestures she used whenever she talked about sex. He realized that he had adopted these as his own, and he came to see them as illogical and unhealthy. After he gained this insight, he practiced talking differently to himself and to his wife when the topics of sex or body elimination were brought up. He worked to bring a touch of humor into the conversation as well as interest and excitement rather than shame and disgust. This took much effort and work on Doug's part, but with the passage of time the newer emotions became dominant and the older ones receded into the background and bothered him only occasionally.

Inappropriate uses of shame and disgust perpetuate vertical movement and give the one using them a superior, powerful position over those to whom he directs such feelings. Horizontal, respectful, loving interaction with other people cannot exist where shame and disgust pervade the relationship.

Note: Concepts you may want to review are life-style, pp. 48-50; social linkage, pp. 44-45; holism, pp. 50-52; bonding, pp. 52-53; modeling, pp. 53-54; warmth and respect, p. 71; empathy, pp. 71-72; genuineness, p. 71; practice, pp. 54-55.

ACHIEVING FULFILLMENT

THE SITUATION

Dinah was attractive and appeared at first glance to be a woman who knew who she was and where she was going. Her sparkling eyes and straight shoulders were betrayed however by her hands which she clasped and unclasped as she told her story to a marriage therapist.

It took Dinah fifteen minutes to talk about her major concern.

"I don't know what's the matter with me," she said with a catch in her voice. "I love my husband, but I can't respond to him as I would like."

"You say you can't respond to him?"

"Yes, I've done a lot of reading lately and I've come to question whether or not I have ever experienced complete fulfillment in our sexual relations. I guess I really don't know what it is."

"You sound discouraged."

"I guess I am. I wonder if I disappoint my husband, and I also wonder what I'm missing and what makes me so different." She dropped her eyes and busied herself with the purse that lay in her lap.

"It sounds like you are concerned about three things: your husband's feelings toward you, your own feelings of sexual inadequacy, and whether or not you are getting as much out of your sexual relations as you should. Is this right?"

"Yes." She nodded in the affirmative as tears filled her eyes.

"Before we talk more about these things, could you describe the feelings you get when you have an exceptionally satisfactory sexual experience with your husband? This will help us determine whether or not you have been completely fulfilled." (Usually if a woman does not know whether she has or not, she hasn't.) "Please go on. Recall a particularly satisfying experience and your feelings at the time."

"I guess about two months ago was when I had a particularly good experience. I felt warm and loving toward my husband. I just wanted to continue holding him in my arms." She seemed to conclude her comments and began to nervously open and shut her purse.

"Did you feel anything else?"

"No. I remember I enjoyed his lovemaking. I felt very peaceful with him. I guess that was all. Oh, I remember I wished he hadn't turned over and gone to sleep when he did."

"What would you have preferred?"

She looked up quickly and said softly and quietly, "I guess I wanted him to tell me how much he loved me and to continue to hold me."

DISCUSSION

Dinah was not achieving complete fulfillment, but her situation was no different from that of a high percentage of other wives who seldom, if ever, experience it.

It seems that in many cases women do not need to experience complete sexual fulfillment in order to achieve happiness. Many find that sexual intimacies which build up tension without allowing release are still comforting and rewarding. But their relationships can be even more satisfactory as they and their husbands learn to help each other become completely sexually fulfilled.

Further discussion with Dinah revealed that her relationship with her father was somewhat distant. "It seemed like he was never at home. He was always gone on church business or community service projects. He was a big man in the community and everyone else was always calling on him to do things for them. I hardly knew I had a father. In fact, I felt he thought more of everyone else than he did of me. He was too busy to do anything for his family, but not too busy to help anyone else out. All they had to do was call and he'd go running." Dinah clenched her hands and tightened her jaw as she spoke.

"You sound angry."

"I guess I am. I felt I never had a father. He was always away. Other people always came first. I know it was hard on Mother." She thrust her chin forward; a look of defiance crept into her face and then quickly vanished.

"When growing up, Dinah, did you often get the feeling that you had to hold tight or you would lose those you loved?"

Surprise lit up her face, "How did you know?"

"It sometimes happens to those who feel toward a loved one as you have described your feelings about your father. Do you sometimes get these same feelings toward your husband?"

She was quiet for some time and had bent her head way down. She began to cry, then dabbed at her eyes with a tissue, looked up, and continued. "Greg is away much of the time too. He is, I guess, a little like Dad, popular in the community. Sometimes I feel so lonely."

"Do you get that old feeling of wanting to hold tight and not let go?"

"Yes, I do."

"This may be related to your not achieving sexual fulfillment."

"How could that be? I love Greg very much."

"No, I wasn't questioning your love for Greg. It is something else that I was wondering about. In order to be completely fulfilled sexually, a woman has to abandon herself. She has to let herself completely go and lose herself to the experience. It is as though she were to give of herself completely to the experience and to her husband with complete trust in him. We find that many women who do not trust loved ones, or who have not had the experience or faith that their loved ones will always be there no matter what, have a difficult time achieving complete fulfillment in their sexual relations."

The therapist continued, "I guess becoming sexually fulfilled requires that the woman detach her conscious attention from her surroundings, give up her hold on the world. And the woman who has experienced much loneliness and a lack of trust in loved ones finds this difficult to do." The therapist turned to Dinah. "Dinah, could it be that something like this has happened to you?"

"I don't know. I've never thought about it before quite in that way. It seems right to me. I know I've always felt I had to hold tight to things or I would lose them. Greg has sometimes accused me of being possessive, but I try not to be. I get the feeling that other people count more than I do. I had this feeling intensely with my father." She put her hand to her face and waited.

"Are you suggesting that it's not quite the same with Greg?"

"Yes, Greg is really pretty good about including me. Sometimes though . . ." Her voice fell away as she thought.

"Could you get ghost feelings?"

"Ghost feelings. That's a funny thing to say."

"Well, I was thinking that some of these feelings with Greg could be arising from your past. Do you think this could be true?"

"You mean my fear of my father leaving me or liking others more than me has moved into my relationships with Greg?"

"I was wondering."

"You may be right. I get this old fear, and I panic at times even when Greg does nothing to make me afraid he is going to leave me. Many times my feelings are unfounded; I know that."

"As you learn more about your present fear and its origins, you will be able to handle it so that you will feel less need to hold tight. And as you learn to have greater confidence in Greg and to trust him, you will also begin to believe that he will always be there when you need him; you will be better able to let yourself go and thereby become fulfilled."

Following the discussion with Dinah, her husband came in for interviews. He was a husband deeply in love with his wife, but quite unaware of her needs. He was most cooperative and open to suggestions. He agreed to work to make himself more emotionally dependable according to his wife's needs. He decided he wanted to put his interest, love, and loyalty for her first. This meant that he would cut down on his church and community activities and unnecessary vocational activities. He said that he would ask his wife about her plans before he committed himself to any other people. He also agreed to initiate many affectionate acts toward his wife each day.

Time, concern, care, awareness, interest, and open communication are great facilitators to satisfactory husband-wife relationships, which Dinah and Greg discovered as they worked to improve their marriage.

Note: Concepts you may want to review are empathy, pp. 71-72; warmth and respect, p. 71; genuineness, p. 71; life-style, pp. 48-50; social linkage, pp. 44-45; holism, pp. 50-52; belonging, pp. 45-46; practice, pp. 54-55.

A PROBLEM OF IMPOTENCY

THE SITUATION

Jerry jammed his hands deeper into his pockets and shifted in the chair. "I just don't get it. I played basketball and football. I've always been athletic. Not only did girls look up to me while I was in school, but the fellows thought I was pretty sharp too. I never thought anything like this would ever happen to me."

"Would you like to talk about it?"

"I don't know where to begin. I don't know how to tell you. I guess I am ashamed." His strong fingers bit into the chair arms, and he seemed to want to sink deeper into its cushions.

"Sometimes it's easier to talk once you get started."

His face flushed as he began, "I guess it started on our honeymoon. It's a sexual problem. There, I've said it. It went fairly well, but twice I couldn't . . . I couldn't . . ." He paused and groped for the words.

"You couldn't perform? Is that what you were going to say, Jerry?"

He exhaled and seemed to relax, "How did you know?" He looked intently at the therapist.

"Those things happen."

"It was terribly embarrassing. I'll never forget it. I swore to myself it would never happen again, but it has. In fact, I've been married two years now and it seems to be getting worse instead of better." He slumped dejectedly.

"What do you mean?"

"You know, I can't follow through. Sometimes I can't even get started."

"Have you been to your medical doctor?"

"Yes, and he said there was nothing wrong with me. That's why I'm here. I need help."

"You sound pretty discouraged."

"I am. I don't know what to do. I've tried to force myself in order to make it happen, but it hasn't worked. I don't know what to do."

"What do you feel when you try to become sexually intimate with your wife? Can you describe these feelings?"

"I don't know. I get all mixed up."

"Do you feel fear, frustration, embarrassment, anger, hate, hurt, or combinations of these things?"

"Gosh, I'm not sure. They're all mixed up. I need to sort them out." He paused deep in thought as the seconds, then minutes ticked by. Beads of perspiration appeared on his forehead as he wrestled with the problem.

Jerry continued after about three minutes, "I hate to admit it, but I guess I am afraid. That's the first thing I feel. I'm afraid I can't. Then I get embarrassed."

"Do you feel anything else?"

He hesitated, "Yes, I get angry."

"Who are you angry at?"

"I'm angry at myself for being so stupid and I'm angry . . ." He stopped in mid-sentence and looked startled.

"Please go on."

"I'm angry with Ann."

"Why are you angry with Ann?"

"Because I think she secretly enjoys my failure."

"You feel like a failure at such times."

"Yes." He spoke in a quiet tone. He appeared crestfallen, forlorn, and alone.

"It hurts," the therapist interpreted.

"It hurts terribly."

"Tell me about your wife. How would you describe her?"

"She's sharp, you know. She's got brains, looks, the works."

"It sounds like she is rather special."

"She is. We went to the same high school together. All the fellows were out to win her. I was lucky."

"How do you feel around her?"

Jerry looked up as one corner of his mouth gave a barely perceptible twitch. "I feel small, inadequate. Sometimes I feel like a little boy."

DISCUSSION

The therapy sessions continued and included Ann. She was a striking, young, successful, working woman, immaculate in dress and grooming. She sat somewhat stiffly with her hands folded in her lap and seldom moved them. She spoke in quiet assured tones, radiating confidence, self-assurance, and intolerance. She gave the impression of demanding much from herself and other people as well as being intolerant of mistakes and inefficiency. Her eyes wandered over the therapist's cluttered desk and then met his, communicating her disapproval.

It soon became apparent that Ann, in her attempts to *make* a good marriage, was critical of much of Jerry's behavior. She would express her criticism through derisive laughter, a lift of her eyebrow, and statements which compared Jerry to others in an unfavorable light. She tended to be dominating and threatening in her relationship with him.

Both Jerry and Ann wished to improve their relationship with each other. And Ann agreed to work at never criticizing Jerry in anything he did. When he did something she did not like that involved her directly, she practiced telling him how it made her feel so that she gave no hint of ridicule or sarcasm. Jerry also worked to tell Ann when she fell back into her old critical behavior. He worked to be more direct and assertive with her in a kind, gentle manner.

The therapist felt that as Ann became less critical she would be less threatening to Jerry and he would be better able to function sexually. Also, there appeared to be an element of his counterhurting Ann through his impotency. Her criticism of him hurt, and his impotency was frustrating to her. By not satisfying her sexually, he was paid off. He was able to hurt her as he felt she had hurt him. Therefore, as she stopped criticizing him, she became a safer and less fearful person. And he had less need to get revenge through withholding his sexual expressions of affection.

It was also discovered in interviews with Jerry that his mother had been domineering and critical of him. He had always felt small, insignificant, and rather worthless around her. His self-esteem suffered not only because of her harsh comments about him, but also because as a grown man he still allowed her to run his life in some areas.

Jerry discovered that his fear of his mother and the accompanying low self-esteem had generalized to most assertive women he met, including his wife. It was as if he told himself, "All confident women are dangerous. They will criticize me and make me feel worthless and inadequate." Jerry's discovery of his not-quite-conscious pattern regarding assertive women freed him to take a closer look at confident women on an individual basis and to discern those who were critical and those who were not.

He also learned to take more responsibility for his own personal life and Ann's and to keep his mother from interfering and taking over. His success in this area also enabled him to be less fearful of assertive women in general and to think more of himself.

Another approach to the couple's concern that Jerry become sexually able was to help the couple try less hard. They were encouraged to approach intimate relations in an easy-going, relaxed, good-humored manner. Jerry was not to work in order to perform. He was to let it happen naturally. They were to work to please each other sexually, but neither of them was to approach the experience with any set expectations of performance. The goal was to enjoy each other's company. Complete sexual fulfillment was to be a by-product, not the direct goal.

It was important that Jerry behave in a manner that would help him develop a higher level of self-esteem. His effective responses to his mother that kindly but firmly kept her from interfering in their lives were helpful. His open and direct responses to Ann when she forgot herself and became critical also raised his level of self-esteem, as did Ann's efforts not to criticize him and her efforts to pay off his attempts to be more assertive and friendly by listening to, touching, and kissing him at such times.

As Jerry's mother had been critical of him, he had become critical of himself. He, in fact, had adopted some of the phrases she had used in talking to him. He usually talked to himself, using such terms and phrases as "You stupid idiot. Can't you ever do anything right? You're a dumbbell."

Jerry learned to substitute positive phrases for the negative ones. Whenever he caught himself talking to himself negatively, he was to substitute such phrases as "You're O.K., Jerry. You can do it. You're a good guy. You have a good heart."

It was important for Jerry to learn to forgive himself and not be so hard on himself. And as he learned to stand up to assertive women, he learned that by maintaining his integrity with such behavior he was able to be more tolerant of other people and be more forgiving. He learned the great lesson that *the free man, the man who does not betray himself in his relationships with other people, can be forgiving.* The unforgiving are most typically those who betray themselves by letting others demean or abuse them in some way or who behave contrary to their basic value system.

Jerry worked at focusing on his positive traits. He emphasized his good traits and habits rather than his imperfections while working on those areas where he needed to improve. He saw himself in a more realistic way as a man with many fine qualities and some traits that needed to be worked on.

Jerry had also lived a competitive life, always comparing himself with other people. He had marched to the rhythm of other people's drums and had to learn to march to his own, to set his own pace, to measure progress according to his own past performance and not to use the progress of other people as a standard.

Those who are critical and sarcastic and use ridicule in their relationships set themselves up as superior to other people. Among the common fruits of such vertical interaction are self-abasement and general impotency.

As discussed in Learning to Be Patient in Intimate Relationships, many healthy uses of sex can exist between husband and wife. The unhealthy, vertical purposes that many people attempt to achieve through sex include (1) flirting with other people in order to make one's spouse jealous; (2) proving to oneself that he/she is accepted, worthwhile, capable, and/or loved by having extramarital sexual relations; (3) excusing oneself for not meeting the challenges of life ("How can you expect anything of me when I am sexually frustrated, inadequate, biologically incapable, sexually put upon?"); (4) dominating one's spouse by giving and withholding sex as a bribe; (5) counterhurting one's spouse by withholding oneself or by being sexually brutal and perverse; (6) striving for acceptance by bragging of one's sexual activity; and (7) maintaining distance by treating one's spouse as an object or thing.

An individual's life-style tends to be expressed in his sexual activity. His ability to use sex for healthy purposes is a measure of his ability to move cooperatively with other people. On the other hand his use of sex for unhealthy, unconstructive, destructive purposes is a measure of his vertical movement against others.

Note: Concepts you may want to review are empathy, pp. 71-72; warmth and respect, p. 71; genuineness, p. 71; vertical goals, pp. 16-23, 43; bonding, pp. 52-53; life style, pp. 48-50; social linkage, pp. 44-45; holism, pp. 50-52; communal interest, pp. 47-48; self-esteem, pp. 46-47; modeling, pp. 53-54.

PREPARATION FOR MARRIAGE

THE SITUATION

The following situation consists of a conversation between a father and son which, though perhaps somewhat idealistic, represents good communication and the kind of idealism that is necessary for young couples to possess if they wish to have a happy marriage relationship.

Bart sighed contentedly, pushed himself out of a cushioned chair and said, "Dad, it's great to be home. School life is good, but there's nothing like spending an evening at home with the family."

Bart's father looked at his oldest son and smiled. "It's good to have you home too, son. We all miss you."

Bart felt the warmth of his father's response. "Dad, I know it's late and you have a big day tomorrow, but I was wondering," he paused, searching for the words to express what was on his mind, "if we could have a talk?" He then proceeded more quickly as he seemed to find the right words. "I'm really looking forward to marrying Diane next month, but there's so much I don't know. I've read a lot about man, woman, and sex in marriage and have some ideas, but so many of them seem kind of vague and disjointed. I've seen a lot of people become disappointed with marriage after the first year or two. I don't want that to happen to Diane and me. Right now I think we have a really good thing going."

He stopped and waited for his father to reply.

"Bart, it sounds like you are already feeling your responsibilities to Diane and marriage. You have many ideas about what a good marriage relationship entails, but you are still somewhat unsure. Is this right?"

"Yes, that's it."

"Well, how can I help?"

"I'm not sure. Maybe you could just listen and make a few comments like you usually do when I need to work something out. You've always been frank and honest with me, and I've always known how you've felt. You've seldom tried to force your ideas down my throat, and I guess that's why I want to talk to you now."

"I appreciate that, son. Where would you like to begin?"

"I don't know. There are so many loose ends."

"How about starting anywhere and we'll go from there."

"O.K. As I understand it, one of Diane's major goals is to find security. I believe the education and training I'm getting now in specific skills will help me provide for her without too much worry."

"That is important, son. But I wonder if there aren't other things that might be even more important to her."

"Do you mean her feeling that I will always love her and be loyal to her?"

"Yes, I was wondering about that. Economic security is necessary of course, but there are many couples who do not have much money yet they are stable in their love and devotion for each other. They actually experience a security that many wealthy men would give everything to have."

"I want her to feel secure in my love for her."

"And how will you go about this, Bart?"

"I'll give her a lot of affection. I'm a very affectionate fellow, you know."

"Yes, and that's good. But do you think it will be enough?"

"I guess not. I know some couples who seem very affectionate, at least in public, but who are not very happy. I guess they are unsure of the true feelings of their partners. But Diane has a fairly stable personality, and I don't think she'll make it hard for me."

"What are you thinking?"

"Well, I'm thinking of a couple I know. Jack is living in hell. I would hate to be married to a possessive woman like his wife."

"Do you feel that could happen to you with Diane?"

"No, not really. But just for a moment I felt sorry for Jack." Bart got up, went over to the fireplace, and leaned on the mantel. "Dad, I think loyalty plays a big part in helping the other person feel she belongs."

"What do you mean?"

"Many of the guys where I work part time are disloyal to their wives. They call them stupid and really cut them down. They even talk about some things that they have no business talking about. You'd think they want to please their buddies more than their wives."

"What have you learned from this that you can apply to your relationship with Diane?"

"Well, for one thing, I will never talk against her to other people. And rather than going out with the boys as I have done up to now, my first obligation will be to Diane. And," Bart paused and looked over at his father with a twinkle in his eye and a slight grin beginning at the corners of his mouth, "I think I have learned that if you and Mother get into disagreements with Diane, I'd better not support you. My first obligation will be to my wife. Even if she is dead wrong, I won't side with you. I'll probably not stick up for her either in a case like that, but I'll certainly not support you."

Dad chuckled, "Bart, today you sound like a wise old man. There are many who live and die without learning that if a marriage relationship is to be secure both partners must be loyal."

"Diane and I have decided that we are not going to let our children come between us."

"Please go on."

"We are not going to side with the children against each other for any reason. We have also agreed to take time each week for going out together. It will be sort of a special time that will be for just the two of us."

"Um hum. Sounds like you have been doing a lot of thinking."

"I know that self-respect is very important to Diane. I remember the times I have felt small and dumb and how painful it is. I want to be able to help Diane achieve a high degree of self-respect and self-fulfillment. I think by giving her economic security, loving her, and being loyal to her, I will help her to be happy.

"And what about your attitude toward the man's place in the home?" Bart's father paused to let his son think for a minute.

Bart turned abruptly from gazing at the dying fire and faced his father. "That's funny you'd bring that up now. I was talking about self-respect and fulfillment."

"Could there be a connection?"

Bart paused, then laughed a little. He moved to the sofa and sat down next to his father, saying, "I think I see what you're getting at."

Bart's father continued as he laid his hand on his son's knee. "Sometimes it's helpful to stop and consider just how we are supposed to function as husbands and fathers in the home. The man of the house can either build up or tear down the home."

"Dad, I don't want to act like a dictator to my wife even though some of my friends seem to think men are supposed to."

"What comes to your mind, Bart, when you think of a husband being a dictator to his wife?"

"I think of someone who believes he is superior to his wife or at least acts like it. He bosses her around and refuses to encourage her to make decisions on her own. If she has the courage to do so, he is sarcastic with her. He sticks his nose into everything his wife does and then corrects her on everything."

"It sounds as though you have a good understanding of what a dictator does. What are the results of such a relationship?"

"It causes a lot of resentment, anger, rebellion, hate, and even low self-esteem. I've noticed the wives of men who think they are supposed to be dictators. Most of them complain and criticize their husbands. Some of them are disloyal to their husbands and belittle and criticize them behind their backs. Some of these wives even seem listless and haggard. They appear depressed and apathetic, yet they seem to think their husbands are supposed to boss them around. I'll bet that if I were to boss Diane and if she were to let me do so, she would soon lose her respect for herself as well as her respect for me."

"Bart, I know what you mean and agree wholeheartedly with what you've said. Do you think though that husbands deliberately act like dictators so that they can have power over their wives?"

"Not really. I'm convinced that practically all of them want to do what's right. But I believe those who dominate their wives and children do it because they think that the man is the one who is supposed to be the boss."

"Yes, Bart, I agree. It could be that such attitudes stem from the Dark Ages when a man could actually sell his wife and children or beat them to death if he so desired. The irony of this whole business, so it seems to me, is that some men who are trying so hard to be good husbands and fathers are the very ones causing the most unhappiness to themselves and their loved ones. The consequences are women and children who live in rebellion or in apathy. There are even some women I've noticed who exercise control over their husbands. I get the feeling that they fear their husbands will try to control them if they don't get the power first. But, Bart, do you believe there should be a leader in the home?"

"Yes. In order for a family to get along well, there have to be those who will take leadership responsibilities. Both parents should be strong leaders. For example, each of them should know his own mind but not impose his thinking on anyone else. He can make decisions, but also encourage others to help him when appropriate. Each parent will want the children to be able to make good decisions as well. He will be honest, courteous, respectful, and loving with his spouse and children.

"You appear to have done your homework. Have you discussed these things with Diane? Have you talked with her in detail about her expectations regarding her and your responsibilities?"

"Well, we've talked some about them. I know she sees her responsibility as the homemaker. She wants to do the decorating and arranging. She also wants to be a good mother."

"How do you feel about this?"

"Oh, there may be a few things I'll want to have a say on about the house, but generally it can be her thing. Of course I will want to have a say in how we should rear our children."

"Will you and Diane work together to identify and reach agreement on your individual responsibilities?"

"Yes, I guess we should."

"How will you show respect for each other in the responsibilities you each hold?"

"I guess we've talked more about this than we have the responsibilities themselves. For one thing I'll try not to come home and criticize the way Diane has arranged the furniture or the way she is keeping house. I'll try to offer ideas when she asks for them. I have also made a vow within myself to support and encourage Diane in her work by recognizing her accomplishments and expressing my appreciation. You know, Dad, I don't think Diane will interfere with me in my occupation. While I've been going to school, she has never meddled with my school work. She has been great to support, encourage, and listen. She has never tried to tell me what to do. I think she will be the same when I get a full-time job after I finish my education."

"And how do you feel, son, when she supports and encourages you in your studies? How do you feel as you realize she respects you in your stewardship by never meddling or bossing you?"

"Oh, it makes me feel just great. I guess I get the feeling she trusts me. This makes me feel worthwhile. I feel good toward myself and toward her. I feel that I can do great things."

"Have you told her how this makes you feel?"

"I guess I haven't as much as I could. I usually sort of hint at it."

"Your telling her would not only compliment her but it would tend to increase that kind of behavior from her in the future, for she would know its effect on you."

"What you say makes sense. Let's turn to something else now. I think Diane and I can work through this business about the man's place in the home. One thing I'm still not too clear on is . . ." Bart paused and looked away from his father. "What I mean to say is sex. I've read a lot, and Diane and I have talked pretty freely about what we expect, but I'm still wondering about a lot of things. I don't quite know where to begin."

"It sounds like you have made a good beginning by talking with Diane about the sexual part of your future relationships."

Bart appeared encouraged by his father's words and spoke with greater confidence. "There seems to be so much contradictory information that is given out now. For example, do you think good sex makes a good relationship, or do you think a good relationship makes for good sex?"

"That's a rough question, Bart. In fact, some people might lead you to believe that it's an either/or situation when in reality it's not. People who have poor sexual relations usually get along poorly in other ways, and those who have a basically good relationship usually have good sex relations. It seems that everything that happens between husband and wife tends to affect or influence every other thing that happens."

"O.K., I'll buy that. It seems to me that women have as much right to experience sexual fulfillment as men. Do you agree?"

"Yes, I do. Women were made so that they could achieve satisfaction as well as men. But many men have for too long achieved sexual fulfillment in a rather selfish way with little regard for their wives in helping them meet their needs. In a good sexual relationship these things are crucial: a good relationship as a foundation; open and continuing communications, especially during sexual relations; some knowledge of physiology; courage to experiment; and humor."

"Diane is a fun girl. She has a ready, pleasant, sensitive kind of humor. I think if we remember not to take ourselves too seriously and to use humor to advantage, we'll have a good life."

"You seem to be on target, Bart."

"These were the things I wanted to talk about. Thanks for helping me."

"It's been my pleasure, Bart. One thing you might consider which we haven't had time to talk about tonight is how your past ways of fitting into our family will affect your behavior with Diane."

"You mean like being the oldest?"

"I was wondering . . ."

"I'll have to watch that I don't move in on Diane and tell her how to run the home. I know I have a tendency to be somewhat bossy, being the oldest and all. I wonder, since she is the youngest in her family, if she will try to get me to make decisions for her when she should be making them herself."

"That could happen to you. You may wish to talk over some of these things with Diane."

"Yes, I think I will. That's a whole new discussion. Well, I think I'll turn in. Thanks again, Dad."

Note: Concepts you may want to review are warmth and respect, p. 71; genuineness, p. 71; empathy, pp. 71-72; bonding, pp. 52-53; life-style, pp. 48-50.

REFERENCES

Adler, Alfred
    1964   Social Interest: A Challenge to Mankind. New York: Capricorn Books.

Allred, G. Hugh
    1968   Mission for Mother: Guiding the Child. Salt Lake City: Bookcraft.

Ansbacher, Heinz L., and Rowena R. Ansbacher
    1956   The Individual Psychology of Alfred Adler. New York: Basic Books.

Bandura, Albert, and Richard H. Walters
    1963   Social Learning and Personality Development. New York: Holt, Rinehart and Winston.

Beier, Ernst G.
    1966   The Silent Language of Psychotherapy. Chicago: Aldine Publishing Co.

Berenson, Bernard G., and Robert R. Carkhuff, eds.
    1967   Sources of Gain in Counseling and Psychotherapy. New York: Holt, Rinehart and Winston.

Bergin, Allen E., and Hans H. Strupp
  1972   Changing Frontiers in the Science of Psychotherapy. Chicago: Aldine
          Publishing Co.

Blood, Robert O., Jr.
  1969   Marriage (2d ed.). New York: The Free Press.

Buckley, Walter, ed.
  1968   Modern Systems Research for the Behavioral Scientist: A Sourcebook.
          Chicago: Aldine Publishing Co.

Cannon, Kenneth
  1968   What You Bring to Marriage. Provo, Utah: Brigham Young University
          Press.

Dewey, Edith A.
  1972   Understanding Our Human Nature. Toronto: printed by Edith A. Dewey.

Dreikurs, Rudolf
  1946   The Challenge of Marriage. New York: Duell, Sloan and Pearce.
          "The courage to be imperfect." Chicago: The Alfred Adler Institute.

Fisher, Seymour
  1973   The Female Orgasm: Psychology, Physiology, Fantasy. New York: Basic
          Books.

Glasser, William
  1965   Reality Therapy: A New Approach to Psychiatry. New York: Harper
          and Row.

Haley, Jay
  1963   Strategies of Psychotherapy. New York: Grune and Stratton.

Hartman, William E., and Marilyn A. Fithian
  1972   Treatment of Sexual Dysfunction: A Bio-Psycho-Social Approach. Long
          Beach: Center for Marital and Sexual Studies.

Klemer, Richard H.
  1965   Counseling in Marital and Sexual Problems: A Physician's Handbook.
          Baltimore: The Williams and Wilkins Co.

Maslow, Abraham H.
  1962   Toward a Psychology of Being. New York: D. Van Nostrand Co.
  1971   The Farther Reaches of Human Nature. New York: The Viking Press.

Masters, William H., and Virginia E. Johnson.
  1966   Human Sexual Response. Boston: Little, Brown and Co.

Ruesch, Jurgen
  1961   Therapeutic Communication. New York: W. W. Norton and Co.

Sicher, Lydia
  1955   "Education for freedom." The American Journal of Individual Psy-
          chology 11 (2).

Trainer, Joseph B.
    1965   Physiologic Foundations for Marriage Counseling. Saint Louis: The C.
            V. Mosby Co.

Watzlawic, Paul, et al.
    1967   Pragmatics of Human Communication: A Study of Interactional Pat-
            terns, Pathologies and Paradoxes. New York: W. W. Norton and Co.

FIVE

APPLICATION: ACHIEVING HORIZONTAL INTERACTION WITH OTHERS

11
MAN
AND SOCIETY

Just as we have the choice to move horizontally or vertically with members of our families, we have the same choice with our neighbors. There is much cooperation and beauty in the family of mankind, but there is also much ugliness and competition in which one person is pitted against another.

Many of the organizations and procedures men have built put great pressure on the individual to move against his neighbor in vertical fashion. Such traditions as definitions of success, rewards systems, zoning laws, unfair distribution of wealth, government licensing practices, differential law enforcement, unequal distribution of political power, competitive leisure activities for participants and spectators, and bureaucratic organizations act as agents to set one person against another.

This chapter presents for your consideration situations that bring about the bitter fruits of vertical movement with one's neighbor and suggestions on how these can be changed to more horizontal movement and its accompanying fruits of greater peace, tranquility, mutual respect, and love.

ROAD TO NOTHINGNESS
THE SITUATION

It was late. Roderick leaned forward, placed his elbows on the beautifully carved desk, and rested his forehead on his fingertips. His den, well furnished, symbolized his success. On richly paneled walls hung record trophy heads of deer and elk. And scattered about the large room were souvenirs representing distant travels. One twenty-six-foot wall was almost completely lined with awards, certificates, and medals testifying to Roderick's many successes.

He felt alarm and terror. "Why does it always have to be like this?" he wondered. "Whenever I'm alone and not busy I feel a great void. At fifty-six I should have learned to cope with these feelings. But they are only getting worse. Why is this so? Haven't I tried to make a success of my life?" These phrases came again to him:

"Hitch your wagon to a star."

"I don't care what you become, but whatever it is make sure you're the best."

"Shoot for the stars, for if you miss them you'll still be shooting high."

"No son of mine will be content with second best."

"My children were born to lead, not follow."

"Only A grades are worth bringing home. If you get a B, you can forget it. If you get a C or less, you might as well go bury yourself."

"Be an executive."

"Associate with those who can do something for you. Don't waste your time with those who can't help move you ahead."

"Put on a show of wealth and success. Others will then tend to believe it is so, and it will be to your advantage."

Roderick slammed his fist on the desk. "I've done all those things. I've been a leader all my life in my vocation, church, and community!" he exclaimed to himself in a tone of despair.

"What's wrong with me? I'm a success. But why am I so miserable?" He spoke the words quietly to himself, but with an intensity that betrayed his helplessness.

He thought of his wife who had been a stranger to him for the past twenty years. They spoke courteously and formally to one another, but as travellers who meet briefly and continue on separate journeys. Their words were civilized, but their minds and hearts were separated. They might as well have lived thousands of miles apart.

He thought of their more intimate moments, which were few— maybe once every two or three months, and knew he made love to someone he no longer understood. Even his children seemed distant. They were like foreigners to him.

He next turned his attention to his colleagues at work. He knew they respected and even feared him. His mood changed as he recalled the last meeting they had together. It never ceased to amaze him how he could intimidate other people if he used just the right approach. He recalled how he had been able to dominate the proceedings with his forceful personality. He knew the power of many words strongly spoken, but was not so aware of how skillful he had become in phrasing his ideas so that other people were led to feel the emotional impact he wanted them to feel rather than to think critically about what he was saying.

Roderick's chest swelled with pride as he thought of many triumphant moments in various meetings he attended where he controlled the proceedings so that the outcomes were as he wished. The feelings of exhilaration lasted only a few minutes, however, and were quickly replaced again by a void.

"Why is it always like this?" he said quietly to himself, "Why can't I find peace?"

DISCUSSION

The tragedy for Roderick is that he will never find peace if he continues moving in the same direction. He can gain all the prestigious positions within his reach, acquire all the wealth within his view, and still not achieve a quiet, stable peace; for his life-style is faulty. He will find peace only when he decides to travel in a different direction.

When Roderick was growing up, his well-meaning parents indoctrinated him with the idea that to be worthwhile he had to be the best at whatever he did. This meant he had to outdo other people. Therefore, anyone who did better than he was an enemy who threatened his self-worth. Roderick had to get ahead of such people in order to feel worthy and acceptable to his parents and to himself.

He also developed a belief system in which he felt he had to attain leadership positions in order to be acceptable to himself, loved ones, and his God. He had built his friendships to achieve such purposes. And as he made friends for what he could get from people, he suspected that they did the same in their professed friendship for him. He doubted deep within himself his capacity to attract people for the sake of friendship alone.

Much was demanded of him when he was growing up, but he was also treated specially. He was his mother's and father's favorite child. He knew it and so did his brothers and sisters. If he pouted or looked sad, he got his way. If he screamed and yelled, he got his way. And if all else failed, he knew he could tell his mother that she did not love him anymore, let the tears stream down his cheeks, and she would give in. He learned in his family how to gain power over other people and continued to develop and refine his techniques as an adult.

His special treatment and his success with power at home bore bitter fruit. He grew up thinking that it was his right to take from other people without considering too much the consequences for them. Also his feeling of worth became connected to the amount of power he was able to gain over others. This had its genesis at home where he perceived he was worthwhile and important to his family to the degree that he was able to get them to do his bidding, usually by yelling, screaming, or crying for his way. He was able to have an emotional impact on his loved ones and to get them to notice him and to give him service. As his parents paid him off for his powerful acts, he learned to believe that he was worthwhile only when he could obtain power over other people.

Roderick refined his power tactics as he grew older and became expert in their use. Few were the meetings he did not control. Few were the outcomes he could not have predicted beforehand.

Always trying to be superior to others contains its own built-in failures. There are always those who will be better, and there are times when one must follow the leadership of another. In like manner, the feeling that one is worthwhile only to the degree that he has power over others contains its own failure. People may give in to those who are power-oriented, but they seldom if ever truly love them. People tend to place an emotional barrier between themselves and those who are power-oriented. As the powerful person senses his alienation from deep, meaningful relationships with others, he typically attempts to bring people closer to him by asserting more power. This drives those who could provide him with deep relationships further from him. His attempts become circular as he drives people further and further from him, including his wife, children, and colleagues.

And there is the danger that he who desires power for the sake of power will always be eager to grab even more. The power-oriented person never has enough. There are always those whom he considers more powerful and more worthwhile, and he must compete with them. Also since the power-oriented person is moving vertically against other people, he feels that he must be continually on his guard against all who might threaten to undermine him. Other people become potential enemies.

Another very important reason for Roderick's not being at peace with himself is his betrayal of basic values. He had been taught not to steal and cheat. Yet, he felt so much pressure to outdo anyone else that he had begun cheating in school to maintain high grades. He had continued this basic practice in his adult life. He colored his reports to provide a more favorable impression of himself to his superiors. He had learned to parade himself and his accomplishments before other people with the main purpose of impressing them, not to present information factually and accurately. In his financial dealings his attitude was not "What is fair and right?" but "How can I get the most without going against the letter of the law or getting caught?"

Outwardly Roderick's most important values had to do with getting ahead of other people, but he had deep-seated values which included honesty and respect for the rights and welfare of his fellowmen. His betrayal of such basic values was bound to disrupt his feelings of satisfaction even though he was not consciously aware of the causes.

In order to find peace of mind, Roderick must learn to move horizontally with his fellowman. This will require much hard work and periods of frustration and discouragement, but if he is persistent, he will be able to learn the necessary new ways of relating.

All people strive to belong to those who are significant to them. This may also include a desire to belong with their God as well as with their family members and friends. Failure to achieve this results in feelings of loneliness, alienation, and nothingness. In order to belong to his God, his fellowman, and himself, Roderick must be true to his basic values of honesty in his relationships with other people. He must also learn to give up his desire to dominate anyone else. He will have to learn that he can be loved and worthwhile without being powerful and that control over other people tends to alienate him from them.

Roderick must also learn that he himself is of value. He does not have to be the best, the most outstanding, or the richest. He can learn that presents, gifts, and power will not buy the love of wife, children, or friends. Warm, empathetic, respectful companionship is of greatest worth.

Note: Concepts you may want to review are vertical goals, pp. 16-23, 43; belonging, pp. 45-46; life-style, pp. 48-50; social linkage, pp. 44-45; bonding, pp. 52-53; modeling, pp. 53-54; communal interest, pp. 47-48; self-esteem, pp. 46-47; genuineness, p. 71; warmth and respect, p. 71; practice, pp. 54-55.

BROTHERHOOD AND WAR

THE SITUATION

As two college-age students were leaving the school cafeteria, one of them made this comment on the war: "I've got a cousin over there. He says it's real fun shooting those gooks." He laughed as he turned his head toward his companion who responded with a chuckle of approval.

DISCUSSION

War seems to bring out the worst in many of us. It is often much easier and safer to turn our frustration, anger, hostility, and hatred toward a far distant fellow labeled *enemy* than to work at solving our problems with spouses, children, in-laws, friends, and other people. Many of us who have low self-esteem also find it easier to direct self-hate toward an enemy than to work through our difficulties in such a way that we learn to think better of ourselves.

The vertically oriented person may even delight in warfare and feel intense hatred for strange enemies. The horizontally oriented person is saddened by war and pulls the trigger and releases bombs with feelings of anguish and sorrow. His heart is full of care and concern, even for his enemy.

Note: Concepts you may want to review are vertical goals, pp. 16-23, 43; communal interest, pp. 47-48; genuineness, p. 71; self-esteem, pp. 46-47; warmth and respect, p. 71; empathy, pp. 71-72.

THE NEIGHBORHOOD HELPER

THE SITUATION

She was small, but a bundle of tremendous energy. She seemed to be here, there, and everywhere, and at almost the same time. No one in the neighborhood could be sick twenty-four hours before Samantha was there cleaning house, offering advice, and taking care of the one who was ill. The following is typical of Samantha's desire to help.

"Well, good morning, Samantha. I didn't realize anyone was up this early."

"I hardly slept a wink thinking about you last night. I rushed over as soon as I could this morning. Now you go right to bed and I'll take over for you." Samantha brushed past her neighbor who stood in the doorway partially blocking its opening.

"Samantha, really I'm not that ill. I think it's just a twenty-four-hour bug. I'm sure I'll be all right tomorrow." She remained standing by the doorway.

"Nonsense! You can never tell about these things. You've got your husband and children to think about. You go to bed. I'll be here and you won't have a thing to worry about." Samantha took her by the hand and led her firmly to her bed.

Later on the same day Samantha counseled her neighbor, "You really should get a different dishwashing detergent. The kind you use leaves spots on your dishes. Now you stay down. I'm going to run over to my place to get my detergent. Now you stay put. Hear?" Samantha almost flew out the door and was back within ten minutes. She busied herself about the kitchen until the breakfast dishes were washed and dried. There was not a spot on any dish. Samantha proudly placed them in her neighbor's cupboard, slightly rearranging one cupboard so that the dishes were placed more efficiently.

For dinner Samantha prepared a special meal for her sick neighbor. She located a tray and expertly arranged everything so that her friend could eat while still in bed. She fussed around telling her what she should and should not eat and how important it was to get plenty of rest.

"Why is it that I resent this woman?" thought Samantha's neighbor. "She is so kind and considerate. Is it that I'm just not appreciative? Is there something wrong with me? I can't help it; I can't stand her coming in like she does. I feel nothing is private when she is around." The neighbor turned over in her bed and stared at designs in the wallpaper as she worked to shut out Samantha's chatter.

DISCUSSION

The tragedy of the Samanthas is that they tend to use the principle of helping one's neighbor as an unconscious strategy for gaining worth and feeling important. In doing so, they assert their superiority over other people.

Samantha grew up in a family where she found her place by taking care of those younger and more helpless than she. As they grew up, she felt threatened and tried to keep them helpless by undermining their attempts to make their own decisions and care for themselves in independent ways. Samantha felt, in her own illogical way, that she could be worthwhile in her family only as long as she took good care of other people. She felt she had to be superior in order to have a place. This feeling generalized to other relationships and found expression as she became sensitive to those in possible need and quickly moved in to help them. She often erred in her perception and moved in where she was not needed or wanted.

Samantha always gave her help in a superior way. She tended to give advice freely and to do things for others that they would just as soon do for themselves. She became known as *Mother* among those who knew her. The name was applied with raised eyebrows and a knowing tone of voice.

She created mixed emotions wherever she went. Those she helped usually resented her because of the superior attitude with which she gave help, the intrusive way she moved in, and her critical comments about the way they had been managing before she appeared on the scene. They felt guilty because of all the help she would give and because of her quick comments such as "But I was only trying to help" when anyone tried to preserve a degree of privacy and independence.

Samantha's major goal was to help others so that she would feel worthwhile and of value. Her compulsion was to be needed in order to belong. This made her relations with other people vertical. Her faulty life-style caused her to feel useless and of no worth around those who were independent, strong, and healthy.

If Samantha is to have any peace of mind and experience good relations with others, she must learn to interact in a horizontal manner. If she can learn that others will like her, appreciate her, and befriend her without her taking care of and doing things for them, she will discover peace and serenity. She must learn to treat other people as equals if she is to find true happiness and contentment and be of greatest worth to her neighbors.

She must also learn to give her help in a horizontal manner only when it is needed or requested and in so doing be respectful of the rights and privacy of those being helped. True assistance to one's friend should leave the friend with greater feelings of love, confidence in her own ability to grow and develop, and a higher level of self-esteem. These are evidences of horizontal relationships. Resentment, anger, depression, guilt, low self-esteem, and a lower level of self-confidence are results of vertical behaviors.

Note: Concepts you may want to review are vertical goals, pp. 16-23, 43; life-style, pp. 48-50; communal interest, pp. 47-48; empathy, pp. 71-72; warmth and respect, p. 71; self-esteem, pp. 46-47.

A PROGRAM THAT ALIENATES

THE SITUATION

He had been running all of his life. But he could not explain the reason even to himself.

He was a religious teacher of youth, well known in the area for his innovative and creative projects to help youth learn. He was a sixteen-hour-a-day man who used almost every hour to develop and implement teaching and learning programs. Even during regular sleeping hours he would awaken with new ideas. They pestered him until he got up, wrote them down, and began their development.

A common theme in all of his programs was competition. He felt the most effective way for his students to learn scriptures, religious history, and doctrine was to set one against the other in games where the goal was to win by showing superior knowledge.

He felt his programs were working well. Students he taught won almost all of the competitive meets they entered. The use of competition to gain religious knowledge had expanded far beyond his classroom. He had developed a pool of over fifty different kinds of competitive activities to stimulate learning. Many teachers were asking for his game plans.

And yet, in unguarded moments he was haunted by doubts. They lasted for only fleeting moments at any one time, for he had learned to push down anything that threatened to disrupt his drive to move ahead.

If one were able to view this teacher and his students during unguarded moments, he would view such things as a beautiful young girl crying quietly while performing under pressure. He would see students stomping out of class after losing a challenge, hear them laughing loudly, see them jumping up and down, scowling, frowning, and hear them complaining. He would also sense a tension that is intense and at times excruciating.

DISCUSSION

The purpose of the teacher's competitive games was to stimulate his students to improve their learning of scriptures, doctrine, and history. He was able to demonstrate beyond reasonable doubt the accomplishment of his goal with his top students. Therefore, if one were to observe the accomplishments of a few students, he would be impressed.

But education, especially religious education, is far more than the memorization of names, dates, and events. Real education should be concerned with the total individual, his attitudes, emotions, and behavior beyond simple rote memorization of facts. Comprehensive evaluation of such education concerns itself with how students translate their knowledge into their behavior with one another. And how do students treat one another during competitive games?

During the process of competition some students learned to parade their superiority. Others were experiencing ridicule from fellow students. For some the reward of winning became so important that all means justified the end. Therefore, many experienced rewards for cheating. Others saw them cheat and gain their rewards from the religious institution and felt angry. Many felt that their fellow students were agents who shamed them. Those put on the spot who could not come up with correct answers were usually demeaned by some of their fellow students who were all too willing to answer for them in order to show their own superiority.

During the competitive process they were also learning the excitement of winning and the fear of losing that had little bearing on basic religious beliefs. In addition they were learning behaviors of discourtesy that undermined their fellow students' confidence. The goal was to win the game and defeat others, and many in every class learned subtle and vicious strategies that would shake their fellow student's confidence in themselves and make them unsure and hesitant. This increased the chances of winning for those who learned to employ such tactics against other people.

Quite often in competition the same students tend to win and the same students tend to lose. The winners usually remain winners while the losers remain losers. As a result many students tend to equate religious matters with failure whenever competition is used to stimulate their learning.

What are the emotions of students when they are involved in competitive situations? This question has great implications, for what is it that students are really learning in the process of competing? Panic, fear, shame, embarrassment, anger, and even hate are common emotions to those involved in competition. Also closely related are feelings of self-doubt and even low self-esteem. Not only do the losers feel these emotions, but also the winners. Emotions of care, love, concern for others, and courteous respectful behavior tend to be far removed from those involved in such vertical interaction.

What do principles of learning (see pages 52-58) suggest to us about the learning of students who are involved in competition with their fellows in a religious or any other setting? First, the principle of bonding suggests that to the degree students feel fear, panic, shame, embarrassment, anger, hate, self-doubt, and low self-esteem, they will tend to bond such feelings to those teachers and institutions employing competitive tactics. In other words students will experience these same feelings whenever they are around such teachers and institutions. Such feelings can even become bonded to religious as well as other buildings so that when some people approach a church house, they again feel the negative feelings they experienced previously. As a result they will tend to avoid such buildings, people, and organizations in order to escape these bad feelings. Whenever competition is emphasized in religious settings, many people become trained to stay away from religious institutions or else they approach such institutions with mixed feelings. Second, in the process of competing to acquire knowledge, students experience and thereby learn to strive for superiority over their fellowmen, to parade their own knowledge at the expense of others, to develop techniques for putting others down, to undermine the progress of others, to be discourteous, and to even cheat. They learn that their fellowman is an enemy against whom they must be on guard. Their values tend to become distorted since their objective in life is to walk against their brother rather than hand in hand with him. Rote memorization of dates, events, and ideas usually does not last as long as those things one actually experiences firsthand. This suggests that negative relationships and accompanying bad feelings are the things which students will tend to learn whenever competition is used.

How then are teachers to teach? A teacher should first understand himself. The teacher referred to previously had been competing all of his life. He had never been sure of his parents' love. He felt somewhat alienated from them and felt that he had to prove himself over and over to them. He had competed with his brothers and sisters for his parents' love and affection. He strove mightily to outdo his brothers and sisters, to point out their faults and weaknesses to his parents, and to parade his own superiority. This life-style he took into the classroom. And as he strove to teach well, to have the approval of his supervisors as well as his parents, he imposed his own competitive behaviors on his students.

Teachers can do several things to encourage horizontal relationships in the classroom. First, they need to understand themselves in order to avoid the pitfalls of the negative aspects of their own life-styles. Second, teachers must also be aware of students' behavior with one another as they gain knowledge. It is at the interpersonal level that knowledge should be applied. The teacher should always be ready to stimulate courtesy, respect, cooperation, and mutual encouragement among his students. By-products of such behavior are care, love, concern, high self-esteem, and self-confidence. Third, teachers must emphasize the application of basic principles to everyday life outside of the classroom as well as inside. Religious teachers and students should, for example, encourage concern for other people by practicing working through interpersonal problems in productive ways, tutoring those who need help, assisting the widowed and orphaned, visiting the sick, and working to improve the social and physical ecology of their surroundings. The by-products of such activities will most often be feelings of self-worth, oneness with mankind, and a quiet joy. Security and serenity will also be common companions.

Note: Concepts you may want to review are life-style, pp. 48-50; vertical goals, pp.

THE CLASSROOM:
IMPLICATIONS FOR TEACHERS AND CLASS MEMBERS

THE SITUATION

Bill pulled himself up to his full six-foot height, shot a challenging look at the rebellious class member, and said in a sarcastic tone of voice, "Ben, if you had read the lesson beforehand you would not be asking such questions."

He immediately sensed the whole class pull back from him and, feeling the threat and not knowing what to do about it, he hurried on in his lesson presentation. He heard himself reading and talking to the class and felt as if he were separated from them by a heavy fog. He tried to do a better job by giving more information in a rapid, business-like manner.

In his own mind he seemed to be fading in and out of the picture. He heard himself talking to them, speaking the words almost mechanically with his mind on the job of teaching one minute and on questioning what was going on the next minute. Such phrases as the following found their way in and out of his consciousness as he continued to teach: Why did Ben put me on the spot again with his question? Why do they ask so many questions when I've got so much material to cover? I work hard to get all my facts and stories. Why don't they appreciate my efforts? You'd think they would realize that I am the teacher, not they.

DISCUSSION

Bill was a responsible individual whose definition of teaching was a vertical one. Being a child who had experienced much responsibility when taking care of those smaller than himself, he approached his teaching assignment in the same manner. He felt that he had to know all answers, that he had to be the repository of all knowledge, and, semiconsciously, that class members should defer to him. The tone he set was of a superior person preaching to his inferiors. Class members naturally rebelled and, through many subtle and overt means, communicated their displeasure. Some slept, others looked out the windows or up at the ceiling, and others, like Ben, baited him.

Bill had a good, quick mind, but in order to be more effective as a teacher, he had to learn to relate to his class members in a horizontal, equalitarian manner. He had to learn to share the responsibilities of the lessons with them, to let them help him carry the burden. He had to learn to listen respectfully to their comments and to give up verbal and nonverbal signals that communicated, "I am superior to you."

As he struggled to learn to relate more horizontally in class, Bill found greater satisfaction in teaching. And he sensed that those in his class also enjoyed it more.

For those who are presently teaching, the following more detailed discussion of teaching guidelines is presented. The purpose of these guidelines is to assist you in structuring your class and presenting yourself and lessons in such a manner that class members will be encouraged to achieve desired class objectives.

One of the most critical components of the teaching-learning processes is the teacher. The effective teacher encourages learning by being warm and friendly, understanding, empathetic, sincere, honest, relaxed, a good communicator, well organized, confident in himself, able to smile readily, competent, approachable, able to admit to imperfection himself, and ready to admit that he does not have all of the answers. Probably no teacher exhibits all of the above qualities, for everyone is subject to inadequacies and mistakes. One effective way to improve, however, is to concentrate on improving in one area each week.

Closely related to these twelve traits of the effective teacher is the general attitude with which he approaches his class. If he tends to be autocratic, as indicated by the vertical movement column on the following chart, he will tend to exhibit the attitudes and behaviors listed there and get the suggested responses from class members. However, to the extent that he establishes a horizontal movement with them, he and they will tend to have a more enjoyable and productive series of experiences.

It is recommended that you go over the chart and become familiar with the differences between the two kinds of relationships. All of

Teaching/Learning

Vertical Movement   **Horizontal Movement**

Characteristics of Teachers

authority figure . . . . knowledgeable co-worker
superior . . . . equality and mutual respect
imposes own will . . . . encourages self-determination
has the answers . . . . search together
dominates . . . . guides, resource centered
I am the boss . . . . we are working together
over-powers . . . . influences
demands . . . . wins cooperation
restricts choices . . . . encourages freedom of choice from alternatives
pressures . . . . stimulates

Characteristics of Class Members

dependent . . . . interdependent
will not risk . . . . will risk
fearful of help . . . . request help
distrust . . . . trust
discouraged . . . . encouraged
rebellious . . . . friendly

Class Atmosphere

room on pedestal only for superior . . . . room for all — no pedestal
tradition bound . . . . innovative
perfection now . . . . improvement
rigid . . . . flexible
personal . . . . objective
mistake centered . . . . strength centered
punishment centered . . . . consequence centered
prestige centered . . . . situation, problem, people centered
competition . . . . cooperation

your lesson plans and teaching strategies should be such that they will stimulate horizontal interaction. In fact your success will probably be directly related to the degree that you are able to foster such relationships during the lessons.

The effective teacher is able to make the material relevant to the needs and interests of his students and to present it in novel and stimulating ways. The following are ideas and methods for accomplishing these purposes.

- An effective teacher actively involves his class members in the lesson presentation whenever possible.
- He deals with the realistic, concrete experiences of life whenever his subject matter allows.
- He encourages class members to read assigned reading before class.
- He stimulates members to share success experiences whenever possible.
- He has class members simulate husband-wife and parent-child interactions by having them role-play real-life situations when appropriate in order to help them come up with successful solutions.
- He will occasionally use panel discussions if these are appropriate.
- He will use visual aids (e.g., writing on the blackboard) whenever possible and appropriate.
- He will follow up by having members in a class on human behavior who committed themselves to work at changing behavior report their results.
- He will use a variety of techniques for helping class members learn new ideas.

Note: Concepts you may want to review are life-style, pp. 48-50; vertical goals, pp. 16-23, 43; communal interest, pp. 47-48; warmth and respect, p. 71; empathy, pp. 71-72.

ALIENATION OR ALLEGIANCE: A PROBLEM FOR THE COURTS

THE SITUATION

He put on his black robe. When he was younger his shoulders were straight and extended, but now they sagged as if weighted down with the years he had spent making difficult decisions. His eyes moved down over the day's schedule of cases, and he sighed as he recognized the names heading the list.

The Honorable Mr. Smith entered his courtroom and proudly responded to the opening ceremonies. He had known extreme poverty as a child and had fought his way from the wrong side of town, through prejudice and ignorance, until he had arrived at, in his opinion, the right side. He considered himself a self-made man and believed that everyone else could accomplish what he had if they had the same courage and determination.

He looked over the two youths before him and tried to hide his revulsion. Both were from affluent families. His lower lip stuck out, betraying his thoughts. "This is the third time this one has been here and the second time for the other. Too much too soon," he muttered to himself. "If they had struggled like me, they wouldn't have such weak characters."

He read the charges and listened to the prosecutor state them at the same time, his lower lip protruding even farther. His jaw tightened. He raised his eyes and peered through bushy eyebrows into the mocking eyes of the blond youth.

"Haven't I seen you in my court before?"

"Maybe," the youth sneered, meeting his gaze.

The Honorable Mr. Smith fought to control himself. In his youth he would have responded to such an insult by physically beating the offender until he had cried "Uncle!"

He averted his eyes from the youth, fastened them on the list of charges, and asked without looking up, "And what do you have to say for yourself? Did you or did you not participate in breaking car windows in a used car lot, causing five hundred dollars damage?"

"If you say so, I guess we did" was the sneering response.

Again the judge fought to control himself. The case continued until both admitted their guilt. Now it was time for them to be sentenced.

The Honorable Mr. Smith paced the floor of his chambers. What to do? This was the big question. His gut-level reaction was to crush them as he would have if they had sneered and mocked him in his

298

youth. But he fought this feeling down. The questions I must ask
are: What is best for them? What will make them change? How can
they be won over to society rather than alienated from it? He quick-
ened his pacing as the questions came to him.

DISCUSSION

The courts have a tremendous potential for good or for evil. They can,
through their fair and reasonable administration of justice, win the
allegiance of citizens or alienate them. To the degree that court officials harass and punish or seek for revenge and seek to hurt accused
citizens, to that same degree they will encourage certain citizens to
disassociate themselves from judicial institutions. They may even become alienated from the larger society. The Honorable Mr. Smith
could become sarcastic with the two youths and sentence them for the
purpose of hurting them, but this is not the wisest solution.

In contrast, courts will tend to win the allegiance of citizens when
justice is administered in a fair, friendly, and reasonable manner, and
when the emphasis is on restitution, not punishment. Mr. Smith was
demonstrating this approach when he refused to become upset or angry
with the youths when they responded sarcastically. Rather than trying
to hurt them, he would, for example, help them arrange to pay for the
damages by their working at the used car lot where they broke the
windows or some other place of their reasonable choosing. The youths
would be kept under the influence of the courts until full restitution
would be made.

There are definite reasons why anger and punishment do not
correct the behavior of many of those coming before the courts. There
are those who feel that life is unfair, that people are out to get other
people, and that power is important. When judges get angry and pass
sentences where punishment is emphasized, they tend to meet the expectations of such people and thereby stimulate them to continue thinking and acting as they have been. A prestigious judge's angry responses
to mocking eyes and sarcastic comments are great payoff for the
power-oriented criminal. He expects punishment; and when it comes,
he is paid off and thus is encouraged to continue the same behaviors.
His goal may be to be notorious and infamous, and a judge's preaching
coupled with newspaper articles on his crimes and unruly actions in

court enable him to achieve this goal. The judge and reporters become ignorant allies in his attempts to pursue his purposes.

Such an individual may feel that the only way he can belong is to be noticed for his nefarious acts. Society must win the allegiance of such men by helping them learn that people will not pay them off for their notorious acts. They will receive payoff only for their constructive, cooperative behaviors.

As in the case of the Honorable Mr. Smith, a judge's personality may pay off an accused man. Mr. Smith's goal was, in many ways, similar to that of the two youths. He had wanted power over others and had found ways of asserting it through his role as judge. The one youth sensed his vulnerability and with mocking eyes and sarcastic tones called into question the judge's authority and power. Mr. Smith's first impulse was to get angry. If he had, the youth would have gained power over him and achieved his goal.

Judges should know themselves and how their behavior on the bench contributes to or detracts from the horizontal movement of those appearing before them so that they can relate horizonally with them and thus be helpful.

Permissiveness is never a good alternative in the treatment of criminals, whereas firm and friendly treatment that emphasizes restitution rather than punishment is horizontally effective. In many cases the criminal will have to be locked up so that society can be protected from him. But this can be done with friendliness, rather than with anger and hostility. While he is confined, those working with him should constantly work to help him relate horizontally with his fellowmen.

Note: Concepts you may want to review are life-style, pp. 48-50; social linkage, pp. 44-45; holism, pp. 50-52; vertical goals, pp. 16-23, 43; communal interest, pp. 47-48; belonging, pp. 45-46; bonding, pp. 52-53; warmth and respect, p. 71; empathy, pp. 71-72; genuineness, p. 71; natural consequences, pp. 85-86; logical consequences, p. 86.

PRISON: A TRAGEDY

THE SITUATION

Gale had always been treated as a special person. He was a dark, handsome young man of slender build who had a way with most women. His mother had spoiled him to a formidable degree. What he could not get from her with flattery and sweet words he got through skillfully executed tantrums. He learned that these same behaviors would work with other people. As a result he developed a life-style of taking rather than giving. He looked upon himself as someone who was indeed special with rights and privileges to which only he was entitled. He expected people to serve him, to respond to his wishes and commands. He expected the most favored portions at meals, the best clothes, expensive gifts, and he usually got them.

One technique he used with others (which was learned and re-fined at home) when they did not give him his way was to hurt them and/or make them feel guilty (see the discussion on counterhurting, pages 20-22). This worked wonderfully with his mother. He thought nothing of lashing out at others who did not give in to him and blaming them for his own mistakes.

Shortly after he finished school, Gale took a job with a large firm. Every day he handled large sums of money.

He was with the firm two years when his feelings of frustration and anger reached a crescendo because he was considered by the management as simply one of the employees and was not given special privileges nor advanced in rank rapidly. Gale felt this was unfair and was deeply hurt. Hadn't he always been special? Wasn't he better looking than the others? Couldn't he talk to the women customers better than anyone else in the company? These were typical of the thoughts that went through his mind many times a day, day after day.

His thoughts gradually changed. "I'll make you pay; you just wait; I'll get even." And he began taking money from the funds entrusted to his care. He felt at first that he was taking only what was rightfully his since he believed he was being paid only a fraction of his real worth. He also felt secretly glad that he was getting even with them for all of their slights and unfair treatment. These feelings were coupled with the conviction that if he were found out, he would be forgiven. Had not his mother always bailed him out before?

However, events did not go quite as he planned. His thefts were discovered and within six months he was tried, convicted, and sent to prison. His mother could not save him.

Gale said a tearful goodbye to his young wife and his mother before he climbed into the van which took him away. He was a confused, bewildered young man. He thought, "This cannot be happening. There is some mistake. Surely they will stop the van and let me out before it gets there." But they did not.

Having been over-protected and pampered, Gale was ill-prepared for the challenges and dangers of prison life. His was the typical prison. Habitual criminals and first-time offenders were put together in the same cells, exercise yards, work details, and mess halls. Veteran rapists, murderers, homosexuals, and sadists mingled freely with the young and naive.

Gale was in prison less than a week when he sensed that the warden and his guards were not the only group exercising control over the prisoners. It was in his second week that tragedy struck.

He was on a work detail with several of the prisoners when the one who seemed to be boss, a big six-foot two-inch veteran of many years in prisons, began to make sexual advances. Gale pretended to ignore him. The man's sweet talk changed to anger, then rage, and he knocked Gale down. Gale had never been in a physical fight in his life and, being frail, felt himself no match for him. He trembled with fear and cowered when he fell. The man then leaned down and talked kindly to him.

"I'm sorry I lost my head. All you need to do is be nice and you'll get along fine. I'll protect you. You'll see. You'll need me in a place like this."

He lifted Gale as easily as a man would lift a child and set him on his feet. Gale continued to ignore the so-called boss as he continued to make sexual advances. Suddenly, Gale saw him double up his right fist, and that was all he remembered for a time.

He awoke and knew the other man had had his way.

The weeks stretched into months and Gale learned to fit in to the prisoner's structure. He traded his beauty, fear, and self-respect for a degree of security provided by his protector.

At first their relationship had been forced, but the Wolf, as the man was called, was kind to Gale. Gale learned to respect him in a sense and to be thankful for his protection against all of the other bullies. He was Wolf's property and no one bothered him except Wolf.

As time passed, home, wife and mother seemed like a far distant dream to Gale. Prison life was the only reality he knew. Here and now only was important.

His wife's visits were unsatisfactory to both. At first he was ashamed. He could not tell her what had been forced upon him. He began to feel angry with her but didn't know why. He then felt a cold detachment. And as his term drew to a close, he knew he could never go back to the families he knew. Where could he go? He did not know.

DISCUSSION

This is a story repeated over and over in the prisons throughout the land. The philosophy behind our traditional laws and prisons is that the way to stop crime is to hurt criminals. If they suffer enough, they will stop committing criminal acts. It is punishment, and it has been generally ineffective.

Our prisons have been and still are universities for criminals. These institutions tend to alienate prisoners from their families and from the larger society. Some prisoners are forced and coerced by other inmates into acts that are completely contrary to their basic values. Prisons are spawning grounds for innumerable acts of injustice and evil.

Too many of those who enter prison naive and hopeful leave full of self-disgust, distrust of others, and anger toward their fellowman. Many who enter prison full of hate and anger toward society find ample evidence in prison to justify their life-styles. Rather than helping them become responsible, loyal citizens, our prisons, because of their rules, physical settings, structures, and traditions, are geared to estrange, alienate, and dehumanize. As a result they have failed. The high recidivism rate provides us with ample evidence that this is so.

Those in prison are our fellowmen with rights to progression and development. Rather than desiring to humiliate, punish, and get revenge, those who set up laws for and work in our prisons must desire to help prisoners learn how to behave horizontally, to bring back into full fellowship those who have transgressed.

In order for this to be accomplished, our laws, courts, and prisons will have to (1) emphasize restitution where possible; (2) allow each inmate whenever possible to continue close contact with his family (husbands and wives should have extended visits in private each week; this will help them continue to identify with the real world outside of their prison walls, and problems of homosexuality will be greatly diminished); (3) carefully segregate inmates to protect those who would fall prey to the ruthless appetites of the more powerful; (4) employ judges, wardens, and guards who genuinely care for other people and who can communicate this care within the necessary limits of fairness, justice, and firmness (they must not be vindictive, brutal, or sadistic since these attitudes tend to dehumanize and perpetuate criminal behavior); (5) provide a system of justice that is equal for all (too often we have a justice for the wealthy or those with powerful connections and another for those who are poor and lack such connections, but our laws must be fairly and equally applied if they are to win the allegiance of our citizens, including those convicted of unlawful acts); (6) provide training and licensing practices that will enable people to return to full, productive citizenship (training may include the development of skills that can enable one to get along respectfully with others as well as skills that can enable him to get good jobs; furthermore, ex-prisoners must have access to licensing that will allow them to practice their vocations).

There are no simple answers to the problems of correcting the behavior of lawbreakers and helping them want to be law-abiding, useful, and constructive citizens. The old ways have not worked; new ways must be found. Concepts that may help point the direction include:

- Estrangement begets alienation.
- Anger begets anger.
- Hurt begets hurt.
- Punishment begets revenge.
- Brutality begets brutality.
- Belonging begets loyalty.
- Fairness begets allegiance.
- Respect begets respect.
- Caring begets caring.

304

- Love begets love.

Note: Concepts you may want to review are life-style, pp. 48-50; social linkage, pp. 44-45; holism, pp. 50-52; natural consequences, pp. 85-86; logical consequences, p. 86; communal interest, pp. 47-48; bonding, pp. 52-53; warmth and respect, p. 71; genuineness, p. 71; empathy, pp. 71-72; modeling, pp. 53-54.

TITLES AND BROTHERHOOD
THE SITUATION

The social group, which was an affluent one, was largely made up of professional people. The following conversation took place in one of their meetings.

"I think we should show greater respect for one another."

"What do you mean, Philip?"

"Well, I've been thinking. We have many in our group who have spent long years in intensive study and I believe we should recognize that. For example, we have many college professors, medical doctors, and dentists among us. I think it is all right to call them by their regular names, but wouldn't it be showing even greater respect to preface their names with the title of doctor?"

The rest of the meeting time was taken up by a rather emotional and at times heated discussion on the propriety of the suggestion. A large part of the group argued with intensity in favor of its adoption, and another part argued with equal intensity against it. They could not reach a decision and decided to drop the issue for a while.

DISCUSSION

As one considers the propriety of calling a person in his group by his professional title rather than by his name, he needs also to consider the reasons certain professions use titles. Some of these reasons are public knowledge, others are not. Some of the more public reasons have to do with identifying the service the individual can perform and expressing respect for his training and service.

The not-so-public reasons may include placing the professional on a higher pedestal than other people and giving him more status than those he serves so that he can have more power and influence over them. These reasons also include attempts for instilling in clients a deference to the professional so that the quality of services he provides and the fees he charges are seldom questioned by his clients or patients.

The professional title designates not only a service but tends to divide and separate one man from another and to place one above another. Superior-inferior vertical relationships are emphasized, and equality and oneness within the great brotherhood of man is undermined. Perhaps there should be no place in social groups with equalitarian ideals where professional titles are used.

Those who insist on professional titles outside of business and professional settings where they are commonly used actually do harm to the concepts of equality and oneness.

Note: Concepts you may want to review are vertical goals, pp. 16-23, 43; communal interest, pp. 47-48.

THE BOARD

THE SITUATION

The seven board members surrounded the heavy rectangular desk in strict seniority order. The chairman, who had been longest with the firm, sat at the head of the desk, with the next senior member on his right and the rest in descending order of seniority around the table. The members were typical of those who have shaped themselves into the bureaucratic mold required by the firm. They were those advanced in positions of responsibility.

This board meeting offered an observer good insight into the members' relationships with each other. The business of the day was the advantages and disadvantages of locating a branch of the firm in a foreign country. The rest of the board meeting proceeded as follows (each board member is identified by number according to his seniority).

"Well, Number Seven, what do you believe are the main advantages of locating a branch of the firm overseas?" Number One spoke the words with barely a hint of sarcasm. He shifted in his massive chair and let his eyes gaze at the intricate carvings on the high ceiling. His manner seemed to communicate at best, "We'll tolerate your response," and at worst, "Here we go with more dribble."

Number Seven shifted uncomfortably in his chair and met the gazes of those waiting for him to answer. Number Two appeared the mirror image of Number One in his expectations. Number Three was close in appearance, but appeared hesitant, while Numbers Five and Six appeared to share the discomfort with Number Seven.

Seven coughed nervously and proceeded to answer in the forceful, articulate manner he had taught himself in his long climb up the bureaucratic ladder. His hands trembled slightly and his neck flushed close to his collar. Finally he stopped. He thought to himself as the meeting continued, "Why do I feel they don't really care what I say? Why do I feel so bad when I participate with these men? What has happened to my feelings of worth?"

Number One asked each the same question. As each responded, Number One showed progressively more interest, until the peak of interest was demonstrated when Number Two responded. There was a tendency for Number One's interest and disinterest to be mirrored in the nonverbal responses of the listeners.

The meeting proceeded. If an observer had counted the number of times the chairman had spoken to each one, he would have seen that he spoke to those with greatest seniority most and those with least seniority hardly at all. This was a general trend as members carried out the same pattern of conversation among themselves.

DISCUSSION

One of the common vehicles for perpetuating vertical relationship is the system of seniority. It is an anathema to the ideas of equality and oneness that are so basic to horizontal movement. Concomitants of the seniority system include feelings among some employees that they are, at best, fourth-class citizens. Resentment and anger often follow such a system, as well as doubts about one's own worth. Other concomitants include arrogance among the senior members, demonstrated by their not listening to the others, not really caring, and being puffed up by what they believe is their own importance. It is difficult for men in such a system not to become sycophants. Mediocrity tends to be the fruit of such a system, especially if it operates over a long period of time. Any new ideas are typically crushed by those with age, tradition, and power on their side.

Among boards operating in the horizontal fashion are attitudes of courtesy, respect, and concern for each member. A member's ideas are listened to in a courteous manner no matter how long he has been on the board. And ideas are considered according to their value regardless of the contributor's age, time with the firm, race, or ethnic origin. There should also be a natural shifting in seating arrangements from meeting to meeting that would effectively symbolize equality in relationships. Such meetings, if they are really horizontal in nature, are conducted with good fellowship and no condescension toward any person.

Note: Concepts you may want to review are vertical goals, pp. 16-23, 43; communal interest, pp. 47-48; self-esteem, pp. 46-47; warmth and respect, p. 71.

PLANNING A COMMUNITY
THE SITUATION

Ken, a muscular six-foot two-inch successful business man, was called by a religious group to provide his recommendations for the design of an educational community in a far distant land. The committee intended to meet the educational needs of the local people by drawing up plans for a school board office, a superintendent's residence, teacher's residences, and schools. Ken was pleased and somewhat flattered that the committee would turn to him and was determined to fulfill his assignment to the best of his ability.

He returned to his office in the evening to work on his assignment. He chose his office because he had found that while he was there he was mentally set for work and was able to produce a great deal. He also disliked taking work home since he preferred to keep his home free from pressures of work so that he could devote his undivided time and energy to his wife and children.

Ken entered the large office building of which he was a strong, integral part and quietly and with dignity recognized the respectful greeting of an attendant who called him by name, prefaced with Mr. He walked briskly past the rows of resting elevators with their open doors and around a corner to a door marked Private Elevator. This was the elevator used by only the president and vice-presidents. Ken was filled with satisfaction and pride as he firmly pressed the button labeled "23," the floor second from the top. He was reminded of the first day he joined the powerful inner circle of the company's management team five years ago and wondered if he would ever not thrill to the deferential way his subordinates treated him.

The elevator smoothly and quietly deposited him at his floor. As the door slid silently open, his eyes caught the familiar sights of the cubicle reserved for the junior vice-presidents. He walked through this section on the twenty-dollar-per-square-foot carpet and entered the hallway reserved for the senior vice-presidents. He stepped onto the thirty-dollar-per-square-foot hall carpet and his hand gently caressed the beautiful and expensive wood lining on one side of the large hall. A few more steps and he arrived at his door. As his key searched out its opening, Ken's eyes wandered to his name embossed in gold on the heavy oak door. He grunted in satisfaction as he read "Senior Vice-President—Plant Operations Section."

He opened the door and walked to his desk, a massive but beautiful piece of furniture placed directly in front of large windows reaching almost to the floor. Before pulling the drapes, Ken looked out upon the city, just awakening to the evening. He had always enjoyed looking at cities at night, and his eyes lingered on the neon signs blinking on and off and the street lights that were now turning on. His hand finally found the button and the drapes closed silently as the electric motor did its job.

He opened his briefcase and spent thirty minutes refreshing his memory on the needs of the proposed community. He studied with rather intense interest a three-dimensional map of the area before launching into his preliminary work. Time passed quickly while he buried himself in his work. At twelve-thirty he glanced at his watch, yawned, placed his completed first rough draft into his briefcase, and returned home.

Ken climbed quietly into bed trying not to awaken his wife. He lay for long minutes going over the initial draft in his mind. He turned over and tried to get to sleep, but he only tossed and turned. Two hours passed, but sleep did not come. Something kept bothering him about his plans. They did not seem right. Yet he felt they had to be. Hadn't he incorporated twenty-five years of professional experience into them? He went over them again in his mind.

He pictured in his mind's eye the school board office on the topmost hill like a white pearl in the sun above the other buildings in the complex. Next he pictured the superintendent's home that he had designed to be placed on the second highest hill. The house was to cost several dollars a square foot more than any of the other residences and was to symbolize the high status of his position. He then pictured the schools and noted with pleasure the principal's office with carpet, a desk, and chairs more costly than any of the other offices. Thinking of the principal's office brought to mind the principal's home that would be built. Ken painted it in his mind, placing its image onto the three-dimensional map until it came to rest on the fourth highest hill. He then thought of the recommended costs. He had recommended that the principal's home cost several dollars less per square foot than the superintendent's, but several dollars more than the teachers' houses.

He pictured the community as it would be when finished, with the superintendent's more expensive home isolated and looking over the other houses, the principal's less expensive house separated from his teacher colleagues' and on a high hill, and all the teachers' houses bunched together in a low valley. He surveyed all of this again and tried to fight down the uncomfortable feeling welling up inside.

"I've designed this with the best of my knowledge," he thought to himself. "It is basically a sound plan. It is in the best of business tradition. It must be right; why then am I so disturbed?"

DISCUSSION

Ken was caught in a trap. His business experience told him to draw up the plans so that those with different positions in the community would be identified by a differential allocation of material goods. In business this approach is used to demand or manipulate for differential status, prestige, and power. Its effect is to isolate one man from another, create divisions among people, and stimulate envy, greed, resentment, and hostility. In such a hierarchy the individual is stimulated to move vertically against his fellowman rather than to move horizontally with him.

The conflict gnawing at Ken was the result of discrepancies between the business ethics of his plans and the religious ethics he believed in. He had roughed-in plans that would stimulate business objectives for increasing status and prestige and thereby the power of those holding responsible positions; but these objectives were contradictory to his religious objectives for stimulating equality and unity among the people.

310

To solve his conflict, Ken could focus first on his religious objectives of unity and equality and then design the community in such a manner that these goals would be encouraged by his plans. For example, Ken may decide that isolating the superintendent's and principal's houses from the others and elevating them differentially would create distance in interpersonal relationships. Providing more expensive furniture, carpets, and drapes would stimulate greed, envy, and division and should be avoided.

Every position is valuable and important. It is important that unity and equality among people be emphasized, not the artificial status that is too often applied to various positions.

If status and prestige are not to be emphasized in the plans for houses, does this mean that each is to be exactly the same? The answer to this is a resounding no. Man's environment would be a dreary place if each residence were a carbon copy of all others. The houses could be built in such a manner that each would be unique in appearance but similar in cost per square foot. Some could be larger than others so that the needs of larger families or the entertaining requirements of the superintendent and principal could be satisfied. House preference would be based on floor plan, type of architectural design, color preference, and space needs rather than the neuroticizing and divisive goals of greater wealth, status, prestige, and power.

Note: Concepts you may want to review are life-style, pp. 48-50; social linkage, pp. 44-45; holism, pp. 50-52; vertical goals, pp. 16-23, 43; bonding, pp. 52-53; communal interest, pp. 47-48.

CITY ZONING

THE SITUATION

Jonathan, a successful businessman and now successful politician, had just won a seat on the town council. His slogan had been "Progress for our town through attracting light industry." But a covert part of his platform was "Let us zone this town to protect our homes."

Jonathan had just built an expensive house on the east side of town. It was a beautiful home and he was determined to do everything in his power to maintain and enhance its value. He decided that his best strategy was to gain a seat on the town council and help write zoning laws. He saw people of different ethnic and socioeconomic backgrounds moving in the direction of his block and was anxious to stop them, because he feared that they would then diminish what he had worked so hard to obtain for his children.

He spent several nights writing and polishing a revised zoning code. According to his code, only houses of a minimum large size and with certain large values would be allowed in those sections of town he wished to protect.

DISCUSSION

One of the greatest evidences of a vertical society is zoning laws which separate brother from brother on the basis of such things as wealth. This vertical situation is perpetrated for the purpose of financial, prestige, and status gains at the expense of one's fellowman. The very act of zoning on a socioeconomic basis communicates "You are not good enough to associate with us." The physical distance imposed stimulates estrangement and estrangement breeds suspicion. Other attitudes which result are contempt, condescension, greed, resentment, hostility, alienation, and superiority.

Such zoning tends to lock people into groups. There is less personal interaction between groups, resulting in fewer exchanges in marriage, less education for the lower socioeconomic group, and less sharing in the economic wealth of the community. There also tends to be little political power exercised by those in the lower socioeconomic group. They tend to believe the indirect communication of "You're not good enough"; as a result they give up and most often do not take advantage of their political rights.

In the ideal town run on horizontal principles wealth would be shared equitably. This would allow every man to be accepted on the basis of his character, not his wealth, name, or position. In a society moving in the horizontal direction, the humble home could exist side by side with the wealthy. There would be free and easy social interaction among various groups and all would gain, regardless of socioeconomic situation. Each man would be accepted and respected on the basis of his behavior and the fact that he is a member of the human race. There would be no cliques or divisions based on socio-economic vertical games.

Children's schools would reflect their parents' attitudes. There would be no cliques to exclude and hurt people. The name-brand clothes game, where one can only belong to certain groups if he wears the right clothes labels, will not be played. The measure of a town's vertical life-style is the extent to which adults zone out their fellowmen and create divisions and the extent to which their children form cliques at school based on material goods, prestige, and status. In contrast, the measure of a town's horizontal life-style is the extent to which all of its citizens are included in its groups, free and easy social interaction exists among all its members, and children in the schools and churches are free from exclusive cliques and groups.

In the horizontal community each person keeps his yard and house neat and clean regardless of size. Each concerns himself with making his place an attractive part of the community. Yards and homes are not allowed to run down since each individual feels obligated to help his neighbor contribute to the appearance of the community. This is actually easy to do, for when people feel they belong and are accepted, they tend to contribute constructively to their community.

Where there are no exclusive zoning laws, older people can settle throughout the community. Aged persons in a neighborhood have many assets, among them a mellowing, maturing, and stabilizing influence on other people and the ability to give wise counsel. Children usually benefit a good deal from associations with the aged person who expresses care, love, understanding, and support. He contributes much to the growing child in the process of developing love for his fellowmen. As a result life often means more to him as he associates with other people. He also tends to feel greater personal worth.

Note: Concepts you may want to review are communal interest, pp. 47-48; belonging, pp. 45-46; social linkage, pp. 44-45; holism, pp. 50-52; self-esteem, pp. 46-47; bonding, pp. 52-53.

COMPETITIVE SPORTS

THE SITUATION

The referee called a foul on a visiting team member. This was followed by yells and shouts of glee from the hometown crowd as they exhibited their delight.

In this close league game, the referees worked under a good deal of strain. Their facial muscles were tight and their faces became red then gray. They perspired not so much because of their physical activity, but more from the emotional pressure caused by the crowd and team members.

A rabid fan jumped to his feet and shouted advice and insults to the referees, coaches, and players. His neck and face were red and his neck muscles protruded. He clenched his jaw and fists as he expressed himself in loud, boisterous, derisive tones.

A technical foul was called on the opposing team and the home crowd went wild with joy. Then a foul was called on a home team player. His face was contorted with rage as he shot both of his hands high in the air.

The referee again blew his whistle. The crowd rose to its feet in anger as a favorite hometown player was assessed with a foul. A coat came sailing out from among the spectators and landed squarely on top of the referee's head covering him to his waist. He fought to get out from under it as a large part of the vast crowd of spectators laughed, hooted, and clapped their approval. He immediately imposed a technical foul.

During a later game, after a referee gave a call with which he violently disagreed, a visiting coach got up from his bench so that the spectators could see him, turned and faced the hometown fans, raised his hands high above his head, and bowed from the waist three times in mock supplication. The mammoth hall rang with boos and hoots from the partisan crowd.

In another school district, after many violent fights among students from opposing schools, interschool basketball programs were closed down because of student hostility and anger, which threatened to get completely out of control.

Several middle-aged men who were members of a local religious sect had decided to play basketball in the meetinghouse gymnasium as part of a physical fitness program. They divided into two teams. One night tempers flared and before the evening game was finished, two of the men fought each other with doubled-up fists.

In one well-publicized, closely contested collegiate basketball game the fans threw peanuts, peanut sacks, pennies, and cups on the playing floor during the closing seconds. Immediately following this a visiting player went in for an easy lay-up. He was instantly clobbered by a home player. Another home player made a gesture to help him and, when he had risen part way, drove his knee into his groin. He lay back writhing on the floor. Another home player rushed over and stamped on the neck and head of the helpless, unconscious visitor. The fight mushroomed, with both fans and players entering the fray. It was finally stopped when police reinforcements arrived.

It seems that fights have always been part of the college basketball scene for it thrives on physical contact and emotion. This is true of much of the general competitive sport scene.

One competitive swimmer told with pride how he psyched out his greatest rival and undermined his confidence by sitting extra close to him, staring at him, and following him everywhere he went, even into lavatories.

DISCUSSION

The oft-stated purpose of competitive athletics is to build character. The model athlete is portrayed as a gracious winner and a good loser. He is charming, sociable, casual, and cool. He wins because he has greater ability than others.

The ideal too often has little resemblance to real life, however. Winners are often those who have an intense desire to appear better than their fellowmen, to outdo other people, and to make them look worse than themselves.

Competition encourages dishonesty. As pressure mounts, many resort to unscrupulous methods to gain advantages over their opponents. Fear, anger, frustration, exhilaration, and depression tend to be common emotional concomitants for those heavily involved in competitive activities. These emotions are sure evidences of vertical relationships.

There is really very little evidence that competitive activity builds individuals who grow and develop in their love for their fellowman. But there is much first-hand evidence that the exact opposite is true. The next time you go to a competitive game ask yourself the following questions. What emotions do I have toward my fellowman while I am watching this game? Is there a spirit of brotherhood with us? Don't be surprised if your answers startle you.

The consequences of competitive activities and more specifically those related to competitive sports were well demonstrated in an experiment by Muzafer Sherif and colleagues (Bernard, 1969) who took a group of normal boys and arranged to have them participate in a tournament of games. This included baseball, touch football, a tug-of-war, and a treasure hunt. This placed the boys in situations where some won and some lost, classical win-lose competitive situations. The experimenters graphically described the intense hostility among the boys.

. . . *good feeling soon evaporated. The members of each group began to call their rivals "stinkers," "sneaks," and "cheaters." They refused to have anything more to do with individuals in the opposing group. The boys . . . turned against buddies whom they had chosen as "best friends" when they first arrived at the camp. A large proportion of the boys in each group gave negative ratings to all the boys in the other. The rival groups made threatening posters and planned raids, collecting secret hoards of green apples for ammunition. To the Robber's Cave came the Eagles, after a defeat in a tournament game, and burned a banner left behind by the Rattlers; the next morning the Rattlers seized the Eagles' flag when they arrived on the athletic field. From that time on name-calling, scuffles, and raids were the rule of the day.*

. . . *In the dining-hall line they shoved each other aside, and the group that lost the contest for the head of the line shouted "Ladies first!" at the winner. They threw paper, food, and vile names at each other at the tables. An Eagle bumped by a Rattler was admonished by his fellow Eagles to brush "the dirt" off his clothes* [Bernard 1969, p. 456].

Another test was conducted to determine if this hostility could be diminished through "mere interaction" in pleasant social contacts.

. . . *we brought the hostile Rattlers and Eagles together for social events: going to the movies, eating in the same dining room, and so on. But far from reducing conflict, these situations only served as opportunities for the rival groups to berate and attack each other* [Bernard 1969, p. 457].

It appears that pleasant social contact alone is not enough to reduce hostility among antagonists with a history of competing against one another.

The hostility was reduced however by several strategies that required the boys to work cooperatively in order to accomplish their objectives. One such strategy was the interrupting of the boys' water supply by the experimenters. The boys volunteered to search out the problem and correct it. In this situation there were no winners or losers; all were needed, all could contribute. The consequences of such strategies were:

> . . . *The members of the two groups began to feel more friendly to each other. For example, a Rattler whom the Eagles disliked for his sharp tongue and skill in defeating them became a "good egg." The boys stopped shoving in the meal line. They no longer called each other names and sat together at the table. New friendships developed between individuals in the two groups.*
>
> *In the end the groups were actively seeking opportunities to mingle, to entertain, and "treat" each other. They decided to hold a joint campfire. They took turns presenting skits and songs. Members of both groups requested that they go home together on the same bus, rather than on the separate buses in which they had come. On the way the bus stopped for refreshments. One group still had $5 which they had won as a prize in a contest. They decided to spend this sum on refreshments. On their own initiative they had invited their former rivals to be their guests for malted milks [Bernard 1969, p. 456].*

The challenge appears clear. Those who wish to foster brotherhood, equality, and oneness will do so to the degree that they avoid win-lose competitive activities and encourage cooperative activities instead in which each member can make a worthwhile contribution.

Note: Concepts you may want to review are vertical goals, pp. 16-23, 43; modeling, pp. 53-54; bonding, pp. 52-53; communal interest, pp. 47-48.

ROBBING OTHER PEOPLES' IDEAS

THE SITUATION

He was moving up fast in the organization. His hours were long. He seemed to be operating under a full head of steam, proceeding at an exceptionally high rate. But in spite of his drive and successes he continued to feel inferior and inadequate. He was respected by some of his colleagues, but others were suspicious of him.

Rob was desperate in his drive to succeed. The means he used to accomplish his end goals were not weighed carefully. The important thing to him was whether they contributed to his status and prestige. The following samples of his behavior are rather typical of his methods to gain his ends.

Some of the firm's junior officers were meeting with others from different departments. During a coffee break, as discussions continued informally, a junior officer from another department told in some detail of his boss's plans to radically alter their department's organization to make it more effective. This was overheard by one of Rob's junior assistants who told Rob about the plans. Rob felt the plans were sound and immediately took steps to implement the changes in his department, with one or two minor revisions from the original plans, before the other department could implement them. Rob accompanied the changes with much publicity for the ears and eyes of his senior officers, to whom it appeared that the ideas were all Rob's. No credit was given to his colleague in the department where the ideas originated.

Rob was also adept at muscling in and making almost any project in which he participated his own. Frank, one of his colleagues, had cultivated a relationship with an important officer in a firm that consumed the items they produced. The organization's team was to visit the firm for the purpose of further cultivating relationships and signing a large contract, and Rob was invited along as a supporting member of the team. It was soon apparent that Rob was using his tremendous energy and needs for success to move in and take over from Frank in the discussions. The team returned home before signing a contract, with the understanding that the discussions would be continued by phone. The first phone call Rob's organization received was placed by Frank's friend in the other firm and was for Frank. He was sick at home that day, but Rob happened to pass the secretary who was handling the call. He heard her state the name of the city from which the call was originating and knew what it was about. When the secretary told the caller that Frank was sick, Rob quickly told the secretary to transfer the call to him in his office. He very deftly structured the discussion so that all future calls would go to him. He, in effect, moved in and took over, stealing his colleague's many hours of cultivating relations with an important official in the other firm and using it for his own power, prestige, and status. When the contract was fully signed, he took the credit.

Not only did Rob borrow designs from others and move in on their projects, making them his own, he also even adopted their ideas and phrases and spoke them as though he had originated them himself. This was apparent in not only formal, but also informal settings. A colleague would make a perceptive, analytical statement about what would improve the organization in an informal discussion with Rob. Later the colleague would be astounded to hear Rob expressing his ideas to others using the very phrases he used in describing them to Rob. Rob would usually present them as his own at the next formal meeting of the organization. At a party someone would make an astute comparison or analogy of situations and would be amazed to hear Rob telling another small group the same things using the same words as though they were his own. One other trait of Rob's was to demean before other people those colleagues whom he felt were potential rivals to his climb up the organization's ladder of success.

In spite of Rob's many successes, his feelings of inadequacy, inferiority, and general dissatisfaction with himself were keeping him in a perpetual state of turmoil.

DISCUSSION

Rob lived in the shadow of an older brother whom his parents felt was more successful. It seemed to Rob as he was growing up that no matter how hard he tried, his older brother did things better than he and was better accepted by his parents. The shadow Rob lived in was dark and long and dramatically affected his behavior. He hurt deeply as he felt his parents' greater love for his brother. But he continued to struggle to do better and greater things so that he would be accepted as well as his brother. In fact, his drive was to be better and do greater things so that he could displace his brother and become the more preferred son. He was only dimly aware of this goal, however.

This same behavior he brought to his vocation, using his vocation as a vehicle to achieve his goals. It was so important to him to have a preferred place with his parents that this end justified almost any means. He would rob or steal the ideas from anyone if he could present them as his own and thus gain more prestige and status. However, Rob had traded the achievement of these immediate goals for long-range, more satisfying ones. He was still feeling inferior and dissatisfied because he was moving vertically, not only against others but against himself. In other words he was selling himself short.

As Rob borrowed ideas, plans, and phrases from other people and used them as his own, he was in effect communicating to himself, "Rob, I don't believe in you. You have to steal from other people." And since he did not give anyone credit for the ideas he borrowed, he was betraying his basic values. All of this increased his feelings of inferiority and dissatisfaction with himself, rather than diminishing them.

Rob needs to realize that he cannot force his parents to like him. He needs to decide that if they relate vertically by preferring an older brother, this is their hang-up. All he can be responsible for is being a competent husband, father, and citizen. If they like him as he is, all is well and good. If not, he has done all that he can do, and he can rightfully feel at peace with himself.

He will not find peace and satisfaction with himself by striving to force his parents to prefer him. Even if he were to achieve a preferred place, he would always be afraid that his brother's shadow would lengthen and he would again be less preferred. The only way to achieve the fruits of positive interaction is for Rob to move horizontally with other people.

Note: Concepts you may want to review are life-style, pp. 48-50; social linkage, pp. 44-45; holism, pp. 50-52; belonging, pp. 45-46; vertical goals, pp. 16-23, 43; communal interest, pp. 47-48; genuineness, p. 71.

REFERENCES
Adler, Alfred
  1958   What Life Should Mean to You. New York: Capricorn Books.
  1964   Social Interest: A Challenge to Mankind. New York: Capricorn Books.

Allport, Gordon
  1958   The Nature of Prejudice. New York: Anchor Books.

Allred, G. Hugh
  1966   A study of the personality traits and classroom verbal behavior of senior

320

high school student teachers. Doctoral dissertation, University of Oregon, Eugene, Oregon.

1968   Mission for Mother: Guiding the Child. Salt Lake City: Bookcraft.

1960-   Personal observations of human conditions in Canada, New Zealand, and
1973   the United States. File in possession of G. Hugh Allred, Brigham Young University, Provo, Utah.

1972-   Personal observations, Brigham Young University Marriott Activities Cen-
1973   ter. File in possession of G. Hugh Allred, Brigham Young University, Provo, Utah.

Bandura, Albert, and Richard H. Walters
    1963   Social Learning and Personality Development. New York: Holt, Rinehart and Winston.

Barrett, William
    1962   Irrational Man. New York: Anchor Books.

Beier, Ernst G.
    1966   The Silent Language of Psychotherapy. Chicago: Aldine Publishing Co.

Bernard, Harold W.
    1969   Readings in Adolescent Development. Scranton, Pennsylvania: International Textbook Co.

Brosnan, Jim
    1971   "What we're losing by our craze for winning." Today's Health (May):17-19.

Davidson, Henry A., et al.
    1960   "Should Johnny compete or cooperate?" NEA Journal 49 (October): 30-32.

Dreikurs, Rudolf
              "The courage to be imperfect." Chicago: The Alfred Adler Institute.
    1958   "The cultural implications of reward and punishment." The International Journal of Social Psychiatry 4(3) (Winter).

Frankl, Viktor E.
    1963   Man's Search for Meaning: An Introduction to Logotherapy. New York: Washington Square Press.

Haines, Donald Bruce, and W. J. McKeachie
    1967   "Cooperative versus competitive discussion methods in teaching introductory psychology." Journal of Educational Psychology 58(6) (December): 386-390.

Holt, John
    1966   "The fourth r—the rat race." The New York Times Magazine (May 1): 146-151.

Johnston, Norman, et al.
    1962   The Sociology of Punishment and Correction. New York: John Wiley and Sons.

Korn, Richard R., and Lloyd W. McCorkle
1963   Criminology and Penology. New York: Holt, Rinehart and Winston.

Maslow, Abraham H.
1962   Toward a Psychology of Being. New York: D. Van Nostrand Co.
1971   The Farther Reaches of Human Nature. New York: The Viking Press.

Matson, Floyd W.
1966   The Broken Image: Man, Science and Society. New York: Anchor Books.

May, Rollo, et al.
1961   Existential Psychology. New York: Random House.

Nelson, Janice D., et al.
1969   "Children's aggression following competition and exposure to an aggressive model." Child Development (December): 1085-1097.

Reed, William F.
1972   "An ugly affair in Minneapolis." Sports Illustrated (February 7):18-21.

Sage, George H.
1968   "Team morale and the problem of intra-squad competition." Athletic Journal 49 (November):44-45, 61.

Shapira, Ariella, and Millard C. Madsen
1969   "Cooperative and competitive behavior of kibbutz and urban children in Israel." Child Development (June):609-617.

Schollander, Donald A., and Michael D. Savage
1971   Deep Water. New York: Crown Publishers.

Sicher, Lydia
1955   "Education for freedom." The American Journal of Individual Psychology 11 (2).

Szasz, Thomas S.
1961   The Myth of Mental Illness: Foundations of a Theory of Personal Conduct. New York: Harper and Row.

"The fanatics."
1970   Newsweek (May 4):67-68.

Weinberg, Carl
1965   "The price of competition." Teachers College Record (November):108-114.

Wolfgang, Marvin E., et al.
1962   The Sociology of Crime and Delinquency. New York: John Wiley and Sons.

SIX

A
SUMMARY

12
IDENTIFYING MOVEMENT AS HORIZONTAL OR VERTICAL

It is, at times, a somewhat difficult task for us to determine whether we are interacting in a vertical or a horizontal manner. Included in this final chapter are specific verbal responses, nonverbal responses, feelings and attitudes. These are divided into vertical and horizontal categories according to where they typically tend to occur. Reflections of young adults on their home life conclude each of these sections. The accounts are written by university students. When they gave their permission for their thoughts to be printed here, they requested that their names and other identifying factors be omitted.

By becoming more aware of feelings and attitudes, you can sharpen your insights concerning the kind of relationships you are involved in at any given time and thereby learn to actively work for more horizontal interaction with other people. This should help you achieve greater serenity, greater respect for yourself and other people, and a renewed zest for living.

It is usually unwise to use an isolated bit of behavior to classify a relationship. You will find that your classifications will be more accurate as you observe similar and repetitive patterns of behavior.

IDENTIFYING VERTICAL MOVEMENT
VERBAL RESPONSES
- Don't be so impractical.
- You always seem to be wrong.
- Must you be so stupid?
- Does Jane have a room as messy as yours?
- Don't you ever think?
- You are ridiculous.
- Wash your face. You look like a pig.
- It's just where you left it.

326

- When are you going to learn to do things without being told?
- Do you want me to hit you?
- You're the most gutless person I've ever seen.
- How can you be so childish?
- That isn't right. Let me do it for you.
- How can you be so bad?
- You always do poorly.
- You should be ashamed of yourself.
- Don't be so silly.
- Don't you know better?
- You're not big enough.
- When are you going to grow up?
- You are so immature.
- When are you going to get some sense?
- You Dumb-Dumb.
- Why don't you be a good boy?
- Speak only when you are spoken to.
- Just try that once more and you'll wish you hadn't.
- You are as narrow-minded as ever.
- Why don't you think before you jump?
- Another poor mark! You'll never make it.
- Leave him alone.
- No one else could have made such a poor job out of it.
- Do it again and I'll give you something to really cry about.
- Can't you spell that easy word?
- I'll give you to the . . .
- You're the laughingstock of the whole neighborhood.
- You are cheap and no good.
- Can't you ever say, "excuse"?
- Don't be so rude.
- It is so simple that any child could do it.
- You haven't even tried.
- Show 'em up.
- Do you want me to smack you?
- A good thrashing will straighten you out.
- We have the best . . .
- We live in the best . . .

- No one can do it as good as . . .
- I know this is not your best effort.
- I wonder how you ever made it through grade school.
- You know better.
- Is that the way I taught you to drive?
- You're a liar.
- Once a thief always a thief.
- I told you at least ten times to do it.
- Quit acting like a baby.
- You act like a spoiled brat.
- You cause problems wherever you go.
- I don't want to see you.
- You chew like a camel.
- You look like a horse.
- If you had an ounce of brains, you would . . .
- You stupid oaf.
- How about answering right just once?
- You will always be a failure.
- You never make any sense.
- Were you born or hatched?
- If you ever listened, you would know.
- Why can't you be like . . . ?
- Becky could .... at your age.
- Why can't you be as nice looking as . . . ?
- I knew when I gave you this to do, you couldn't do it.
- You never think.
- You're like a bull in a china closet.
- You make me sick.
- Let's face it, you're just not too capable.
- You're a bore.
- You never change.
- You do nothing right.
- Do you realize you're the slowest in . . . ?
- Be careful.
- What's the matter with you?
- Stop sitting there like a blob.
- What a stupid way to . . . ?

- Who did this? Your baby sister?
- Where are your brains? A moron could have done better.
- You should be ashamed of yourself.
- Do it to please me.
- That was a lousy decision.
- Didn't I warn you it would turn out that way?
- Father knows best.
- Maybe next time you'll listen to me.
- That man is watching you. You had better shape up.
- If you want my love, you'll . . .
- You are now worthy of my love.
- That's good. Your brother can now follow your example.
- You make me happy when you do what I say.
- I'm older; therefore . . .
- Don't be such a fool.
- I know a way to do it that makes your methods obsolete.
- Don't talk back to me.
- Quit complaining.
- You'll be sorry.
- Respect your elders.
- You'd best get someone with more sense than you to tell you what to do.
- My experience tells me that your best bet is to . . .
- When I was your age, I . . .
- Your thinking is muddy.
- You're wrong.
- Look here, Mr. Know-it-all.
- You're just jealous.
- You'd better tell me all about it; I'll find out anyway.
- It seems I've heard that same old song before.
- Just forget it!
- You never were any good.
- Here, let me do it for you.

NONVERBAL RESPONSES

- Arched eyebrow
- Slap across the face

- The stare
- Nose in the air
- A smirk
- Derisive laughter
- Pointed finger
- Shaking fist or finger
- Head in the air and marching away
- Curled lip
- Head drawn down between shoulders
- Teeth bared
- Tongue stuck out
- Nose thumbed
- A hiss
- Pounding fist
- Looking down nose at another
- Looking up and down from head to toe
- Sitting apart from
- Tongue clucks
- Looking to (one part of a larger group) in a knowing way
- Displaying possessions
- Perfect dress and grooming (not a hair out of place)
- Rigid posture
- Clothes which set one apart
- Shoulders rounded
- Not noticing others (demanding that other people speak first)
- Look of disinterest
- Eyes averted
- Walking away
- A snicker
- Hand over face
- Teeth gritted
- A sneer
- Eyelids partly closed or shut
- Chin sunk on chest
- Sly smile
- Close scrutiny of another's living room
- Standing on higher ground than anyone else

- Extensive accumulation and display of material goods
- Protection of one who can work things through
- Redoing something done by someone else
- Whining
- Crying
- Pouty face
- Building alliances and cliques
- Competing
- Comparing
- Quarrelling
- Fighting
- Being disloyal
- Using sarcasm
- Getting revenge
- Emphasizing mistakes and inadequacies
- Dressing better than anyone else
- Dressing more poorly than anyone else
- Being punishment-centered
- Retying shoelaces
- Combing someone else's hair when he is capable
- Straightening another person's clothes
- Picking lint off someone's clothes
- Helping another person get dressed when he is capable
- Feeding another person when he is capable
- Rearranging another person's personal articles (i.e., husband rearranging his wife's clothing in her chest of drawers)

FEELINGS AND ATTITUDES

FEELINGS OF

- Irritation
- Annoyance
- Anger
- Pity
- Hurt
- Vengeance
- Fear
- Hate

- Alienation
- Anxiety
- Misery
- Sadness
- Disinterest
- Depression
- Apathy
- Resentment
- Jealousy
- Envy
- Triumph over others
- Inferiority
- Superiority
- Better than
- Lower than
- Low self-esteem
- Low morale

DESIRE TO

- Gain power
- Be preferred
- Punish
- Embarrass
- Humiliate
- Retaliate
- Subdue
- Suppress
- Force
- Threaten
- Admonish
- Warn
- Dominate
- Order
- Command
- Exhort
- Moralize
- Preach

- Always advise, tell what to do
- Lecture
- Judge
- Blame
- Criticize
- Ridicule
- Shame
- Analyze
- Sympathize
- Pity
- Probe
- Interrogate
- Hold a grudge
- Hurt
- Make excessive profits
- Get undue service
- Take advantage of
- Put responsibility for one's own actions on others
- Avoid making one's own decisions
- Avoid pulling one's fair share of the load
- Reward
- Bribe
- Make one's advantage a disadvantage for other people

REFLECTIONS

- *Monday mornings were hectic for our family with all of us going to school and having to have our P.E. suits cleaned and ironed, our books ready to go, lunches packed, etc. Mother did all this for us— helping us find lost items, making sure that each one of us was ready to go on time—but a lot of yelling and threatening went along with it, and I know that it absolutely wore her out and sometimes us too. I really feel badly about those times I got out of doing the dishes or helping clean. I didn't feel good about it then, either, but I feel worse now. Our mother would just threaten that she couldn't and wouldn't stand for us not helping, and then she would do it all herself. I don't think it helped our family become closer, and now I wish she had really set up some limits and had made us stick to more responsibilities.*

● *My mother does have her share of fears that come across as don'ts. Don't be late. Don't touch the dog. Don't get too near the water. Don't go into the deep end of the pool. Don't touch the vases and figurines. Don't jump on the bed. If we did one of those things, she was sure to get a migraine headache.*

● *My mom is a great worrier and does little. She anticipates problems that never exist and worries about those she can't do anything about. She worries about everything she can't see an immediate solution to. I think as children we realized this and really got her involved with us. We would argue, and she would come running and take sides. If you talked back or questioned her, she was sure you were being impudent and you got a lecture. She goes by first impulses, and now we know more how she'll react to what we do than I think she knows what we'll do. A lot of talking goes on but little is said. After awhile we turn her off.*

● *My father never complimented me when I did well, but merely commented on my poor marks and what he felt they meant. His approach was, "A C is the smartest of the dumbest, and the dumbest of the best." ...I can never change my father's ideas, but I can say that, had he commented on my poor grades in this manner, "We are concerned and hope that this hasn't discouraged you from trying to do your best," then less depression and anxiety would have been aroused. To this day, I would be less depressed and worried about tests and what will happen if the results are low.*

● *Since we are all girls [seven] and are relatively close in age, we are a very competitive family. If someone does something that is good, someone will always try to make it sound as if it isn't really that special. We tend to blow out someone else's candle in order to make ours shine brighter. We're so concerned with each other that we don't try to improve ourselves. My parents tend to increase this atmosphere by comparing the kids. This only adds resentment, and we try even harder to make others feel bad. An example of this was a dance recital the whole family attended to see my sister perform. She did a* very good job and Mother and Father were saying how pleased they were with her. Another sister said, "She wasn't really that good because she didn't do a solo number." Usually my parents' reaction was to reprimand the child who was knocking the other child.

• I remember making things at about eight years old and Mom always saying, "Get this junk picked up in case we get company." ...I remember when we were old enough to sew our own clothes, we had to do it exactly like the pattern. If we liked the dress and wanted long sleeves instead of short—too bad.

• We talked little about how we felt. We did not "hate" anyone, we were told; but I knew I did and so did my sister. We didn't talk about why we felt the way we did when we were angry. My mother is very free about stating that she doesn't like so-and-so one day and yet going off to coffee with her the next. Whenever my mother starts this now, all three of us shut her off and have little respect for her judgment of people.

• If they [our parents] decided to go on a picnic, we all had to go regardless of what other plans we'd made the week before. We didn't take friends. I enjoyed going on the spur of the moment—it's fun— but I didn't like the compulsion of "You have to go or you don't love me," or taking a friend and knowing my mother wished she wasn't there.

• They [our parents] didn't listen to our ideas or points of view and this really made me feel awful, especially when I learned that you wash knives and forks last, measure liquids in one type of measuring cup and dry ingredients in another, or when I knew a quicker and better way to put in a zipper. My mom could always discredit me, and the same thing happened with my sisters. If a mistake was made like spilling the sugar or breaking a milk bottle, it was always, "I told you so," or, "You shouldn't have been there anyway," and on and on for an eternity it seemed. It did no good to apologize and try to make restitution. Instead it was, "Go away, I'll clean it up." The incident was bound to pop up three days from then, and she'd go all over it again. It only made me feel angry towards her because there was no way to make it right again. I always felt, "Why tell you anything at all?"

- *Whenever we said something mean about someone, my mother would always turn right around and say something nice about that person.*

- *Comparisons among the four of us were made very often by my parents and other relatives. I recall being aware of our differences very early. Competition was highly valued, and we were frequently pitted against each other in physical contests or mental reasoning games. Unfortunately for the second child, who nearly always lost, the results were emphatically impressed upon us. I feel that such pressures on each of us to compete in the family fostered some very unpleasant rivalries. Even now, after living away from my sisters for six years, it is nearly impossible for me to relax with them.*

- *Dad would do anything for the church. He spent hours and hours at his church office, and I feel he neglected his home and family to do so. He paid an extra offering to his church and gave many donations to one fund or another. I remember one night when there was an auction for a new church building. Daddy gave all of his purse, his age twice: $100, then $200 more, $75 for a watch, and a promissory note of several hundred dollars for the next year. The next day I begged him for a $9 cheerleading outfit! We had strict limits on "sensual desires for personal gratification...."*

- *Mother always had this dream about me helping her in the kitchen and both of us working "right along-side each other." She could never understand why I wasn't breaking the door down to cook dinner or do the dishes. Yet whenever I made endeavors to help her out, she would always complain (and still does to this day) that my efforts were pretty puny and that I should help her more. She was never satisfied. I got the distinct impression that it was impossible to satisfy her, so I stopped trying.*

- *My mother ... would let everyone make her decisions for her and thus kept everyone involved with her. She was always a sacrificer; this kept people in her debt. She obeyed my father completely, but she would then tell us kids and other people derogatory things about my father to get even with him for his strictness and to gain our complete love and others' sympathy. She never took responsibility for anything; she accomplished this by her use of indecisiveness and her obedience to my father—so she always had someone else to blame if things went wrong.*

• *Looking for mistakes—especially my father glorified in it. My parents only looked for the mistakes. I think this stemmed from the fact that my father always had to be best. While I was at home, I never once heard anything good about myself or anything I had done. I was twenty-one before I was even aware that there was anything good about me. If I made a mistake, it would be public knowledge. Then for months afterwards my parents would continually remind me of it. A phrase I probably heard a dozen times each day would go something like this, "Can't you ever do anything right? Why can't I count on you to do a decent job?"*

• *Father was the central figure at home. He was waited on by Mother, me, and my two sisters. He was a perfectionist. He felt that he never made a mistake, and he thought he was perfect and knew all. Any mistakes he did make were credited to someone else. His perfection made him impatient with us. He wasn't the type to do things himself in order to have them done the way he wanted them done. He just harped until things were done and harped some more because they weren't exactly as he'd have done them. He then said, "I should have done it myself." We were made very anxious by his attitude. We could never count on having done something that would please him. In the teen years the eldest and youngest began to rebel. They did the opposite of what they knew he expected. My older sister married a fellow totally opposed by our parents. The younger one married at eighteen, against the wishes of our parents, who had no time to complain since the announcement came only a few hours before the ceremony. She has now brought her young family into harmony and agreement with Mother and Dad, but the older one remains in open rebellion.*

• *I have been expected to meet the standards and achievements which my older sister met, and I truly resent this. In fact, to this day it is obviously a stumbling block in the progression of our relationship. I feel its effect in the comparison of our husbands and even in our future children and the way we will handle them. I don't feel that I can ever measure up to her in my entire family's eyes, though I feel* that my husband and our marriage are most successful and completely fulfill my needs.

- My father and I were sitting on my grandmother's sofa drinking postum, and I accidentally spilled my cup. My father, realizing that I had damaged his mother's sofa, immediately got up and started to yell at me. At the time I remember feeling that he wanted to be sure that my grandmother knew who was to blame.

- My father made all the decisions for everyone. He tried to make sure that none of us made a decision for ourselves. He would say, "You are just a snot-nosed babe-in-arms and you don't know what is best for you!" If we tried to make a decision for ourselves, we were belittled, and our stupidity for making such a foolish decision was pointed out. My father wouldn't listen to any of our reasoning or why we thought a certain decision should be made. If we still had the courage to try to carry out our decision, we had to face his wrath for not following what he had said (which is frightening in and of itself). Next, if our decision should turn out wrong, then we would hear about our stupidity and foolishness in the decision we made. "I told you so" was expressed generously; and if we decided to try to make another decision, we would be quickly reminded of the foolish decision we made that didn't turn out. If a decision did turn out, which didn't happen very often because we had so little experience in making decisions, my parents would say that they were amazed that it could and wouldn't mention it again. Needless to say, we almost programmed them out of our lives because of the difficulty that we encountered.

- As a result of Dad's forceful physical and verbal discipline, there were triggered many power struggles between Dad and the children. The oldest girl had power struggles for independence and respect from Dad. The second girl had a struggle over dating, the car, and attending church. This was the most severe battle in the family. It lasted for several years and partially ended when this daughter married while still in high school. I was the third child, and the first son and I had a power struggle with Dad for independence and his respect for me. All the other children seemed to be involved in these struggles with Dad, with the exception of the youngest daughter. *Dad usually initiated these struggles with forceful criticism and punishment when we did things that did not please him. He never really talked to us with an understanding voice. He held us under and suppressed our feelings of independence and self-worth and inhibited the expression of our real thoughts and feelings.*

• *I never did talk with Father much. If we talked at all, it was only about material, external things, and then only briefly. We never shared our real feelings and emotions. He did not care about sharing these things, and he might even hurt my feelings by harshly criticizing me. This was the attitude that I seemed to associate with my father. . . . Whenever I wanted to ask Father something, it was not easy. I would usually get Mother to talk to him first, then I would behave extra well, and then I would ask him myself. . . .*

• *My mother is an easy mark for pity, making it easy to blame others, like the teacher because you have too much homework. . . . Tears get most anything.*

• *This type of discipline was even more strictly imposed in our family than in most because my father was a dominant and very achievement-oriented person. He gave the orders, and we all obeyed because we respected his authority. We also were very afraid to sass or talk back to our parents for fear of punishment from our Dad. . . . I'm quite shy and very obedient to authority, but I'm also aggressive and dominating.*

• *I feel that because of my second brother's untimely passing at age 16, some dramatic changes occurred in the way my parents raised me. I think my mother particularly became quite permissive with me, and I became the typical spoiled youngest child, and in many respects was treated as an only child in the family since my oldest brother had married and was on his own. I was pampered and given many things which I really didn't need. . . . I became a mama's boy, and if it were not for my oldest brother occasionally taking me to Scout camps, I would have had greater difficulty developing. . . . If I wanted something from Mother, I would continue to coax and plead until finally any or all resistance she might have had would be completely broken down, and I usually got my way. Looking back at this, I think there* were times when I really wanted Mother to stand her ground and be firm with me, but she could not do this because perhaps she felt she had to make up for my brother's death.

- The Golden Rule was not always followed in my home. The children were taught to obey this rule, but at times Father especially seemed to disregard it. For instance, he wanted it quiet when he watched TV and got very upset if the door of the TV was bumped partly shut accidentally. However, if someone else was watching TV or playing records, he often wasn't aware that we wanted these same considerations from him.

- Father was very impatient with Mother and frequently yelled at her for various reasons. When Father couldn't find some papers he wanted, of course Mother had misplaced them or, worse still, had thrown them away. When Father couldn't find his clothes brush in his drawer, Mother would find it in the back of the drawer, and it would be her fault. She had hidden it from Father. If the family was late for church, it was because Mother wasn't ready on time.

- When we were small, I remember that Mother made an effort to talk to us about our day. But as I reached high school and college, it seemed that when I wanted to talk, she was busy and wouldn't really hear what I was saying. Then when she wanted to talk to me, she would try to force me to talk, which resulted in my silence.

- We were seldom praised or encouraged for what we did. I will never forget the only time I remember my father praising me. I had given a speech in a meeting. Afterwards many people came up and said that it had been a great talk and were very complimentary. On the way home that night my father said, "I think we can be proud of our daughter tonight." That was the only time he ever said anything to praise me that I can remember.

- Mom and Dad had many ways of building up feelings of inferiority in us children. When we would make mistakes, they would often react by calling us names. I have been called a goon and harebrain many times and have learned to hate those names. Most, if not all, of our family members suffer from a lack of self-worth and have feelings of inferiority. We are not open in the expression of our *emotions and feelings. We tend to be afraid of our real selves and revealing our feelings for fear we will be ridiculed or hurt. In compensating for these feelings of inadequacy, many of us have become either loudmouths and show-offs or have withdrawn. . . .*

- *My parents always emphasized their personal authority over me, and I was constantly reminded of this by their frequent use of the principle "Honor thy father and thy mother." I was never allowed to challenge that authority. Because of the barriers between me and my parents, I constantly sought their approval.*

- *I married early in life in a desperate search for love, affection, and the kind of acceptance that I never really experienced at home. I used marriage to get away from the constant bickering between my parents.*

- *In spite of the fact that my parents loved each other and enjoyed an intimate relationship, they fought and quarreled often. They had established a pattern of bickering and . . . picking at one another, a habit which persists today. The children kid them about it now, but all recall the times when heads were smothered in pillows at night to keep from hearing the angry voices. I remember feeling very frightened and insecure during those fights. Sometimes Mother would have a sinking spell when she wanted to escape or avoid the problems. Other times she would run out of the house and walk for hours until Father went after her. We sometimes wondered if she would come back.*

- *My parents believed that children had no right to talk back at any time, because to do so was showing disrespect for their authority. There were several times when I felt that the punishment they gave me was unfair and unjust. I remember one time when I expressed my resentment after one of those experiences and how my father came up behind me and planted a firm kick on the seat of my pants as I went down the basement steps. Needless to say, that didn't help my feelings any.*

- *I hadn't realized until now how much my parents looked to the success of their own children as a measurement of their own success or failure as parents. Their great desire to not be failures in the home made it difficult for such overly conscientious parents to make mistakes, or for their children to make mistakes for that matter.*

● *In my family there was no mutual respect. We children were treated as possessions. We were never able to say how we felt about things—never had a voice in things concerning the family or even our private lives for that matter. We were humiliated and made to feel ashamed because there wasn't anything good about us.*

● *My dad told me to drive the car to the far right when pulling up to a stop sign. Then some time later when he was driving, he drove the car to the center of the street, and I asked him why. He told me to keep my mouth shut and not to question his driving.*

● *Many experiences I had with my dad showed me he was quite inconsistent in what he said and what he did. Consequently, I learned not to question or do what he did, but do what he said. This I did but with anger and hostility and mistrust for my father. I also grew to dislike his paddling us.*

● *Dad once told my brother to go get the mail from the mailbox, which was about a fourth of a mile from the house. My brother went over to Dad and told him that he did not want to do it, so Dad had someone else do it. A few days later he asked me and I told him the same thing, but I got paddled. At this time I felt really hurt, not necessarily because I got paddled, but because my dad paddled me and not my brother. After that I felt my dad favored my brother over me.*

● *Because my mother didn't like the role of homemaker or her role as mother, she usually worked and stayed away as much as possible (I wondered if she was avoiding Father's criticism). As a result of this, from the time we were very little, she would have us do all the work so she wouldn't have to be bothered. From the time I was a sophomore in high school until I left home after I was twenty-one, I had to do all the shopping and fix all the family meals. This really interfered with my social life and friendships because I always had to hurry home to fix dinner. Also my mother didn't like to clean house, iron, mend, etc. So I was stuck with all the jobs as a homemaker when I was in my teens. She forced us to do those things that she didn't care to do, and she didn't care that we didn't like to do them any more than she did.*

IDENTIFYING HORIZONTAL MOVEMENT

VERBAL RESPONSES

- Um hmm.
- Please go on.
- It seems you are saying . . .
- That's great.
- You really worked hard.
- It seems to me . . .
- I could be wrong, but . . .
- My feeling is that . . .
- Have you considered . . . ?
- You can do it. All you need is a little more practice.
- You are pretty sharp.
- How did it make you feel when . . . ?
- I like you.
- You are easy to like.
- What could you do differently to make it turn out as you would like it?
- What do you think you should do to make restitution?
- I enjoy being with you.
- I believe that . . .
- You are improving.
- What is great about you is that you're always right there trying.
- You are a sincere person.
- You are the kind who cares. This will help make your relationships with others more meaningful.
- It is a pleasure to be around you.
- You make things so interesting.
- You learn fast.
- You show great imagination.
- Your efforts really help out the family.
- What would we ever do without you?
- How were we ever so lucky to have you?

- That is pretty original.
- That was courteous of you.
- As you mature in your behavior and values, you will find happiness.
- Work to behave in such a manner that you will like yourself.
- That is something to think about.
- Things will work out! Just keep trying.
- Let me see if I understand you. You believe that . . . ?
- You have a good heart.
- You can be trusted.
- You can learn to gain the trust of others.
- You have a pleasant attitude.
- You're getting it.
- You are perceptive.
- You are thoughtful.
- It may be hard, but you can do it.
- You have the ability to work it through.
- Things will work out for you.
- You have a clear head.
- You feel bad now, but time is a great healer.

NONVERBAL RESPONSES

- Arm on other person's shoulder
- Arm around other person's waist
- Eyes on other's eyes and face with friendly expression
- Relaxed facial muscles
- Smile
- Relaxed posture
- Cheek pressed to cheek
- Fingers through hair
- Being comfortably close
- Hand on head
- Focus on individual, not his clothes
- Quiet, relaxed tone of voice
- Nod of the head
- Pleasant, attentive expression
- Taking time for others
- Listening to others—considering their ideas and needs

- Hand in hand
- Hugging
- Hand touching hand
- Shaking hands
- Squeezing arm or hand
- Walking with
- Putting face next to face
- Cupping face in hands

FEELINGS AND ATTITUDES
FEELINGS OF

- Care and concern for other people
- Generous friendship with self and other people
- Love
- Fondness for other people
- A reasonable degree of trust in other people
- Optimism toward other people—expecting good from them
- Peacefulness
- A desire to see that justice is done
- Security
- Self-worth
- Openness
- Equality
- Cooperation
- Mutual respect
- Zest for living
- Courage

DESIRE TO

- Use natural consequences
- Use logical consequences
- Focus on people, not their material wealth or lack of it
- Focus on providing a warm, friendly atmosphere when entertaining, not on the perfection of the meal
- Display about the same quality and quantity of material things as friends and neighbors (do not attempt to display superiority in material goods)

- Give unobtrusively
- Work primarily to assist other people rather than to get more than they in the form of material wealth
- Entertain people for the purpose of bringing joy to self and them, not for the purpose of getting ahead
- Be a friend to other people with no strings attached
- Befriend other people regardless of race, occupation, ethnic background, or socioeconomic status
- Seek to serve people, not to acquire positions of status
- Structure cooperative activities rather than competitive games when entertaining other people
- Cheer other people on to greater growth and development
- Make one's own advantage also an advantage for other people
- Share wealth

REFLECTIONS

- *Through my parents' example I learned to love work. We always did things together. Daddy and my brother would do the farm work (which included Mother's and my help), and Mother and I would do the housework. Work was fun most of the time. I never remember my mother working when she wasn't singing, and that singing together made our work a lot more fun. Both my parents enjoyed their work, and they gained much pleasure from it. As a result, their attitude rubbed off onto my brother and me, and we also enjoyed the work to be done. . . . Another excellent technique that my mother had was that while we worked, we could talk. Mother always understood me and was always willing to listen.*

- *I'm reminded of the time when I started college. It would have been so easy for my parents to have given up on me. They wanted me to go to a university, but I had decided to go to a business college, so that's where I went. After I got there, I wanted to quit and go home. Because of my parents' encouragement, letters, and their coming to see me, I made it through one quarter. My mother kept telling me that she knew exactly how I felt but that I could stick it out one quarter. With her encouragement and confidence in me, I was able to. The next year I went to a university. It would have been so easy for* my parents to have said, "If you'd have gone there in the first place like we wanted you to. . . ." They never said anything like that, for which I am very grateful.

● There has never been anything that I couldn't talk to Mother about. Some of our best discussions took place while we did the work. As a result of this, Mother has not only been my mother but my very best friend who always understands.

● I will always appreciate the example my parents set as far as church is concerned. My parents always went with me to my meetings. It was just something that was done. Whenever the young people's group had an affair where the parents were invited, they were always happy to go. Daddy was always willing to go with me, too. This meant a lot to me.

● Some of my best memories are of the times when all the members of my family would go on a vacation, go bowling, go to the farm, get together the week before Christmas to make cookies and candy. These helped our family to love each other and to care more deeply about each other. The only thing I regret was that we had as few of these experiences as we did.

● Mother was very wise in the way she helped and taught me to make decisions. For quite a while I couldn't even decide on the pair of shoes to buy. I literally made Mother make the decision for me, but it wasn't long until Mother put a stop to this. She would give me counsel, and to a small degree, her opinion, but the final decision I had to make. . . .

● When I was quite young (*still in grade school*), my mother would go to meetings and leave me in charge of the home. This wasn't quite as easy as it sounds because I lived on a farm, and in the summertime you have the house to keep, the yardwork to do (and we have a huge lawn and lots of flower beds), hired men to cook, wash, and iron for, plus any errands that need to be done. This was a big responsibility for me but I will never forget how it made me feel. It made me feel like a worthwhile person. It made me feel really good inside to be able to carry the responsibilities that Mother gave to me. It makes *you feel good to know that your Mother trusts you with such a big responsibility.*

● *When I really felt like I had failed miserably, my dad didn't always sympathize with me. Sometimes he was quite stern and he'd say, "Sally, quit your damn crying!" He would proceed to tell me how it wasn't the end of the world, and how these hard knocks made you stronger if you got back up on your feet and kept fighting. He'd say, "Sally, I don't care how many times you fail, just as long as you keep right on trying and hanging in there. Someday you'll come out O.K. if you just keep plugging through all your discouraged moments." At the time, I thought he was just a little heartless; but darn, I don't think I would have made it through some of the rough spots without him there telling me these things.*

● *"Now it is your very own decision. Make it as you may, but as you make your bed, you must lie in it." This was my parent's way of saying that we must suffer the consequences of our decisions.*

● *The thing I like and admire most about my parents is the amount of trust they have in me. As long as I can remember, they have given me things to do and trusted me to do them. When I was little, it was just things like riding my bike to the store to get something, or cleaning house, or other errands like these. It made me feel important to think that my parents would trust me to do these things. As I grew older, they trusted me more and more. For instance, I was really impressed when, at age fifteen and a half, my parents trusted me with the car as soon as I got my license and let me take it a lot to go with friends, etc. They trusted me in dating situations during the summers when I went away to work. They would tell me what a good head I had and how much common sense I used. I asked my Mom once why she trusted me so much and didn't worry about me and what I would do when I went out of her influence. She said, "Why shouldn't I trust you? I've never had any reason not to, and I trust you like I trust myself." She said she knew me well and just knew that I had been straight all my life and she had no reason to believe that I would change now. I was really flattered. I mean I just wanted to be supergood after that. I think it's excellent to trust a person so much. I plan to do the same with my children.*

348

• *I feel very fortunate to be in the family I'm in. I have always felt very secure at home, and I know that I'm loved there. I trust and love my family more than any of my friends and would tell them anything before I would my friends. My parents always stick together and never get too upset with things. For instance, tonight I'm superupset because campus police just called and want me to come in and discuss the three parking tickets I got last September. I had my Dad's car here for the first week, so I just parked it in the visitor's lot and didn't sign the tickets and send them in. I didn't think it was any big deal to park in the visitor's lot when it wasn't even my car and I only had it for a few days. Everyone told me to sign a phony name or just throw them [the tickets] away, because they would never check on them. So I threw them away and never thought another thing about them until today when campus police called. They finally chased me down, and now I have to go in and explain the situation. I figured out that all three tickets came to $57, and that's quite a sum to come out of a college girl's pocket. So I was just sick, and my roommates and I have been sitting here for two hours making up some pretty fantastic stories of how my Mom was here and she got the tickets and never bothered to mail them in. Well, I knew all along that I would end up just telling the plain old honest truth, but I just couldn't quite bring myself to admit it, so I called home just to see what my parents would say I should do. Well, without even thinking twice they said, "For pete's sake, tell the truth." In fact they were rather amazed that I could make up such a fantastic story. They proceeded to tell me how $57 was a very cheap price to pay for honesty and how if I was dishonest with the law once that would just make it easier for me to do it again. It was just so reassuring to hear them say that; I was greatly relieved to know that they were still there working together and that they were behind me and loved me. It's great to have such groovy parents.*

• *I can hardly remember a time when I was going out that I didn't come to my mom's room to tell her that I was home and to tell her what type of evening I had had, good or bad. This usually led to a discussion which brought my sister out of her room also. This type of relationship seems to have given us all security in our home.*

REFERENCES

Allred, G. Hugh
  1968   Mission for Mother: Guiding the Child. Salt Lake City: Bookcraft.

Dreikurs, Rudolf, et al.
  1971   Maintaining Sanity in the Classroom. New York: Harper and Row.

Lowe, Raymond N.
  1965   "Talking as Motivation." Dittoed classroom handout, University of Oregon, Eugene, Oregon.

Madsen, Clifford K., and Charles H. Madsen, Jr.
  1972   Parents Children Discipline Boston: Allyn and Bacon.

Maslow, Abraham H.
  1971   The Farther Reaches of Human Nature. New York: The Viking Press.

Ruesch, Jurgen, and Weldon Kees
  1956   Nonverbal Communication: Notes on the Visual Perception of Human Relations. Berkeley: University of California Press.

Sicher, Lydia
  1955   "Education for freedom." The American Journal of Individual Psychology 11 (2).

Smith, Judith M., and Donald E. P. Smith
  1966   Child Management: A Program for Parents. Ann Arbor, Michigan: Ann Arbor Publishers.

INDEX

The following index consists of topic, name, and concept entries, with the main focus being on concepts. There is some departure from the traditional manner of indexing; more inclusive page numbers are referred to than is normal. This has been done primarily to include the case studies and relate them to key concepts and should be of particular value to the student and the instructor. Some pages referred to in the index do not contain the actual entry, but they do contain related information. In these cases, the reader will be interpreting the information on those pages and relating it in a meaningful manner to the concept appearing as an entry in the index. This process should enable the reader to further enhance his understanding of and insights into the main concepts discussed throughout the book.

Bedtime, problems at, 204-6
Bedwetting, 206-9
Behavior, 116
  change of, 90-94
  communicative, 60
  deflecting, 118
  destructive, 192-94
  differential, 80
  horizontal, 45. *See also* Cooper-
    ation, Horizontal movement
  irreverent, 140-42
  models of, 9
  patterns of, 31
  vertical, 45-46. *See also* Com-
    petition, Vertical movement
  goals of, 16-23
Belonging, 45-46
  case studies involving, 106-7,
    114-17, 120-22, 132-34, 155-
    59, 167-75, 185-88, 192-97,
    206-9, 244-49, 260-63, 281-
    86, 296-99, 310-12, 316-19
  goal of, 40
Bernard, 315-16
Bickering, 340
Birth order, 48-49
Body language, 59
Bonding, 52-53, 252-53
  case studies involving, 104-5,
    107-9, 140-42, 147-51, 157-
    63, 170-72, 178-79, 194-95,
    249-59, 263-75, 281-86, 289-
    92, 296-304, 307-16
Boss, desire to become, 16, 18-20,
  145

Bossing behaviors, list of, 18-20
Breath holding, 98-99
Budgeting, 178-79

C

Childrearing principles, 85-87
Children
  foster, 49
  handicapped, 49, 144-45
  only, 49
  treating, as a group, 119
City zoning, 310-12
Clowning, for attention, 64,
  201-2
Communal interest, 47-48
  case studies involving, 129-31,
    134-37, 163-65, 194-95, 209-
    11, 225-32, 237-42, 244-57,
    263-68, 281-319
Communication, 44, 59-68, 69-81,
  338
  content aspect of, 61-62
  hinting in, 70
  horizontal, 70-76
  nonverbal, 44, 62-63, 69
  relationship aspect of, 61-62
  stimulation of, 138-40
  vertical, 69-70
Comparison, of family members,
  335
Competition, 10-11, 14, 47-48,
  289-92, 314-16
  in the family, 333-34, 335. *See
    also* Vertical movement
Competitive games, 291-92

Competitive activities, 133
Compromise, 79
Compulsion, 334
Concession, 79
Conflict
destructive, 77
habitual, 77
hidden, 77-78
resolution of, 78-79
by children, 120
case studies involving, 137-
40, 182-85, 229-32
spiraling, 77
vertical, 77-78
Congruence, 151-53. *See also*
Genuineness
Consequences
logical, 86-87, 115-16, 141-42.
See also Logical conse-
quences, case studies in-
volving
natural, 85-87, 154. *See also*
Natural consequences, case
studies involving
Contact comfort, 94-95
Content aspect of communication, 61-62
Cooperation, 27, 45, 47-48, 133.
See also Horizontal movement
Cooperative activities, 133
Counterhurting, 16, 20-22, 77,
78, 216, 218, 244-49
behaviors, list of, 21-22
Courtesy, 241-43
Courts, 296-99

Creative power, 37, 38, 135
Criticism, 12-13, 23-24, 32-33,
55-56, 163-65
suggested reaction to, 160-61
of spouse, 225-29, 238-41, 247-
49, 253, 265-68
Crying, 16, 99-101

D
Decisions, 346, 347
Destructive conflict, 77
Dictator, husband as, 271-73
Differential behavior, 80
Disabled, appearing, 16, 22-23
Discipline, 55-56, 196-97, 219,
337-38
Discouragement, 16
Dishonesty, in relationships, 11,
14
Disloyalty, to spouse, 225-29
Dormitory living, 130
Dormitory sleeping quarters, 129
Double bind, 252-53, 259
Drug abuse, prevention of, 194-
95
Drug abusers, background of,
195

E
Eating, protracted, 113-14
Eating schedules, 95-97
Education, 290-92
Emotions, 75-76
Empathy, 71-72
case studies involving, 118-20,

354

Time-out room, 129, 130-31, 141, 211
Titles, professional, 304-5
Toilet training
difficulty with, 106-7
reversion from, 107-9
as status symbol, 104-5
Traffic violations, 176-77
Trust, 29, 71, 262, 347
lack of, 70
Twins, 49

V
Vertical behavior, 45-46. *See also* Competition
goals of, 16-23
case studies involving, 102-13, 120-24, 126-28, 151-53, 170-77, 189-97, 199-209, 211-12, 225-36, 243-54, 263-68, 281-99, 304-10, 312-19

Vertical communication, 69-70
Vertical conflict, 77-78
Vertical movement. *See* Competition
consequences of, 12-15
desires of, 331-32
feelings of, 330-31
nonverbal responses indicating, list of, 328-30
in relationships, 9
verbal responses indicating, list of, 325-28

W
War, 286
Warmth, nonpossessive, 71
case studies involving. *See* Respect
Wetting, bed, 206-9

Z
Zoning, city, 310-12